BOOKS BY ANNE-MARIE SLAUGHTER

Unfinished Business

*The Idea That Is America: Keeping Faith with Our Values
in a Dangerous World*

A New World Order

Unfinished Business

Unfinished Business

Women
Men
Work
Family

Anne-Marie Slaughter

RANDOM HOUSE CANADA

Unfinished Business is a work of non-fiction. Some names and identifying details have been changed.

A portion of this work was originally published in *The Atlantic*.

Library and Archives Canada Cataloguing in Publication

Slaughter, Anne-Marie, author
Unfinished business : women men work family / Anne-Marie Slaughter.

Includes bibliographical references and index.
Issued in print and electronic formats.

ISBN 978-0-345-81289-6
eBook ISBN 978-0-345-81291-9

1. Work-life balance—United States. 2. Work and family—United States.
3. Women employees—Family relationships—United States. 4. Women employees—United States—Social conditions. 5. Sex role—United States.
I. Title.

HD4904.25.S58 2015   306.3'6   C2015-904588-6

Book design by Susan Turner

Printed and bound in the United States of America

10 9 8 7 6 5 4 3 2 1

Penguin
Random House
RANDOM HOUSE CANADA

For my three men:
Andy, Edward, and Alexander

CONTENTS

"IT'S SUCH A PITY YOU HAD TO LEAVE WASHINGTON"

IN DECEMBER 2010 I WAS WORKING ROUND THE CLOCK WITH MY team on the Policy Planning Staff of the State Department to finish a major eighteen-month project for Secretary of State Hillary Clinton. It was bitingly cold; as one of my colleagues and I walked home in the early morning hours, we would turn up our collars against the wind and play the endless Washington parlor game of speculating on who would take which job as people came and went after the midterm elections. I kept quiet, but I had been getting unmistakable signals that I could be in line for a promotion myself—to one of a tiny handful of higher positions. I was excited—and deeply conflicted.

I had been working for almost two years as the first female director of policy planning, reporting directly to the secretary of state and responsible for helping her develop and implement big-picture frameworks and strategy for U.S. foreign policy. When Secretary Clinton, a woman I greatly admire and a truly wonderful boss, had called two years earlier to offer me the position, a foreign policy dream job, I immediately accepted. At the same time, I told her that I could only stay for two years. That is the normal period academics receive as public service leave from their universities; if they stay away longer they must give up lifetime tenure. Still, both my husband, Andy, and I expected when I went to Washington that if the opportunity arose for me to stay on in a higher position, it would be very tempting. I had been a professor my entire career, but foreign policy was my lifelong passion.

This was my moment to "lean in," to seize the advantage of being in the right place at the right time and propel myself forward. I certainly had no guarantee I would get the promotion if I put myself in the pool, but I had a reasonable chance; the job I wanted was yet another one that no woman had ever held. I would also have a chance to continue advancing an approach to foreign policy that I believed in strongly and that had become a signature of Secretary Clinton's tenure.

The woman I always thought I was—the career woman, the law professor, the dean, the undergraduate who planned to go to law school as a route to the State Department—would have said yes, without hesitation. But while the professional side of my life was moving forward, the personal side was more complicated. When I first took the job at State in 2009, Andy and I decided it would be much better for him and our two sons if I commuted to Washington every week rather than uprooting the family. The boys were ten and twelve at that point, in fourth and sixth grades in schools and a community they loved and in which they were deeply rooted. They heartily agreed; as upset as they were to hear that I was headed to Washington, when I suggested that everyone come with me their reaction was essentially "Bye, Mom!"

Andy is a tenured professor of politics and international affairs at Princeton. He has always been home more than I; my previous job as dean of Princeton's Woodrow Wilson School of Public and International Affairs and my various foreign policy activities required much more travel than his work did. And even when I was home, my computer was never far from reach. Indeed, in first grade our older son was asked to draw his family; he drew me as a laptop—not a woman sitting at a laptop, but a laptop itself! Still, at that point my office was only a mile from home and their school; I was able to be at teacher's conferences and school and sports events, and the academic schedule also meant that even if I was gone or very busy for stretches, we could always manage catch-up time where we could take a vacation or hang out at home together. I was very present in the boys' lives and considered myself incredibly fortunate that I could be both an engaged parent and a committed professional.

Because Andy and I had somehow always made it work, I assumed we would again simply adapt to new rhythms. But the change was wrenching. Over the span of two weeks, between the time Secretary Clinton offered me the job and I started, we went from a world in which my office was a ten-minute walk away from home to a world in which I left the house at five A.M. Monday morning and came back late Friday afternoon or evening. This schedule was not unusual among political appointees in the Obama administration; I knew a number of other women and men who had left their families behind in New York, Pennsylvania, and even California. Moreover, high government officials who have their families right there in Washington do not see them very often; the hours are punishing, precisely because of the importance of the work. World events will not wait on family schedules; crises pile on top of one another and can disrupt even the most cherished family celebrations. As for vacations, I got one vacation day a month, generous by U.S. standards, but by June I still had barely enough for a week away.

As a professional, I reaped the benefits as well as the costs of my choice, which Andy certainly understood and supported. But for our sons, the costs were immediate and large. My younger son—only ten—would cry on Sunday nights when he knew I had to leave the next morning. Once I opened my mouth to try to comfort him and he yelled out, before I could say a word, "I don't want you to go. And I don't care about the country!" I had ex-plained to him earlier that he was serving his nation just as I was, something Secretary Clinton also told him when she met him, but he had had enough.

Our older son tried to be mature about my leaving, even of-fering to take over responsibility for the breakfast smoothies I made every morning. He understood how much I wanted the job. He also understood something more universal about my new po-sition; early on in my commute, when I was still learning the Washington ropes and was frustrated enough to have said some-thing about quitting and coming home (not really meaning it, of course), he looked at me and said, "Mom, you can't quit! You're a role model." He had heard that from someone, probably the mother of one of his friends, and already had internalized it.

He was proud of me but also newly in middle school, with new friends and more demanding classes, and suddenly all his routines were disturbed. And as puberty hit, he turned into a creature so familiar to many parents: the sulky, taciturn kid who responds in rude monosyllables when he responds at all. His friends changed, and over the next eighteen months he started skipping homework, disrupting classes, failing math, and tuning out any adult who tried to reach him. He fought with his father and did his best to ignore me completely. By eighth grade his behavior had escalated; he had been suspended from school and picked up by the local police. I received several urgent phone calls—inevitably on the day of an important meeting—that re-quired me to drop what I was doing and take the first train back home (Secretary Clinton and her chief of staff, Cheryl Mills, were always understanding, but it put a strain on my office).

Plenty of parents assured me that my son's behavior was typ-ical, that nothing I was facing was particularly unusual. Teenagers rebel; parents of teenagers tear their hair out. And Andy was there, after all, doing his level best as the home parent. Still, my son was constantly on my mind. As much as I loved the work I was doing, I would get a call or a text with the latest upset and wonder why on earth I was sitting in D.C. when my son needed me in Princeton.

I played with various scenarios, wondering if I could perhaps eke out one more year in D.C. but knowing that any of the jobs I might be considered for would require Senate confirmation, which could take three to six months, and that Secretary Clinton would rightly expect a two-year commitment, until the end of President Obama's first term. I thought about asking my husband and sons to move to D.C. after all, but that would have left Andy commuting back to his job in Princeton and would have completely uprooted the boys in ways I truly thought would be very bad for them, particularly our younger son. We had moved to Princeton in the first place precisely because of the quality of the public schools and the kid-friendly nature of the community.

Money was also a consideration. I had taken more than a 50 percent pay cut to go into government and was now paying rent on a tiny studio apartment in D.C. as well as commuting expenses. If the family moved down with me we would be able to rent our house in Princeton, but then Andy would be commuting and we would be saddled with all the costs of a move and life in a more expensive city.

Deep down I knew the right choice was to go home, even if I didn't quite recognize the woman who was making that choice. So I did. Secretary Clinton gave me a wonderful going-away party that will be one of the things I'll remember when I look back on my life. My entire American family—parents, siblings, aunts, uncles, and cousins—came, four of them from as far away as Hong Kong. Andy and the boys were there, beaming, with an audience of so many dear friends, old and new, to see me receive the Secretary's Distinguished Service Award, the highest honor the State Department gives. Amid the speeches, jokes, and gifts from colleagues I had come to love and admire, it never occurred to me that I was "quitting" or "dropping out." Just making a decision to move sideways rather than up.

I packed up my apartment the next day, a Friday, and was back in the classroom teaching at Princeton by the following Tuesday. As I recovered my own balance after the grueling Washington schedule, and as our family righted itself, some fundamental changes took place. I went back to teaching, writing, and speaking as a professor and foreign policy commentator, a more than full-time schedule but a wonderfully flexible one. Now, however, I realized in a way that I never had before just how essential that flexibility had always been in allowing me to be both a mom and a career woman.

Equally important, small things that I had previously taken for granted suddenly seemed much more precious. For the first six months at home I bounded out of bed and made some kind of homemade cooked breakfast for the boys: muffins, scones, pancakes, waffles, hash browns, eggs, you name it. Andy had gotten the boys up, fed, and off to school every day for two years; he rolled over that first morning I was back and said, "Your turn." After a while, though, he did gently suggest that perhaps I was overcompensating just a bit for my absence. In fact, my cooking was as much for me as it was for them. One of the things I never expected about being a mother is the sheer elemental pleasure I get out of watching my sons eat food I have cooked. It must be some very deep evolutionary urge. Regardless, I was home, and I couldn't have been happier.

As the months passed, I started asking myself deeper questions. My decision to leave government was based on my love for and responsibility to my family. But still I thought I would try for another foreign policy job if President Obama were to be re-elected. If you are a political appointee and your party is in power for eight full years when you are at the height of your career, that's your time to reach for the stars. When I left in 2011, I certainly was not ruling out trying to come back in 2013.

But I kept wrestling with myself. Even if I were lucky enough to have the chance to go back to government, leaving again would mean missing the last two years my oldest son would be at home and missing my younger son's transition to high school. It had never occurred to me not to put my career first, as long as my family could handle it, but now I had to be dead honest with myself. This crisis had forced me to confront what was most important to me, rather than what I was conditioned to want, or perhaps what I had conditioned myself to want. That realization led me to question the feminist narrative I grew up with and have always championed. I began to wonder why success as a woman, or indeed as a man, meant privileging career achievement above all else.

I had always believed, and told all the young women I taught and mentored, that women could "have it all," meaning simply that they could have careers and families in the same way and at the same levels that men do. Men who are presidents, CEOs, directors, managers, leaders of all kinds have families too. Women surely could do the same, I told my students—they just had to be committed enough to their careers. But here I was, as committed to my career as I had ever been, making a choice I had never expected to make and being certain it was the right one.

For someone who grew up in the 1970s, shaped by and devoted to the opportunities, power, and promise of the women's movement, deciding to choose family over career felt like heresy. But an event in May 2011, four months after I left D.C., made me see this entire set of issues in a different light. I was invited to

Oxford University to give the first Fulbright Lecture on International Relations. At the request of the event's organizers, I agreed to talk to a group of Rhodes Scholars about "work-family balance." Attending was a group of about forty talented and self-assured young men and women in their mid-twenties.

What poured out of me was not really a talk but more a set of frank reflections on how unexpectedly hard it had been to do the kind of job I wanted to do as a high government official and be the kind of parent I wanted to be at a demanding time for my children. As many women and men have told me since, it may have been naïve of me not to expect this tension, given my commute, but I had simply assumed that my family and I would make it work the way we always had. I concluded by saying that my time in office had convinced me that further government service would be very unlikely while my sons were still at home, even if my party remained in power for another six years.

Somewhat to my surprise, the audience was rapt and asked many thoughtful questions. One of the first was from a young woman who began by thanking me for "not giving just one more fatuous 'You can have it all' talk." She had clearly heard plenty of those and was deeply skeptical. Most of the young women in the room planned to combine careers and family in some way, but they were starting from a much more informed place than I had been in at age twenty-five, when I had simply assumed that I could pursue my career full tilt and a husband and family would just magically follow. Regardless of their achievements at such a young age, these women and many of the men in the audience already assumed that juggling work and family was likely to be hard, even if rewarding. They wanted to hear about real experiences and trade-offs from people who were in the middle of that juggle, words of wisdom or advice that might help them plan for or at least anticipate the road ahead.

Around the same time, I started to notice that the reactions from men and women closer to my own age were decidedly different. After a couple of months, I realized that the problem was not that I had come back to the university per se, but that I had come back because of my kids. When people in Princeton and New York asked why I had come back to teaching, I could simply have said that my two-year public service leave was up, reminding them that Larry Summers left the administration after two years as well to resume teaching at Harvard. But I was determined to assert my family as an equally important consideration in my choice to come home. As dean of the Woodrow Wilson School I had always been deliberately public about going home at six o'clock to have dinner with my family or needing to change my schedule to accommodate my kids' school events or parent-teacher conferences. In the same spirit, I would often respond to the question of why I had left the State Department by saying, "My husband and I have two teenage sons who definitely need hands-on parenting, and they will only be at home for a few more years."

Suddenly, the person I was talking to would have a very different perception of me. The reactions ran the gamut from "It's such a pity that you had to leave Washington" to "I wouldn't generalize from your experience. I never had to compromise and my kids turned out great" to the many little signs that my interlocutor was reassessing whether I was really a "player."

In short, even as a woman who was still working full-time as a tenured professor, I had suddenly become categorized and subtly devalued as just another one of the many talented and well-educated women who showed great promise at the start of their careers and reached the early levels of success but then made a choice to take a less demanding job, work part-time, or stop working entirely to have more time for caregiving. I continually sensed that I had disappointed the expectations of the many people in my life—older women, my male and female peers, even a few friends—who had somehow invested in the arc of my career.

All my life I'd been on the other side of this exchange. I'd been the woman smiling the ever so faintly superior smile in the face of another woman telling me that she had decided to take time out to stay at home or pursue a different, less competitive career track to have more time with her family. I'd been the woman hanging out with the dwindling number of friends from college or law school who had never compromised our career aspirations, congratulating one another on our unswerving commitment to the feminist cause. I'd been the one telling female students and audience members at my lectures that it is possible to have it all and do it all regardless of what job you are in. Which means I'd been part, albeit unwittingly, of making women feel that it is *their* fault if they cannot manage full-time careers and climb the ladder as fast as men while simultaneously maintaining a family and an active home life (and be thin and beautiful to boot). The more I thought about it, the more it seemed to me profoundly wrong that the millions of women and a growing number of men who made choices similar to my own should not be affirmed and even celebrated for insisting that professional success is not the only measure of human happiness and achievement.

In 2012, I wrote a piece for *The Atlantic*, putting down all the thoughts about women and work that had been simmering in my brain. The article was called "Why Women Still Can't Have It All," a title I was soon to regret but that undoubtedly sold more magazines than the more accurate but decidedly less catchy "Why Working Mothers Need Better Choices to Be Able to Stay in the Pool and Make It to the Top." Within five days, the online version had received more than 400,000 views; a week later that number had reached a million; today it is one of the most-read articles in the 150-year history of *The Atlantic*, with an estimated 2.7 million views. Clearly, it seemed, a sizable group of women and a growing number of men wanted another round of the now fifty-year-old conversation about what true equality between men and women really means.

In the months that followed, I received hundreds of emails from people who had been moved by my piece. Jessica Davis-Ganao, an academic who is raising two young children, one with a genetic disorder, while trying to get tenure, wrote, "I just read your article in *The Atlantic* and had to close my door because I couldn't stop crying. You have articulated a struggle I have been waging for the past few years." Another comment that has stuck in my mind came from a mother who said I had "given her per-mission" to stop working and stay home with her kids for a while, something that she had truly wanted to do but had not dared.

The welcome was not always warm, however. I was accused of perpetuating "plutocrat" feminism—that I'm only concerned with the high-class problems of powerful women like myself. Some critics took issue with the entire concept of "having it all," calling it perfectionistic folly to imagine that we can have big ca-reers and be highly devoted parents at the same time. Other crit-ics claimed that my article would undermine the years of historic, hard-won gains of women in the workplace.

I soon got a chance to engage both criticism and praise di-rectly as I traveled the country, gave speeches, listened to ques-tions, and grappled with answers. Gradually, I allowed myself to break free from an entire set of deeply internalized assumptions about what is valuable, what is important, what is right, and what is natural. The process was like going to the optometrist and having her flip the lenses in that little machine, with the letters on the far side coming in and out of focus until gradually what had been a complete blur becomes sharp and startlingly clear.

Feminist pioneers like Betty Friedan and Gloria Steinem broke free of stifling stereotypes that confined women to a world in which their identities were defined almost entirely by their relationships to others: daughter, sister, wife, mother. The movement Friedan and Steinem led, following in the nineteenth-century footsteps of Susan B. Anthony, Elizabeth Cady Stanton, and their fellow revolutionaries, takes its place with the civil rights movement, the global human rights movement, the anti-colonial movement, and the gay rights movement as one of the great struggles for human freedom of the twentieth century.

But it is a movement that remains unfinished in many ways. And at the turn of the twenty-first century, I am increasingly convinced that advancing women means breaking free of a new set of stereotypes and assumptions, not only for women, but also for men. It means challenging a much wider range of conventional wisdom about what we value and why, about measures of success, about the wellsprings of human nature and what equality really means. It means rethinking everything from workplace design to life stages to leadership styles.

I want a society that opens the possibility for every one of us to have a fulfilling career, or simply a good job with good wages if that's what we choose, along with a personal life that allows for the deep satisfactions of loving and caring for others. I hope this book can help move us in that direction.

But one step at a time. To get there, let's start with the world as it is, not as many of us would like it to be.

Unfinished Business

Part I

Moving Beyond Our Mantras

WHEN BETTY FRIEDAN WROTE *THE FEMININE MYSTIQUE,* SHE TItled her opening chapter "The Problem That Has No Name." She described it as "a strange stirring, a sense of dissatisfaction, a yearning that women suffered in the middle of the twentieth century in the United States." She began to believe that it laid in the "discrepancy between the reality of our lives as women and the image to which we were trying to conform."

Friedan purported to speak for all women but was actually chronicling the emotional distress of millions of suburban housewives. Her audience was large enough to help launch the second wave of the feminist movement—no small achievement. Still, the world she described was certainly not the reality for millions of other women who had neither time nor inclination to grapple with an idealized vision of femininity. They were already in the workforce by necessity rather than choice.

For my part, I grew up in a white upper-middle-class suburban household, albeit at a time when that still meant staying in roadside motels, riding Greyhound buses, and learning alongside the children of plumbers and electricians as well as doctors and lawyers. I have been well educated and faced a horizon of expanding opportunity as a member of the America that has steadily grown richer over the past three decades, rather than the America that has stagnated and fallen behind. I live in a version of the nuclear family—two married heterosexual parents, two biological children combining the DNA of both parents—that is now a minority of American families.

In the process of writing this book, responding to reflections, questions, and critiques from many different people from many different backgrounds, I have realized time and again just how much my own experiences inevitably shape my assumptions about how others think and feel. As I have tried to put myself in others' shoes, I have confronted again and again the obvious but too often overlooked point of just how much *money matters.* Money gave Andy and me the ability to afford excellent daycare when the kids were young, a full-time housekeeper as they grew older, the comfort of living in a neighborhood with great public schools and libraries.

Money buys a safety net, relieving stress and providing resources and resilience against the buffets of fate. Yet millions of American families are working as hard as they can without the resources to absorb even one unlucky break. Their "family choices"—whether and how much to work versus whether and how much to stay home to care for children or parents—are not really choices at all; they are driven by economic imperatives. As I challenge my own long-held beliefs, I continually remind myself that my story is not theirs.

I emphasize this point because if we want to move forward—for women and men, for our workplaces, and for our society as a whole—we must first step back and take a hard look at what we reflexively believe to be true. We must question the conventional wisdom, aphorisms, memes, and stories that inform or justify our choices and shape our worlds. We have to ask ourselves why we are so certain of our often-buried assumptions about the way things are, both for ourselves and for millions of others whose lives we can only try to imagine.

We can only change and bring about change if we can genuinely open our minds to new thoughts and possibilities, for everyone.

1

HALF-TRUTHS WOMEN HOLD DEAR

As a professor who had thousands of meetings with students and gave hundreds of lectures over twenty years, the single question that I heard most frequently, hands down, was from young women asking me how I managed to balance work and family. Even after foreign policy talks at other universities, once the audience had thinned out a young woman would invariably raise her hand and ask me what advice I would give to women seeking to have a career and a family at the same time. I am hardly alone in this; any of my female colleagues would say the same thing. We understand why these young women ask us this question and feel proud that they are looking up to us.

But the answers are complicated. I could have told my students that the only way I had managed to have a high-powered career and a husband and two sons was by being a tenured professor at a top university married to another tenured professor at the same university. But that could be deeply discouraging, and it's not the whole truth; drive, hard work, and good fortune each played a role in charting the course of my career. Moreover, many other women manage to combine careers and family successfully in less flexible and fortunate situations.

Later on, I could have said to any of the young women I met

in Washington, "Look, I'm on the edge of perpetual crisis here. My teenage son is having all sorts of issues; my husband and I are desperately trying to figure out how to manage him while I'm gone five days a week; I'm torn up inside and asking myself daily whether this job is worth the personal cost." But that too would have been pretty discouraging and, again, not the whole truth. My situation could have been very different if my kids were not teenagers; if they were not sons battling over every little issue with their father; if my oldest son had not found himself far too familiar with the Princeton police station. I could also look around D.C. and see other women who were doing what I was trying to do, including a commute, without the same difficulties.

So what to say? My truth has multiple parts, and it's only my truth. Still, I'm a feminist, and one of the central tenets of my life has been to believe and live the proposition that women can have full-fledged careers just like men without giving up the joys of family life. For me, at least, that's what it meant to "have it all." (As we'll discuss in chapter 2, I am now quite ambivalent about the phrase, but I will continue to use it here as a shorthand for this idea.) So it's not surprising that I, like virtually every other woman I know in my generation, typically fell back on a set of standard mantras, as if chanting them enough would make them true.

Three of the most common are:

1. "You can have it all if you are just committed enough to your career."
2. "You can have it all if you marry the right person."
3. "You can have it all if you sequence it right."

These are not lies. They are true in part, but they are not the whole truth. They offer the comforting illusion that having a career and a family depends on choices *you* make. In fact, though your choices are certainly important, life has a funny way of intervening. Look back ten years. Has your life gone exactly according to plan over the past decade? *You* also have a funny way of changing. At twenty-five, when I was married for the first time, I thought only about my career. If you had asked me, I would have said I wanted children, but in what seemed like the very far away decade of my thirties. At thirty-five, when I married again, having a baby suddenly became almost all I could think about. I spent two years agonizing that I might have sacrificed being a biological mother to my career—a choice that I never intended to make.

In my view, these mantras are not enough. It is important to encourage younger women, but it's equally important to acknowledge the reality that many women have lived. To be honest about all the couples who assumed when they started out that both partners would have equal opportunities both to parent and to pursue their professional aspirations but then discovered that two full-time careers and two or more children, often together with responsibilities for older relatives, simply did not work.

By telling the whole truth, we can get those couples to talk much more frankly and directly about choices and trade-offs before they commit to each other. We can change what young women look for in their mates. And above all, we can map a more accurate landscape of obstacles and barriers to true equality, so we can then set about knocking them down.

HALF-TRUTH: "YOU CAN HAVE IT ALL IF YOU ARE JUST COMMITTED ENOUGH TO YOUR CAREER"

OVER THE YEARS, I'VE HAD a growing awareness that many older women, often in the pioneering generation just ahead of me, are increasingly judgmental about the choices younger women are making. The experience that crystallized this realization came after giving a lecture on foreign policy at a prominent foundation in New York. I was surrounded afterward by a small cluster of older women who complimented me on the lecture and praised my commitment to a foreign policy career. In the same breath, however, they lamented the seeming lack of drive of many younger women they knew, who were "dropping out" of their careers.

There it is. The assumption that women are dropping out because of a lack of drive or ambition rests on the deeper assumption that these women could have high-flying careers if they just wanted them badly enough. If they were really committed to their careers, they would work around the clock, no matter what the cost.

In other words, if you are prepared to do whatever it takes to advance in your career, including rarely seeing your children, then you can indeed have a career and a family too. Many male CEOs or senior partners would say that is exactly the sacrifice they have long had to make to rise to top jobs—jobs that demand constant travel and availability to clients 24/7. Walter Blass, who was the Peace Corps country director for Afghanistan in the late 1960s and then worked in strategic planning for AT&T, wrote me an email where he outlined the sacrifices he made for his career. "I was leaving most of the responsibility for raising our three children to my 'non-working' wife. She was quite explicit in criticizing me while we were overseas for my 12-hour days worrying about the volunteers, and not spending enough time with her or attention to our kids," Blass wrote. Later, at AT&T, when he had crazy hours during a nine-month strike, "My then 12-year-old daughter wrote a poem about how she and her siblings knew they had a father because I left my dirty socks and underwear next to the bed."

But here's the rub. The men who have chosen to make that trade-off over the decades have almost always been supported in that decision by wives or partners who have either been full-time or at least lead caregivers, as Walter Blass's wife was. That means that a rising corporate executive, consultant, academic, surgeon, or lawyer has been able to devote himself to his career in the knowledge that a loving parent is caring for his children and doing everything possible to ensure that they flourish. As much as he may wish he had more time to spend with them, or lament that his relationship with them is much more distant than he would like, he at least knows that they are in good hands. Moreover, the entrenched social structure of women at home and men in the office reinforces his choice. He is doing what he is supposed to do: supporting his family by providing for them financially and thereby allowing his wife to provide for them physically and emotionally.

A rising career woman with a family does not face the same set of choices. Relatively rare is the husband who agrees to stay home or be the lead parent so that his wife can advance her career. He may support her completely in her career goals, but not to the point of giving up or significantly compromising his own. But someone must take care of the children, or aging parents, or a sick relative. In the most frequent case, instead of being faced with the choice that ambitious career men have traditionally faced—working 24/7 and seeing little of their children but still having them cared for by a parent—an ambitious woman faces the choice of working 24/7 and having neither parent available for the children. Even if she can afford round-the-clock childcare, a big if, that means no parent is reliably available for school plays, sick days, homework help, and late-night hard conversations about everything from being teased at school to adolescent love.

That is a far harder choice. In that situation, knowing your presence might help a child, parent, or spouse thrive and that you are stuck in a meeting, or working another late night, doesn't feel like choosing to sacrifice "time with your family," something you wish you could have but are denying yourself, for the sake of your career. It feels like sacrificing your loved ones' well-being for your own aspirations.

After my lecture in New York that night I went to dinner and sat across from two women in their early thirties who spoke to me about their inability to find role models among the older women they worked with, explaining that they did not want to marry their jobs. Kerry Rubin and Lia Macko, two young New York career women who wrote *Midlife Crisis at 30*, made the same point in memorable fashion: "If we didn't start to learn how to integrate our personal, social, and professional lives, we were about five years away from morphing into the angry woman on the other side of a mahogany desk who questions her staff's work ethic after standard 12-hour workdays, before heading home to eat moo shoo pork in her lonely apartment."

It is exactly that perception of the trade-offs between work and family that is widely shared by millennial women. They see that ambition and commitment are essential to climb to the top of their professions, but they do not see how to create room for family at the same time.

But What About the Success Stories?

AFTER ANOTHER TALK ON WOMEN and work I gave to a group of New Jersey women, a woman in her sixties came up and told me, in an oddly assertive tone, about her daughter, a lawyer with three children who managed to commute into New York every day, advance in her firm, and still be there for her kids when they needed her. I smiled and congratulated her on her daughter's be-half, although I couldn't quite understand the fervor or the edge in her tone. Later it hit me that she believed I thought women can't ever actually manage to do it all, thereby denying the reality of her daughter's life. She was essentially shaking her fist under my nose, pointing out to me that her daughter was in fact doing what I supposedly said she couldn't do. From her perspective, every woman like her daughter who was managing to make a ca-reer and family work was somehow proving me wrong.

So what about the women who are making it to the top in many professions and do have families? Let's look at the facts: women make up 6 percent or so of Fortune 500 CEOs. Twenty percent of U.S. senators are now women. More broadly, roughly 15 percent of corporate "C-suite" (meaning top executive) posi-tions are now held by women, alongside about 20 percent of law firm partners, 24 percent of full-time tenured professors, and 21 percent of surgeons. The numbers from other professions are rather more dismal: 8 percent of the most senior bankers on ex-ecutive committees in investment banking firms (and half of those are heads of human resources or communications), 3 percent of hedge and private equity fund managers, 6 percent of mechanical engineers, and 8.5 percent of the world's billionaires.

These numbers may not be where we ultimately want them to be, but still, they show that it is possible for a significant num-ber of women to make it to the top today. The strong desire to follow in their footsteps explains the success of Facebook COO Sheryl Sandberg's *Lean In*. Sandberg herself has had an extraordi-nary career; she is genuinely motivated by the desire to see thou-sands more women make it to the top and millions rise higher than they are now. She had the courage to become an avatar for a revived feminism in an industry where blending in with the boys has been the key to survival. And she's given us a new vocabulary: Are you leaning in or leaning back?

I have seen some of the positive results of *Lean In* firsthand. A Princeton friend with whom I had worked in various capacities on campus ran into me at a summer barbecue and wondered aloud whether she should go for a top job, musing that perhaps it was her "lean-in moment." I encouraged her to go for it; she did and got it. Would she have put herself forward without *Lean In*? Perhaps—but certainly thinking about her decision in the wake of the book made a big difference. Even closer to home, three of my female employees at New America, where I am currently president and CEO, asked me for raises after reading *Lean In*. As one said, she knew she had to "lean in and do it." When I see examples like these, I smile and tip my hat to Sheryl.

For young women, what is most attractive about the "lean in" message is that it tells them that the fate of their careers and families is within their control. That is the kind of message Americans, particularly, love to hear; it's the kind of spirit that led our ancestors to believe they could come to this country, make their fortunes, and remake their lives. It's the message any young person coming out of school and looking forward to her life wants to believe. It's the reason that optimists do better in life than pessimists. It's a source of both hope and resilience.

The problem, though, is that it's often just not true. We often cannot control the fate of our career and family; insisting that we can obscures the deeper structures and forces that shape our lives and deflects attention from the larger changes that must be made. Plenty of women have leaned in for all they're worth but still run up against insuperable obstacles created by the combination of unpredictable life circumstances and the rigid inflexibilities of our workplaces, the lack of a public infrastructure of care, and cultural attitudes that devalue them the minute they step out, or even just lean back, from the workforce. Other women have decided that their life ambitions should include spending time with and caring for those they love while they can, even if it means deferring professional achievement for a while.

Sheryl Sandberg and I agree on many things. We both encourage women to speak up and take their place at the table; we both want to see many structural changes in the workplace. To some extent the difference between us is largely a matter of which side of the equation to emphasize—a difference that, on my side, at least, is a function of relative age. I would have written a very similar book to *Lean In* at forty-three, Sandberg's age when she published her book. My kids were very young and I had never met a work-life challenge that I could not surmount by working harder or hiring people to help out. By fifty-three, when I wrote my article, I found myself in a different place, one that gave me insight into the circumstances and choices facing the many women who have found that for whatever reason, leaning in simply isn't an option.

On another level, however, the differences between Sandberg and me are more fundamental. We have similar backgrounds in many ways, but our careers have led us on very different paths. Sandberg focuses on how young women can climb into the C-suite in a traditional male world of corporate hierarchies. I see that system itself as antiquated and broken. When law firms and corporations hemorrhage talented women who reject lockstep career paths and question promotion systems that elevate quantity of hours worked over the quality of the work itself, the problem is not with the *women*.

Sandberg argues that "women will tear down the external barriers [to women's advancement] once we achieve leadership roles. We will march into our bosses' offices and demand what we need. . . . Or better yet, we'll become bosses and make sure all women have what they need." I agree that having more women at the top will make a difference and have been fortunate enough to work for two great female bosses—Princeton president Shirley Tilghman and Secretary Clinton—who did indeed do everything they could to create conditions conducive to the advancement of women. On the other hand, almost every time I give a talk someone raises her hand and tells me she has a female boss who's much tougher and less accommodating of work-family conflicts than many male bosses in the office. It's human nature to absorb the values and practices of the system that we survived and succeeded in and to demand that others make it the same way. So it's not surprising that some of the women who made it to the top in a system that demanded they compete on exactly the same terms as the men who had full-time spouses at home may see less need for change than many of their male peers.

Lean In tells you how to survive and win in what is still fundamentally a man's world, while making what changes you can when you reach the top. That is important, but much broader social, political, and cultural change is also necessary. It cannot be achieved within the system, corporation by corporation, one progressive female CEO at a time.

We must rework our society so the expense and headache of childcare and eldercare don't sink women and their families, and we need to remodel our workplaces so that our employers no longer assume that a lawyer or businessperson can be available 24/7 to answer email or that a restaurant worker or clerk can be available 24/7 to staff a shift. This kind of change goes far beyond feminism. If we can adopt policies and practices that support and advance women at every level of our society, we will make things better for everybody.

Fear or Fate?

MY HUSBAND TAUGHT ME TO act like a man. Early on in our relationship, we were both young professors who frequently attended the same seminars and conferences. Andy, a powerful speaker and assertive debater, would listen to me make my arguments. Afterward, he'd point out all the ways in which I'd undercut myself: the typically feminine tropes of speech and posture that signal lack of confidence and thus diminish others' confidence in you.

The most common mistake I made was to start a comment on a speaker's presentation by saying something like "I'm not an expert, but I think . . ." In Andy's memorable phrase, "If you start out by telling everyone you don't know what you are talking about, why on earth should you expect them to listen to you?"

I have since spent years monitoring my own female students and mentees and passing on the lessons I learned: teaching them to be the first to raise their hand after a speech or lecture, because that way they are bound to be called on; to speak confidently and assertively; to look for the weak points in arguments and ask questions probing the basis for a particular assertion rather than immediately responding with a counterassertion that can be brushed off. But fear can always creep back in. Even after a decade of making my living as a professor, dean, and paid public speaker, when I found myself, at the age of fifty, sitting around the table at the State Department at Secretary Clinton's early morning meeting, surrounded by people who had served in government before or worked for her before, I felt that old self-doubt stirring once again. It took months before I could speak up as confidently and clearly as I normally do.

I can attest firsthand, then, that fear can be a major obstacle holding women back. Banishing those doubts, however, can promote a virtuous circle: you assume you can juggle work and family, you step forward, you succeed professionally, and then you're in a better position to ask for what you need and to make changes that could benefit others. As someone who was able to control my own time, as a tenured professor, by the age of thirty-five, and who made it to a leadership position as dean of Princeton's Woodrow Wilson School by the age of forty-two, I know that the faster you can become the boss, the easier it is to fit work and family together. And believing that you can be the boss is an important part of getting there.

What happens, though, when life intervenes? As much as we try to make our own luck, a concept that I suspect is uniquely American, how often have you heard that getting a particular job is a matter of "being in the right place at the right time"? When I came out of college, I had planned my entire career around the idea that I would work for a big New York law firm doing international practice, make myself indispensable to a partner who had served in government and was likely to go in again, and then follow him to Washington as a special assistant of some kind—a path that was well trodden in those days. Little did I imagine that I would discover that I really did not like big-firm law practice or that I would marry a man who at that point was firmly rooted in Boston.

These are relatively benign examples of the unexpected circumstance that the ancients called fate. Though you can't plan for them in advance, they can have very big and very real consequences later on. Suppose the twists and turns of your life include late marriage, no marriage, divorce, or infertility. A miserable economy, a boss who just doesn't recognize your merits no matter how confidently you assert them, a job and a spouse that are not in the same place, a child who needs you more than you expected or whom you want to be with more than you expected, parents who need care. Illness, unemployment, debt, disasters both natural and man-made.

A resilient system is one that can handle the unexpected and bounce back, that anticipates the possibility of many different paths to the same destination. Confidence and conviction are important elements of personal resilience. But even for those of us who are optimists, assuming that life will go your way is not a recipe for success. Build in the expectation of setbacks and unpredictable events; prepare and plan for them. That includes a realistic assessment of your own capabilities; if you need eight hours of sleep, surviving on five hours a night is not a sustainable life proposition. If you are not the world's most organized human being, then trying to run an office and a household at the same time is likely to be a prescription for great stress, not to mention dropped balls. If you are a creative person, cramming every minute of every day with activity, either family or professional, will burn you out quickly.

A key thing to anticipate is the possibility of a tipping point, a situation in which what was once a manageable and enjoyable work-family balance can no longer be sustained—regardless of ambition, confidence, or even an equal partner. In my own life, and in scores of conversations and letters with other women who started out with all the ambition in the world but suddenly found themselves in a place they never expected to be, the tipping point was always a highly individual matter, but it is a frequent enough occurrence to form a clear pattern.

Tipping Over

MANY WOMEN AND MEN MANAGE to juggle two careers and caregiving responsibilities for children and/or aging parents through remarkable organization and time management, often coupled with chronic sleep deprivation. Making it all fit, from baking school cupcakes at midnight to rising at five to get writing or reading done to prep for a meeting or a class, can be exhilarating even if exhausting. When I was a dean, I would often walk down the street to my office (one of the many conveniences that made my life possible) feeling like the luckiest woman in the world, with work I loved and a family I loved even more. My schedule was often so finely calibrated that a kid's ear infection could send a week's worth of appointments toppling into one another like dominoes, and I certainly faced days where I felt like I was letting both my family and my work down. But overall, the satisfactions outweighed the stress, and still do.

Even the most organized and most competent multitasker, however, can reach her limit. Something happens, and the carefully constructed balance suddenly tips. For many women that something is the birth of a second child. Law firms and businesses are well acquainted with the "second-child syndrome," where suddenly a talented woman who was making it work with one child can no longer work full-time or at the same job with two children. Other women manage two children and their careers until a child gets sick or starts having real trouble in or out of school; an aging parent needs care; a partner gets a promotion requiring him or her to travel extensively; a marriage comes apart; or a move requires leaving a vital family support system behind. Alternatively, the woman herself moves steadily up the career ladder until the next job on that ladder requires her to travel extensively, at which point her husband is unable or unwilling to fill the breach.

The tipping point for me was fairly extreme and probably predictable: working in a high-pressure job in another city with two teenagers back at home. Still, I didn't see it coming. As in the cliché about the straw that breaks the camel's back, it's never clear which straw it will be until it happens. Every family's situation is different; some women may be able to handle with ease situations that are too much for others; some women will never encounter a tipping point at all. What matters is that on the precarious seesaw between work and family it is always possible to put enough weight on one side to create a tipping point, most often leaving the woman as the caregiver and the man as the breadwinner.

Listen to a young woman I met while giving a speech to a group of employees at a highly respected bank. Linda, as I'll call her, wrote afterward to tell me she'd reached her tipping point a few days after my speech:

> I resigned yesterday from my job, a job which I love, for the betterment of my family unit. The short of it is that I had a "crisis" child care situation which forced my hand into making a really tough choice. My wonderful nanny made a not so wonderful decision resulting in her losing her license for 7 months. Although I struggled greatly with the challenge of trying to figure it all out on such a tight time frame—the reality was that I could not in good conscience put my 3 young boys (ages 6, 3 and 1) through their fourth nanny change in less than a year. Perhaps they could have been resilient . . . but I wasn't sure if I would be.
>
> Despite having as close to an ideal flexible work arrangement as possible, this temporary derailment caused me to panic, pause, write about 794 pros and cons lists, annoy the hell out of my husband as we had the endless conversation 12 times a day about "am I doing the right thing?," reach out to every woman I know in hopes of finding "the right answer" . . . and then ultimately coming to the realization that being the most stable force in my kids' life is more important

than my professional advancement for today. I can't lie and say that I'm not terrified that I made a totally irrational/short-sighted decision. I am giving up a good thing—and something that I worked hard to get. But I'm doing my best to embrace this leap of faith!

Linda had many different flexible options at work but still hit a tipping point. For many other women, the tipping point is triggered by workplace rigidity. They do not opt out of their jobs; they are shut out by the refusal of their bosses to make it possible for them to fit their family life and their work life together. In her book *Opting Out? Why Women Really Quit Careers and Head Home*, sociologist Pamela Stone calls this a "forced choice." "Denial of requests to work part-time, layoffs, or relocations," she writes, will push even the most ambitious woman out of the workforce.

Carey Goldberg, a talented journalist and author who had a promising career at *The New York Times*, describes her effort to convince the *Times* to allow her to give up her staff position and work on a contract three days a week. Nothing doing; it was either stay on staff or be a pure freelancer paid piece by piece at a very modest rate. So she quit, opting for a three-day-a-week job at *The Boston Globe*. "It hurt to leave the lofty *Times*, but I have not a single regret about that decision. I only regret that I had to make it, that I faced such a stark either-or," Goldberg wrote. Now she works half-time in a job-share arrangement at WBUR's CommonHealth blog.

The stories go on. A young lawyer I know from Virginia was offered a general counsel position, which she determined she could take but only if she could work from home one day a week to be with her two children. Her employer refused. Still another woman wrote,

I aspire to a C-level position, but have had to face up to the very real predicament of trying to climb the C-level ladder with a 2-year-old tugging at my heels. The dilemma is in no way the result of having a toddler: after all, executive men seem to enjoy increased promotions with every additional off-spring. It is the way work continues to be circumscribed as something that happens "in an office," and/or "between 8–6" that causes such conflict. I haven't yet been presented with a shred of reasonable justification for insisting my job requires me to be sitting in this fixed, 15 sq foot room, 20 miles from my home.

As one of my Twitter correspondents wrote in response to Goldberg's story, "There has to be something better than Lean In or Get Out."

Another way to frame the issue is that leaning in when you have significant caregiving responsibilities requires an intensive support structure at home and lots of flexibility at work. Think about simple physics. Imagine a tree leaning over the water or a ballerina on pointe. Lean in too far without a counterweight—an anchoring root system, the supporting arms of another dancer—and you will tip over.

Such a support system is even more essential for the 42 million women in America whom Maria Shriver describes as "women on the brink." These women are on the brink of poverty, "living one single incident—a doctor's bill, a late paycheck, or a broken-down car—away from economic ruin."

Tipping over for these women means that they can no longer care properly for their children—some 28 million—and other relatives who depend on them. They are often working two jobs already and suffering not from too little flexibility but too much, as many low-wage service jobs no longer have a guaranteed number of hours a week. They need reliable work at a decent wage that allows them to save for a rainy day; access to affordable, high-quality daycare and early-education programs; paid days off and family leave for the inevitable times that their children or other loved ones who depend on them are sick or in need; and recognition and respect for the care work they do.

HALF-TRUTH: "YOU CAN HAVE IT ALL IF YOU MARRY THE RIGHT PERSON"

A SECOND POPULAR AND POWERFUL message that many successful women drive home to their younger peers is that the most important career decision you're going to make is choosing the right life partner. You must be sure that he or she will be an equal partner at home so that you'll have an equal chance to take advantage of opportunities at work. Once again, this advice is true in many ways. But it's also not so simple.

I could never have had the career I have had without Andy, who has spent more time with our sons than I have, not only on homework, but also on baseball, music lessons, photography, card games, and more. When each of them had to bring in a foreign dish for his fourth-grade class dinner, Andy made his grandmother's Hungarian *palacsinta;* when our older son needed to memorize his lines for a lead role in a school play, he turned to Andy for help. As academics at wealthy and progressive universities, we were both entitled to maternity and paternity leave; we each took a semester off, sequentially, after each of our sons was born. That meant Andy quickly became proficient at baby care; he could change, dress, feed, burp, and soothe our sons just as well as I could. I travel much more than he does and always have; I could never have done that—or accepted the kinds of jobs that require such travel—without the assurance that a loving and competent parent would be at home.

So I certainly believe that marrying a man or woman who will step up to do what it takes to support your career is essential to fulfilling your professional ambitions and having a family at the same time. The problem is that "fifty-fifty" is just too pat. Life rarely works out that way. And it's much harder to be honest about what it really takes.

"Equal" Isn't So Easy

ALL THESE DISCUSSIONS OF CHOOSING your mate again suffer from the lovely illusion that we can control our lives. As hard as we try, we don't always make the best choices. The divorce rate, which for people in my age group is nearly half, speaks for itself. I was married at twenty-four and divorced at thirty. My ex-husband and I met right after college; we simply grew in different directions as we developed our professional identities. Because we didn't have children, our divorce didn't affect our career trajectories. But if we had had children, we would not have been able to head off to different cities to pursue our respective jobs in law and medicine, much less put in the fifteen-plus hours a day necessary, at least in my case, to get tenure.

So even if you think you're choosing well, you might find yourself single again at some point, often with children and an ex-spouse with whom you must now coordinate your life. Divorced parents who share custody often have more time on their own than when they were together because many couples now divide up the time each spends with their children. But when they have the children, they have far less flexibility to handle a work crisis or sudden trip. And the many divorced mothers who have full custody rather than joint custody are much more likely to be both much poorer than they were when they were married and to have no one with whom to share household chores and caregiving responsibilities.

Even couples who stay together often find they're quite different people in their thirties, forties, and fifties than they predicted they would be when they first married. At a conference in Colorado just a month after my article came out, a woman told me that she'd gone to Harvard Business School and that very few of her female classmates were where they had expected to be in their careers. They had all married men like themselves, who pledged to be equal partners over the life of the marriage. But when equality actually came down to a choice of his career advancement versus hers, he could not actually imagine slowing down and sacrificing his own ambitions.

She was speaking anecdotally, but the figures bear her out. A 2014 study of more than 25,000 Harvard Business School graduates—boomers, Gen Xers, and millennials—found that roughly half the women expected to "take primary responsibility for raising children," which means that they were essentially setting themselves up for carrying a double load while competing with male peers who have more time and energy to spend on work. What's more, the almost three-fourths of boomer women and two-thirds of Gen X women who did *not* expect to be the primary caregiver still ended up in that role. To give men credit, they now do much more housework than their fathers did— enough so that detergent commercials are now being pitched at men as well as women. On the whole, however, women still end up carrying much more of the domestic load.

"Equal" Often Isn't Enough

THE IDEALIZED IMAGE OF A fifty-fifty partnership—where you marry a man who is every bit as successful professionally as you are and shares domestic responsibilities equally—is a lot easier for young women to accept than a much more difficult truth: that many of the women who have made it to the top in business have an *unequal* division of domestic work. Most of the time, these highly successful women have a spouse who carries much more than half the load at home. But while many young women are happy to think about sharing dishes and diaper duties with their husbands, they are much less comfortable acknowledging that if they want to reach the top, their husbands may have to remain in the middle ranks to be able to offer the necessary support at home. They find it difficult to accept the idea that they might be more professionally successful than their husbands, even though the overwhelming majority of men in top jobs have less professionally successful wives.

This is the dirty little secret that women leaders who come together in places like *Fortune* magazine's annual Most Powerful Women Summit don't talk about: the necessity of a primary care-giver spouse. I have never seen a panel discussion titled, say, "Husbands at Home" or heard an interviewer ask a woman CEO about when her husband decided to subordinate his career to hers.

At one such *Fortune* conference, Marillyn Hewson, who was named CEO of Lockheed Martin in late 2012, talked about growing up in Kansas as one of five children raised by a widowed mother. She was inspirational, telling the audience that her mother had raised her to "believe she could be anything she wanted to be" if she just worked hard enough. In an interview in 2005 she sounded a similar note in offering advice to other corporate women: "Bottom line is, do your best and don't set limits on what you think you can do."

But to make it to the top of Lockheed, Hewson held eighteen different leadership roles in the company. On the day she was appointed, the head of a think tank specializing in defense issues who knew her observed: "A reason she's in this job is because she never turned down a promotion." Among the jobs she held along the way were senior positions in Lockheed's aeronautics and internal auditing divisions, requiring her to move around the country from Georgia to Texas to Maryland to New York. Overall, she moved eight times on her way to the C-suite.

Could it really be possible for someone on that career trajectory to be an equal caregiver with her husband? To divide up all the family responsibilities fifty-fifty? Hewson has two sons and a lot of money. But even assuming a great deal of paid help, moving a family requires establishing new relationships with schools, doctors, dentists, coaches, and countless providers of different kinds of after-school activities and lessons. And what of all the games and school events that need to be attended? The long evenings helping with increasingly difficult homework? And how likely is it that your spouse will be able to continue a steady career rise in eight different places not of his or her choosing?

Hewson's secret appears to be her husband, James, who "elected to focus on raising their two sons . . . during [her] rise at Lockheed." He got them through primary and secondary school; by the time Hewson was appointed CEO, both sons were in college. Accounts of Hewson's appointment are full of information about her professional rise and management style, but far less forthcoming about her domestic arrangements. Fair enough; we are all entitled to a measure of privacy with regard to our families. But given that she had children, her husband was as indispensable to her career success as her own drive and determination.

I respect and admire Marillyn Hewson, as I do any woman who makes it to the top job. But it is not enough to tell younger women that they need ambition and confidence, or even ambition, confidence, and a partner willing to share domestic duties. Women who plan to accept every promotion and move wherever the company wants them to go will need a spouse who supports them by taking on the full load, or at least the primary load, at home—exactly as male CEOs have always needed.

Unexpected Desire

EVEN IF YOU ARE COMPLETELY committed to your career, and even if you do have a spouse who is ready and willing to be a lead caregiver, you might still discover that the value you place on career success versus time with your family shifts as the years go by. In an interview with Hanna Rosin about my *Atlantic* article, she told me that she guessed the sentence "I *wanted* to go home" was probably the hardest sentence in the entire article to write. She was right. But though it was very difficult to admit publicly, I cannot choose other than I have chosen while my kids are still at home.

I'm certainly not alone.

Rebecca Hughes Parker, a former big-firm litigator and award-winning broadcast journalist in New York who now edits a legal publication, never stopped working even after having twins and then a third child. Her husband has stayed home with all three daughters as the "hands-on parent," allowing her, in her words, to "reverse the gender roles and be the 'father' who goes to work." Still, she writes in a blog post, even as a "power mom," her trajectory has not been as straightforward as she expected it to be when she came out of law school. She reflects on the extraordinary pull of her children, pointing out that even with a husband who was home full-time, she felt an intense physical need to be with her baby and to be more a part of her children's lives than big-firm litigation hours allowed.

Hughes Parker ultimately asked to reduce her hours by 20 percent and was greeted with the standard "Are you still serious about your career?" question, perhaps precisely *because* her mate was at home. After all, even though many men want to spend more time with their kids, men with wives at home rarely ask for reduced hours. Hughes Parker was and is deeply committed to her career but needed enough flexibility in her life to be with her toddler before work and make enough school events so that missing one was no big deal. She knows she definitely married the right man but discovered she still could not reverse roles completely.

Owning up to this desire feels like coming out of the closet. Abigail Pogrebin, a talented producer and writer, talks about "the ambivalence of motherhood and having a career." She was raised to embrace her career choices but was deeply surprised to discover the pull of her first child once she had him. She said she broke down crying on the tarmac when she was supposed to leave for a reporting trip to Africa; ultimately that pull led her to quit her full-time TV job, which involved a lot of travel, and scale back to writing. "Ambivalence" may seem like a funny term to describe having both a career and children, but it means being pulled in two directions at once. We are pulled not just by duty, but by desire.

HALF-TRUTH: "YOU CAN HAVE IT ALL
IF YOU SEQUENCE IT RIGHT"

WRITING ABOUT MARILLYN HEWSON'S ASCENSION to CEO of Lockheed Martin, think tank head Loren Thompson told a reporter at the *Washington Business Journal*: "If you turn down a promotion in these companies, you get left behind." That, in a nutshell, is why young women should be wary of the mantra "You can have it all; you just can't have it all at the same time."

In theory, it is perfectly possible to fit caring for those you love together even with a high-powered career. Lengthening life expectancies provide plenty of time for education, initiation into a profession, and quick progression up the ladder while work is your primary focus, a slower pace during caregiving years for kids or aging parents, and then a ramp-up into top leadership positions between the ages of fifty-five and seventy-five, or even, particularly for women, sixty and eighty. But we are not there yet. In practice, all too often Thompson's observation holds. Get off the leadership track, even for a short time, and you cannot get back on.

In the past few years, I've met a handful of inspirational women who have succeeded in starting legal careers later in life, whether in their forties or even their early fifties. But their number is dwarfed many times over by the number of women who start as associates in big law firms in their early thirties, put in the kind of performance that gets them on a partnership track, but then shift to part-time work after the birth of their first or more likely second child and take themselves out of the partnership competition for good. In a *New York Times* article about the dearth of female partners, Karen M. Lockwood, a former partner at Howrey LLP and currently the president and executive director of the National Institute for Trial Advocacy, used a term that was coined by Joan C. Williams: "the maternal wall."

Lockwood says the wall is "built on the unstated assumption among male partners that women who return to firms after having children will automatically be less willing to work hard or will be less capable than they were prior to that—resulting in less-choice assignments or less-senior postings."

The obvious answer is to make partner first and then have children. But that choice of sequence often simply isn't up to us.

Family Planning

As I've mentioned, I was first married at twenty-four and divorced at thirty. I remarried at thirty-five. Being single between thirty and thirty-five (those were still the old-fashioned days when it never occurred to me to have a child without a husband) meant that nothing stood in the way of my getting tenure at the University of Chicago Law School but determination and hard work. Andy and I were very much in love, but we were commuting between Cambridge and Chicago. That meant, in the two-week stints between visits, I could stay up and work whenever I needed to. And even on those wonderful weekends we had together, we were still two young academics both trying to get tenure, so we spent plenty of time hanging out laptop to laptop.

It honestly never occurred to me that we wouldn't be able to have children as soon as we started trying, which in our case was immediately after we got married in the fall of 1993. Edward was born three years later, when I was thirty-eight. After six months of trying on our own and eighteen months of various fertility treatments, he was conceived by in vitro fertilization (IVF). Those intervening two years were the worst period of my life. But we were lucky. We got pregnant on our first try with IVF; our second son was conceived naturally soon after we started trying, so by forty I had tenure and two biological sons. (Andy, however, who started teaching after I did and faced a much longer tenure track, was very worried that parenting two young children would make it much harder for him to get tenure.)

Many women of my generation and the generation just ahead of me were not so lucky. According to the American College of

Obstetricians and Gynecologists, the fecundity of women decreases "gradually but significantly" up until age thirty-two, then it starts really going downhill after thirty-seven. Statistically, IVF is also less successful in women as they age. In her book *Creating a Life*, published in 2002, Sylvia Ann Hewlett reported that 42 percent of the women she had interviewed in corporate jobs had not had children by age forty and that most deeply regretted it.

These statistics are why I and so many women like me counsel the younger women in their lives not to wait until their late thirties to try to get pregnant if they can possibly help it. After making this point at a late night pizza and beer discussion with some of my graduate students, one young woman pushed back, telling me that I was effectively advising her, a woman in her early thirties, to "drop out of graduate school and get pregnant." I said no, that actually being in school is a great time to get pregnant if your life circumstances allow, but of course I took her larger point, which was that I was advising her to make a choice I had not made, because my early thirties were a period when I needed to invest in my career.

Which brings us back to the conundrum of sequencing. It is so often simply not within our control, for marital, career, or fertility reasons—not to mention the general folly of assuming that your life will go as planned. Moreover, even when everything does work out, as it did in my case, having children in your late thirties or early forties means that they hit their teens in your mid-fifties. Just as you hit the peak years of your career, when leadership opportunities are most likely to come your way, you discover that in many ways it is even more important to be available as a parent to your teenagers as it was when they were very little.

That is why so many women of my generation have found themselves, in the prime of their careers, saying no to opportunities they once would have jumped at and hoping those chances come around again later. Many others who have decided to step back for a while, taking on consultant positions or part-time work that lets them spend more time with their children (or aging parents), are worrying about how long they can stay out before they lose the competitive edge they worked so hard to acquire.

Up or Out

EVEN IF YOU DO SUCCEED in having the family you want when you want, work is often unlikely to cooperate with your sequencing plan. The real world of current work practices still very much follows the tune of "up or out," of "if you turn down a promotion, you get left behind." I am reminded of a presentation I gave that was sponsored by a large oil company. At the reception afterward a number of women talked about the many great policies that management had put in place to make balancing work and family easier. One of the women who raised her hand said that she was working part-time after having her third child. She said that she had been grateful for the company's willingness to allow her to continue working in a way that made sense for her family. After hearing my presentation, however, she said that her take-away was that she realized that she still wanted to be an executive and was going to recommit herself to that goal.

What she was saying was that by taking advantage of these great policies, she had put herself on "the mommy track," the path of fewer hours and lower expectations. In other words, not the executive track. When she made her decision to slow down, she'd known and accepted that consequence, but now she had some questions. The mommy (or daddy) track is the opposite of the leadership track, but *why?* Working part-time or flexibly or even taking some time out and coming back will understandably put you on a slower track for promotion, but why should it take you *off* the track entirely? Because the deep assumption in the American workplace is that the fast track is the only track. Up or out.

In fact, thinking of careers as a single race in which everyone starts at the same point and competes over the same time period is a choice. It tilts the scales in favor of the workers who *can* compete that way, the ones who have no caregiving responsibilities or who have a full-time caregiver at home. It also means that as a society we lose massive amounts of talent. We lose the distance runners, the athletes with the endurance, patience, fortitude, and resilience to keep going over the long haul. We lose the runners who see a different path to the finish and are willing to take it, even if it is in uncharted territory. We lose the runners who have the temperament and perspective to allow them to see beyond the race.

WHOLE TRUTHS

Now let's look at some whole truths.

You can have it all if you are committed enough to your career . . . *and you are lucky enough never to hit a point where your carefully constructed balance between work and family topples over.*

You can have it all if you marry the right person . . . *who is willing to defer his or her career to yours; you stay married; and your own preferences regarding how much time you are willing to spend at work remain unchanged after you have children or find yourself caring for aging parents.*

You can have it all as long as you sequence it right . . . *as long as you succeed in having children when you planned to; you have an employer who both permits you to work part-time or on a flexible work schedule and still sees you as leadership material; or you take time out and then find a good job on a leadership track once you decide to get back in, regardless of your age.*

As I said at the outset of this chapter, the last thing I want to do is to discourage younger women from pursuing high-powered careers that will catapult them into leadership positions and thereby improve society as a whole. Without a hefty dose of realism, however, we will continue to lose talent as women are pushed off the leadership track after they have children and/or when they spend more time caring for aging parents or other relatives. We will also end up ignoring the reality of the one in three of the nation's women who live in poverty or on the brink of it and who are frequently pushed out of a job and into despair.

On a personal level, the trick is to balance encouragement with expectation. To be clear—to ourselves, our families, and our employers—that putting yourself forward is important at the right moment, but so is pushing back against rules, structures, attitudes, and assumptions that still support a straight-on career path and stigmatize any worker who deviates from it, deferring promotions and bigger jobs to be able to spend time with loved ones. To see the whole picture, not just the shining role models at the top, but the employees, every bit as talented and motivated, who were pushed or shut out of leadership opportunities as their lives took unexpected detours.

Telling whole truths and seeing the whole picture is the right place to start. But we can't do this alone. The men in our lives have their own mantras, serving up their own preferred version of the truth or simply the truths they grew up with. They too need to ask some hard questions.

2

HALF-TRUTHS ABOUT MEN

OVER THE PAST FIVE DECADES, FEMINISM HAS OPENED NEW DOORS of change through the process of questioning our assumptions about women, gender, and the language, categories, and stereotypes that we cling to. It is now time to start questioning our assumptions about men.

The three mantras that I examine here do not pop up nearly as often on the feminist radar as phrases like "You can have it all; you just can't have it all at the same time." But they are often pulled out as trump cards whenever discussions of women, work, and family arise. I have heard them often from men themselves, as well as from women who have absorbed these messages as the accepted order of things. The first one, "Men can't have it all either," immediately deflects attention away from what remains a genuine inequality between many men and many women. The second, "Children need their mother," has taken on the sanctity of mom and apple pie, at least in the United States. How on earth could you challenge that? And the third, "A man's job is to provide," goes all the way back to the Bible.

These statements are also half-truths. But determining what is true, or at least plausible, and what is a mass of sticky, biased belief—like the popcorn glued to the floor of the movie theater—starts the process of unpacking our certainties and convictions. We have to be able to see them clearly before we can begin to dislodge them.

HALF-TRUTH: "MEN CAN'T HAVE IT ALL EITHER"

IN THE LAST FEW YEARS, many people have criticized the entire idea of "having it all." Some criticism came from feminists who argued that Madison Avenue had created the construct of women having it all as a way of selling stressed-out working mothers a bill of goods—literally. Rebecca Traister at *Salon* proposed that we do away entirely with the phrase "having it all," pointing out that it is a frame that inevitably makes women seem selfish and piggish, no matter how much we try to explain that all we are asking for is a career and a family too, just like men have. It is also a phrase that strikes an ugly, unfeeling note at a time when millions of people are struggling to have enough to make ends meet.

To complicate matters further, many men are quick to claim that they don't have it all either. The most common point made is that while women who have careers and families can't pursue their careers as fully as they would like, men who have careers and families can't spend as much time with their families as they would like. That is a trade-off that many men feel they have no choice but to accept.

When I first started hearing men push back, my knee-jerk reaction was to be skeptical. Of course no one has it all, if by that we mean having everything you want and all at once. Still, the entire women's movement was premised on the idea that men in our society have a lot more of "it" than women do; that they have far greater opportunities to flourish both as professionals and in their family roles as sons, brothers, husbands, uncles, and fathers. Indeed, in many societies around the world women still struggle for their basic human rights: to be free from violence, fear, and want; to control their bodies; and to have equal legal status to travel, learn, and pursue their dreams.

Even in a developed, reasonably progressive country like the United States, most women still don't have what most men have. Lilly Ledbetter began work in a Goodyear tire plant in Alabama in 1979 and discovered twenty years later that she had been paid substantially less than her fellow male managers. "I'd known from the get-go that I'd have to work longer and smarter than the men in order to prove myself. But how in the world could I have been paid less all these years?" Looking at a slip of paper that an anonymous co-worker left in her mailbox listing her salary next to those of her male colleagues, she reflected: "I'd wanted so badly to win approval, and I had done so in the eyes of most of my co-workers, who valued my hard work and loyalty—and who gave it back to me. But how dumb I'd been to think that this would counter the hostility surrounding me. . . . Those numbers said loud and clear that it didn't matter how hard I'd worked, how much I'd wanted to succeed and do the right thing: I'd been born the wrong sex, and that was that." That was 1999; as of 2013, over a decade later, American women still earned only 82 percent of what men do for equal work.

So is the claim that "men can't have it all either" just a self-serving fiction? I continue to think that in many societies, including the United States, women are perfectly justified in wanting more of what many men do in fact have. Still, as I listened to men with an open mind, I began to understand the ways in which this view also expresses an important truth—but only a half-truth.

Men Who Try to Have It All May Have a Harder Time than Women

MANY MILLENNIAL MEN ARGUE THAT men and women increasingly want the same thing. A former State Department colleague whom I'll call Steve put it this way: many men in the workplace are "struggling with the work-life balance issue and are reluctant to speak up/rebel against the conventions regarding sacrifice and long hours." His experience has taught him that when men do speak up, they are penalized not only because of a perceived lack of commitment to their careers, but because "they are somehow not 'macho' enough and it works against them when it comes to promotions and career advancement."

This issue seems as stuck as the numbers of women at the top. Consider the experience of an employee at a public utility company who took three weeks off when his second child was born back in 1996. "Comments were made and my work wasn't being covered. . . . It made me feel like I wasn't a 'man' if I choose to stay home and take care of the kids. This same attitude manifests when I ask to take time off so I can take the kids to the doctor." Seventeen years later, in 2013, law professor Joan Williams wrote a piece entitled "The Daddy Dilemma" in which she summarized the conclusions of a host of academic studies: "Men face as many struggles when it comes to using flexible work policies—if not more—because child care, fairly or unfairly, is still seen as being a feminine role."

One of those studies found that men who requested a twelve-week leave to care for a child or elder were more likely to be demoted or downsized because they were seen as more feminine than other men. Another concluded that caregiving fathers had the highest rate of social mistreatment at work among men, chiefly because they suffered the highest rates of "masculinity harassment." Yet a third found that, while men and women valued workplace flexibility equally, men were less likely to seek a flexible schedule if they believed (as many did) that doing so would make them appear less masculine. Overall, the share of companies that offer paternity leave actually dropped 5 percentage points from 2010 to 2014, and 20 percent of companies that are supposed to provide unpaid leave via the Family and Medical Leave Act don't comply with the law when it comes to fathers who want time off. The annals of litigation tell similar stories. In one case, a management trainee was told straight out that he would be "cutting his own throat" if he took paternity leave.

So it's true that many men can reasonably say not only that they don't have it all either, but also that at least some of them pay an even higher price than women do when they try. In the West, at least, a woman who downshifts her professional ambitions for a while may experience an identity crisis when she can no longer define herself primarily in terms of her work, but she is unlikely to face a crisis of femininity.

The experience of many gay men underlines this point. Gauzy commercials featuring same-sex parents notwithstanding, gay men still face enormous social prejudice in their efforts to become parents and caregivers. This point was brought home to me in a blistering but justified letter in response to my *Atlantic* article from Scott Siegel, a former academic who now works for a start-up in San Francisco. He read me, as so many men did, as arguing that the pull of caregiving was felt only by women and indeed as saying that this pull is biological. That is much too strong a reading, but his response is still eye-opening. "You are probably not aware that your piece is being read by the gay community, especially those with children, as saying that 'Oh, well, I don't have those pressures because I'm not a woman—how DARE

HER!' EVERY type of caregiver, gay or straight, faces this difficulty. . . . To say that PRIMARILY WOMEN face the pressure to
'have it all' is itself sexist."

The intensity of his response is driven by his fear that I was
"giving ammunition to those groups who deny and wish to take
away those rights gays and gay families have fought for and received in the last 20 years." I would be deeply upset if my article
contributed to anti-gay discrimination of any kind. But the passion with which Siegel makes his point reminds us of how hard it
still is for gay men to be fully recognized as men—men who are
attracted to other men, but no less men for that. And as men, they
should have the same right to raise a family, to love and care for
children and each other, as any woman does.

Settling

THE THIRD VARIATION ON THE "Men can't have it all either" theme
was articulated on the *Atlantic* website, in a response to my article
by Andrew Cohen, a single father who describes himself as a
"work-at-home dad." He's modest: others describe him as one of
the nation's leading legal journalists, who works for *60 Minutes*
and CBS Radio News. But he describes his life in a way that most
working mothers I know would immediately recognize, the daily
dance of "work and parenting, parenting and work." He tries to
mesh his obligations to his son, and indeed still to his parents,
with the demands of his job: writing all day, overseeing homework and getting dinner on the table at night, while trying to
cram in the rest of life, from laundry to love, in between.

Cohen says that he doesn't know any man who "has it all, or
who says that he does, or who complains that he doesn't." When
he goes out with the guys, they talk about lots of things—work,
sports, women, and, yes, how they can be better parents to their

kids. But they don't talk about "having it all." Indeed, he thinks about his father, who never thought about having it all but rather about "having enough, simply being able to provide for his loved ones."

Does this mean that women really aim higher than men? Are they strivers rather than settlers? In the end, Andy Cohen is arguing just that. He is saying that women of my generation, at least, are simply asking for too much out of life, whereas men have learned to lower their expectations. Millennials too, in Cohen's view, possess a wisdom about their own limits and the limits of life and luck that their elders—meaning my generation—lack.

But hang on. Isn't reaching for the seemingly impossible an all-American tradition? The boys I grew up with were pushed to aim as high as possible. Now that women are striving for what many men had and still have—a high-powered career and a family too—it seems disingenuous to say that they simply want too much.

True and Not True

THE CLAIM THAT "MEN CAN'T have it all either" is complicated. On the one hand, it is important for women to see that many men, today and for decades past, have accepted what they understand to be a role requiring them to trade time at work for time with loved ones. A man may have a family and a high-powered career, but many men wish they were able to spend much more time with that family.

It is also true, of course, that individual men have made trade-offs at the expense of their careers. Perusing a biography of Colgate Darden, a former governor of Virginia and the namesake of the University of Virginia's business school, I was struck by Darden's explanation of his refusal to run for the Senate in 1946, notwithstanding strong public support for his candidacy, on the grounds that he would never see his family. Jim Steinberg, a deputy secretary of state, and Bill Lynn, a deputy secretary of defense, both stepped down from their jobs after two years in order to be available for their children too.

Still, let's not indulge in revisionist history, where we pretend that the trade-off between being a full-time caregiver and a full-time breadwinner was traditionally equal and both sexes would have been happy with more of what the other had. After all, Carl Friedan, Betty's husband, didn't write a book called *The Masculine Mystique* describing a "problem with no name" afflicting men. Men have not complained about being financially dependent, left in poverty when their wives ran off with younger male secretaries. Men have never been regarded as the weaker sex, less capable of reason or brilliance. Men have not had to fight for equal pay for equal work. And men still have far more control over the levers of power and influence in American society than women.

HALF-TRUTH: "CHILDREN NEED THEIR MOTHERS"

I SPEND A LOT OF time being driven back and forth to the train station to catch Amtrak to Washington or New Jersey Transit to New York. One of my favorite local taxi drivers, whom I'll call Steve, is a fount of stories and folk wisdom. He is a little older than I am, with three grown kids and a couple of grandkids. He's devoted both to his wife and to the memory of his own mother. He has very fixed ideas on what men and women are good at, and not so good at. And he tells me regularly, with the confidence born both of conviction and life experience, "Children need their mothers."

What he means is that mothers give children something special, something children cannot live without, something that fathers cannot supply. He means that mothering is distinct and different from fathering, that children cannot fully thrive without their mother's care. He means it as a compliment to mothers—that they provide a special and irreplaceable mother love. But I hear it as a statement of the natural order of things, a mantra that ends any discussion of genuinely equal parenting.

Of course children do need their mothers. And their fathers. And their grandparents, siblings, aunts, uncles, cousins, and close family friends who will follow them on Facebook and look out for them during the years when parental advice, or even conversation, suddenly becomes unendurable. "Children need their mothers" is true. But "Children need their mothers more than they need other loving adults in their lives" is false.

The one time children genuinely cannot do without their biological mothers is during pregnancy. Even surrogate and adopted babies need someone to gestate them. Particularly in the United States, we don't always recognize that enough. Along with Liberia and Papua New Guinea, we are one of the few countries that doesn't offer paid maternity leave. The unpaid leave we do offer only covers women who work for companies that have fifty or more employees and who have been at those companies for more than a year.

Even if you have an understanding employer who provides adequate leave, pregnancy can still throw you—and your career—for a loop. I remember, when I was teaching at Harvard Law School, one of my younger colleagues announced that she was planning to take a two-week maternity leave, much as Marissa Mayer did when she became CEO of Yahoo seven months into a pregnancy. In both cases I thought to myself, *I certainly hope everything goes smoothly, but clearly this is your first pregnancy!* What about an unexpected Cesarean section, as happened with my first son? Or other complications? My experience with our second son, who was born three weeks early, shows that even with the very best medical care available it is still possible to have medical problems that can land you in bed for nearly a month. Virtually every mother I know has a similar story about what she didn't expect when she was expecting.

All that said, after pregnancy, birth, and breast-feeding, nothing a mother does can't be done equally well by a father (and plenty of fathers bottle-feed breast milk to their babies). Yet the stereotypes and cultural expectations about mothers remain outsized when compared to the expectations about fathers, even as we try to challenge them. No one wrote a book called *Battle Hymn of the Tiger Father*. No one wrote a book called *Perfect Madness: Fatherhood in the Age of Anxiety* talking about the unrealistic expectations suddenly placed on fathers. No one developed a theory of good-enough fathering, telling dads they did not need to be perfect parents to create thriving children.

The Oscar-winning movie *Kramer vs. Kramer* addressed exactly this issue. The movie opens with Meryl Streep as a beautiful young mother sitting by the bedside of her six-year-old son, Billy, steeling herself to leave him and divorce his father, played by Dustin Hoffman. At the outset of the movie, Hoffman's character, a successful ad executive, is so preoccupied with work he doesn't know what grade his son is in. But over time as a single parent, Hoffman learns to be a fully engaged dad and takes a less stressful job. Streep's character returns after this evolution and after a nasty custody battle is awarded custody of Billy. Even though she abandoned him completely, the judge believes that the child is best raised by his mother. (Ultimately, Streep gives the child back to his dad, realizing that he's better off with Hoffman.)

Kramer vs. Kramer came out in 1979, more than thirty-five years ago. But astonishingly, in light of the tens of millions of divorces since and substantial changes in the custody laws, we are still clinging to and having to combat the deep assumption that a mother's love and care are somehow better and more essential than a father's, even when that father has time and energy that the mother does not.

And really, what are we to say to gay fathers, if it is only mothers who matter? Despite the fact that numerous studies have shown that children raised by gay parents are just as well-adjusted as children raised by straight parents, our culture hasn't caught up with these truths. Frank Ligtvoet, a gay dad, wrote a moving essay in *The New York Times* about his experience raising a daughter and a son with his partner. Ligtvoet's children were adopted in an open adoption, and their biological mother remains part of their lives and part of their birth narrative. Even so, when Ligtvoet is doing something like picking a sick child up from school, the world looks askance at him. "Every step we as a family take outside in public comes with a question from a stranger about the mother of the children: a motherless child seems unthinkable," Ligtvoet writes.

What children need above all is love, stability, stimulation, care, nurture, and consistency. Those are things that can come from an array of caregivers. Stability is key here, no matter what the parental arrangement is. A study from Ohio State showed that children from stable one-parent homes (homes where the caregiver was always single, from birth) fared as well on test scores as children from stable married homes. Conversely, a 2013 report from the Annie E. Casey Foundation demonstrates that the biggest barriers to a child's social, emotional, and physical well-being are rooted in poverty. It's much easier, though, for pundits to fall back on the crutch of long-held cultural norms—that children need their mothers—than it is to confront and attempt to solve the more serious, endemic issues facing children.

HALF-TRUTH: "A MAN'S JOB IS TO PROVIDE"

THE ORIGINS OF THE DEEPLY held assumption and conviction that it is "a man's job to provide" are actually biblical, from the New Testament. Saint Paul writes to Timothy, a young priest, that "if any provide not for his own, and specially for those of his own house, he hath denied the faith, and is worse than an infidel."

Understood as a command to take responsibility for those you love—those you either brought into the world or who cared for you in various ways—the injunction to provide is uncontroversial. Anyone who cares for anyone else is a provider. We provide love, food, clothing, shelter, nurture, education, solace, support, nursing, stimulation, and many other things for one another's benefit. In an industrial or post-industrial economy, some of us provide income, in the form of money coming in from the outside in return for labor or investment. Others of us convert that income into the necessities and luxuries of life. Without income, there is nothing to convert, but without that conversion, the income itself cannot sustain life.

Understood as a command to men only to provide income for the support of their households, however, Saint Paul's dictum has very different and much more negative implications. There are similar precepts in chapter 4 of the Quran: "Men are the protectors and maintainers of women, because Allah has given the one more [strength] than the other, and because they support them from their means." But why does "providing" or "supporting" mean money rather than care? The production of food rather than the preparation of it? The growing of flax rather than the spinning of it? The purchase of a car rather than the driving of it? The building of a house rather than the making of a home?

Still, the idea that men have to provide is taken literally and quite seriously. Though stay-at-home dads have received considerable media coverage of late, a mere 2 million men identified themselves as such in 2012. Only 8 percent of Americans say they believe that children are better off with dads at home, compared with more than half who say children are better off with a stay-at-home mom. Furthermore, when Pew Research asked the question "How important is it for a man to be able to support a family financially if he wants to get married?" almost two-thirds of respondents said very important. When asked the same question with a gender flip, only a third of Americans say it is very important for women to be able to support a family before she gets married.

These ingrained cultural assumptions, however, do not track with economic reality. The waves of globalization that hit us in the 1990s and 2000s created outsourcing opportunities that hit traditionally male factory jobs much harder than the traditionally female sectors of education and medicine. The resulting shift in economic power from men to women has prompted books like *The Richer Sex* and *The End of Men*. One simple statistic says it all: 40 percent of American women are the primary breadwinners in their families. That number includes single mothers, but it still tracks a major trend.

The even bigger story is the way in which economic trends in the United States since the 1980s have been hard on everyone outside of the educated elite. Most families with two adults have responded by sending Mom to work. Senator Elizabeth Warren and her daughter Amelia Warren Tyagi dubbed this development the "two-income trap." When their book of the same name came out in 2003—more than a decade ago—average mortgage expenses had risen seventy times faster than the average father's income. In the intervening years, fixed costs have risen further; wages have continued to stagnate or even decline; and in the post-recession universe, jobs are even more precarious, particularly for people without a college education. For all these families, it is equally the woman's job to provide, even if she does not necessarily frame it in those terms.

And despite the resistance to the idea of stay-at-home dads, a growing number of men say that they are committed to caregiving. Nearly 50 percent of millennial men say that being a good parent is one of the most important things in their lives, compared with 39 percent of Gen X men. In her book *The Richer Sex*, journalist Liza Mundy talks to many happy stay-at-home dads, like Danny Hawkins. His wife, Susan, is a senior VP with the Henry Ford Health System. Danny used to be in financial services, but he hated the long hours, so he stepped back to take care of the couple's two daughters. "I have told Susie several times that my job is to make her life easier. . . . And I like doing it," Hawkins said to Mundy. Though fewer companies are offering paternity leave, more men are taking advantage of whatever leave is available. According to Mundy in an article in *The Atlantic*, in the decade since the state of California started offering paid paternity leave, "the percentage of 'bonding leaves' claimed by men has risen from 18.7 in 2005 and 2006 to 31.3 in 2012 and 2013."

I would not counsel my teenage sons to make it their life plan to marry a successful woman any more than I would counsel a daughter to marry a successful man as her meal ticket. If things go sour—a lost job, a divorce—a person of either gender who leaves the labor force for a prolonged period of time is vulnerable. But neither would I tell them that it is their job to provide for their families in the sense of bringing in income. I tell them that it is a man's job to provide, and a woman's too. Both are responsible for providing the combination of income and nurture that allows those who depend on them to flourish.

3

HALF-TRUTHS IN THE WORKPLACE

Advice on how to achieve a sane work-life balance has become a cottage industry. Numerous books on the subject have been published within the past few years alone, many of which I've read with pleasure. But they are all aimed at workers, overwhelmingly women, who are presumed to have the responsibility of stretching the twenty-four hours in a day to cover an impossible and never-ending list of things to get done. Why not tackle this issue from a different angle? Perhaps the problem is not with women, but with *work*.

American workers all over the socioeconomic spectrum, from hotel housekeepers to surgeons, have stories about working twelve- to sixteen-hour days (often without overtime pay), experiencing anxiety attacks and constant exhaustion. Public health experts have begun talking about stress as an epidemic. Indeed, the United States is one of the only industrialized countries that does not require paid sick leave, time off during the week, or vacation days.

In 2014 alone, *Huffington Post* founder Arianna Huffington and *Washington Post* reporter Brigid Schulte each wrote a bestselling book about stressed-out American workers, another sign that we're desperate for solutions to our currently unsustainable pace of work. Desperate for solutions, but still trapped in a culture that values quantity over quality, assuming that he who works most works best. Or, less poetically, that he who takes time off is a wimp.

This underlying culture makes a mockery of so many purported work-life "fixes." They are never going to achieve real equality between men and women in the workplace, at the top or the bottom, no matter how hard employers try to make workplaces more family-friendly by adopting policies aimed at women. They will not work because they are at best half-measures based on half-truths.

The first half-truth is that the issue of work-life balance is a "women's problem." If we define it that way, then it is up to women to find or at least implement the solution. The second is that employers can make room for caregiving by offering flextime and part-time arrangements. While these policies certainly represent progress over rigid "all-in or get out" workplaces, they're not nearly enough for many workers with caregiving responsibilities. Third is our assumption that wanting "work-life balance"—or even just wanting a life outside of work—signals a lack of commitment to that work. That assumption reflects a mindset that promotes men with full-time wives and no lives.

Once again, a half-truth is just that—it's not wholly false. But it often obscures a bigger, deeper truth, something that we do not want or do not choose to face. Yet if we cannot even be honest about what the problem is and what it would actually take to fix it, we cannot possibly succeed.

It's time for some truth telling in the office.

HALF-TRUTH: "IT'S A WOMEN'S PROBLEM"

FLORIDA STATE SOCIOLOGIST IRENE PADAVIC, Harvard Business School professor Robin Ely, and Erin Reid from Boston University's Questrom School of Business were asked to conduct a detailed study of a midsized global consulting firm where top management thought they had a "women's problem." The firm had a paucity of women at the highest levels—just 10 percent of partners were women, compared with nearly 40 percent of female junior employees. The firm's brass assumed that their company was shedding women along the way because of work-family conflict on the part of workers who had to care for families, i.e., women. As one partner put it:

> What do I want people to worry about when they wake up first thing in the morning? For Business Development people, I want them to worry about business development. For project managers, I want them to worry about the project. Women are the Project Manager in the home, so it is hard for them to spend the necessary time, energy, and effort to be viewed here as senior leaders.

The plethora of women's leadership groups and support networks at companies across the United States all grow out of the same perception: the lack of women at the top is due to something women themselves are doing or not doing: a lack of ambition, the difficulty of juggling multiple roles at home and at work, or insufficient support from other women.

This depiction of the problem is half true, in that it is indeed a problem that is showing up much more among women than among men. But it is a problem that affects some women much more than others, and it is also a problem for a growing number of men. By thinking of it as a "women's problem" we are missing a much bigger truth.

It's Not a Women's Problem, It's a Care Problem . . .

THOUGH WOMEN HAVE MADE UNPRECEDENTED progress in the workforce over the past forty years, what doesn't always come through in the statistics is the enormous and enduring discrepancy between women who have caregiving responsibilities and those who do not. As I noted in the last chapter, in 2013 women earned 82 cents on a man's dollar. But hidden within that average is a stark difference. Single women without children made 96 cents on the male dollar. Married mothers? They make 76 cents. Indeed, many writers have pointed out that motherhood is now a greater predictor of wage inequality than gender is.

This pattern is even clearer if we look through the lens of age. Girls and young women are surpassing boys in high school, college, and many graduate schools and often draw higher salaries during their early years in the workforce. Overall, women between the ages of twenty-five and thirty-four now make 93 percent of what their male contemporaries do. But those gains dissipate once they become mothers.

To the majority of men and women who think of caregiving as a woman's responsibility, redefining the "women's problem" as a "care problem" may seem redundant. Women are indeed the considerable majority of caregivers in our society. Among parents, mothers spend roughly twice as much time as fathers on childcare. And the typical caregiver of an elderly relative is a woman in her forties who provides twenty hours a week of care to her mother.

Women also face much more cultural pressure to *be* caregivers, and perfect ones at that, than men do. Even in the twenty-first century, America looks askance at any woman who doesn't appear to put her children's care above her professional life. Texas politician Wendy Davis has experienced extreme scrutiny about how and where she raised her children. Her decision to leave them with her then-husband in Texas while she went to Harvard Law School has been held up as an example of her selfishness. In general, men aren't scrutinized in the same way. As a Democratic pollster pointed out in a *New York Times* article about Davis, Rahm Emanuel left his young children behind in Washington while he was running for mayor of Chicago and no one ever said two words about it.

A physician who had two kids during her medical training wrote to me and said she feels like motherhood is the hardest thing she's ever done, in part because of the guilt that comes with it. "There are pressures from many many different sides—for being a 'perfect' mother (from nursing exclusively to making my kids' baby food from scratch!), to being a perfect doctor (well read on the latest studies, engaging in meaningful research, publishing studies). I started my first year of fellowship with a 9-week-old newborn," she wrote to me after my article was published in *The Atlantic*. "I felt guilty for not being a good-enough mom while I was working 80 hours a week and taking overnight calls, and I felt guilty that I wasn't giving 100% to my job." She eventually decided to work part-time so that she could be there to put her kids to bed every night.

When I gave a talk on work and family to a group of young Hispanic men and women who had won internships and fellowships in Washington, a young woman in the audience raised her hand and talked about the way in which her family and community judged mothers, criticizing those who were not home for their children. How, she asked, could she navigate those expectations and still pursue her career? Political strategist Maria Cardona, who was sharing the podium with me and has been an important role model in the Hispanic community, suggested that perhaps she could rely on other women in her extended family to be caregivers. None of us challenged the premise of her question, which was that it is up to women to provide care.

The good news, however, is that the care problem is slowly but steadily becoming a men's problem too. A Wharton School study comparing expectations and attitudes between the class of 1992 and 2012 found that young women today are more likely to anticipate the stress of fitting together work and family than they were twenty years ago. Also noteworthy, however, is that 43 percent of the *men* either agree or strongly agree that their pursuit of a demanding career "will make it difficult . . . to be an attentive spouse/partner," up from 33 percent in 1992. A 2014 study of more than 6,500 Harvard Business School grads over the past few decades also found a significant shift in male attitudes. It showed that a third of male millennial HBS grads expect to split childcare responsibilities fifty-fifty with their partners; that's compared with 22 percent of Gen X men and 16 percent of boomer men.

Think about it. Almost a third to a half of the men in two highly competitive business schools, schools that attract a disproportionate number of alpha males in the first place, expect that family life will have a significant impact on their future success and personal lives. A venture capitalist friend of mine who teaches at Stanford Graduate School of Business reports a similar shift, saying that the attitudes of the young men he teaches have changed remarkably.

In an article for *The New Republic*, Marc Tracy, a twenty-nine-year-old writer, notes that some men his age have begun to have the same kind of full-throated conversation about work-life balance as their female counterparts:

Most men stress over the next step in their professions, with the attitude that if they happen to fall in love and settle down, well, that's great, too. But recently, in many cases inspired by the women in our lives and the conversation they are having among themselves, we have begun to question whether our most basic priorities aren't out of whack, and to wonder whether, for reasons both social and surprisingly biological, we shouldn't be as "ambitious" to have children as we are to land the next great job. Plus, having had children, many of us hope to play a more active role in their upbringing than has typically been expected of fathers. Many of us were lucky to have mothers who, whatever other ambitions and accomplishments they had, clearly took great joy in raising us; some of us were even lucky enough to have similar fathers. Do we want it "all"? Who knows (or cares). But we want that.

A 2013 Pew Research study on modern parenting fills in the statistics: almost as many fathers as mothers bemoan the stress of trying to juggle work and family. Fifty percent of fathers and 56 percent of mothers with children under eighteen at home said that they find it difficult "to balance the responsibilities of [their] job with the responsibilities of [their] family." And an almost equal number of fathers and mothers agreed with the statement "I would prefer to be at home raising my children, but I need to work because we need the income."

In short, both women and men who experience the dual tug of care and career and as a result must make compromises at work pay a price. Redefining the women's problem as a care problem thus broadens our lens and allows us to focus much more precisely on the real issue: the undervaluing of care, no matter who does it.

. . . and a Company Problem

IT'S EASY FOR EMPLOYERS TO marginalize an issue if they label it a "women's problem." A women's problem is an individual issue, not a company-wide dilemma. But again, suppose the problem is not with the woman but with the workplace. Or more precisely, with a workplace designed for what Joan Williams called an "ideal worker." The ideal worker is "the face-time warrior, the first one in in the morning and the last to leave at night. He is rarely sick. Never takes vacation, or brings work along if he does. The ideal worker can jump on a plane whenever the boss asks because someone else is responsible for getting the kids off to school or attending the preschool play." Fifteen years after Williams coined the term, the ideal worker must now also contend with a globalized workplace where someone is always awake and electronic devices ensure that someone can always reach you.

Recall the research undertaken by Professors Padavic, Ely, and Reid at the consulting firm. After careful study, they found that women and men at the firm had equal levels of distress over work-family conflicts and that equal percentages of men *and* women had left the firm in the past three years because they were being asked to work long hours. The firm's key HR problem was not gender, as management believed, but rather a culture of overwork.

The firm's leadership simply refused to accept these findings. They didn't want to be told that they needed to overhaul their entire organizational philosophy or that they were overpromising to clients and overdelivering (for example, making hundred-slide decks that the client couldn't even use). That would require a lot of effort and soul-searching.

What the leaders wanted to be told was that the firm's problem was work-family conflict for women, a narrative that would not require them to make changes in anything *they* were doing or feeling. As Padavic, Ely, and Reid wryly conclude, their attitude required a "rejection [of evidence] on the part of evidence-driven analysts."

Debora Spar, president of Barnard College and author of *Wonder Women*, echoes these conclusions. "'Fixing the women's problem,'" she writes, "is not about fixing the women, or yanking them onto committees, or placating them with yet another networking retreat. It's about fixing the organization—recognizing a diversity of skills and attributes, measuring them in a concrete way, and rewarding people accordingly."

Journalists and media companies are just as guilty of perpetuating the myth of the "women's problem." Issues of work-life balance are discussed at *The New York Times* under the rubric *Motherlode*. Other websites like *Slate* and *Huffington Post* also house smart and worthwhile discussions of work and family in old-fashioned women's sections. If you look at any large business conference, it's the same story: work and family will be framed as a women's issue, never as a mainstream issue. As one of my friends wrote to me,

> I am beyond tired of these critical issues—about work culture, about gender equity, about implicit bias, about how constrained many of the "choices" for both men and women are, about the lack of meaningful family policy, about the way we live, really—always defined through the lens of the harried working mother.

A better lens is that of the harried caregiver, male or female. Best of all would be the lens of the failure of modern American companies to adapt to the realities of modern American life, insisting instead that workers turn themselves inside out to conform to outdated twentieth-century ideas of when and where work should get done.

HALF-TRUTH: "FLEXIBILITY IS THE SOLUTION"

IF YOU ARE A YOUNG woman interviewing with a company, law firm, bank, or university that sees itself as a progressive institution and wants to recruit you, you are likely to be told about their "family-friendly policies." (If you are a young man in exactly the same situation, you are not.) Twenty percent of U.S. companies now offer paid maternity leave ranging from two to twelve weeks; 36 percent allow employees to work part-time for a while without losing their position in the company; some allow them to work from home part of the time on a regular basis; a few let them opt out of the workforce for a while and then still welcome them back in a position that reflects their previous experience.

These policies reflect genuine progress by the women's movement; those of us who have been able to take advantage of them have benefited in many ways that the majority of women have not. My two years working on the inflexible schedule of the State Department—even for a boss I loved and with the understanding that the world certainly would not wait on me—brought home the indispensability of having enough control over your own time to fit your work and your life together. In the academic world, I had that kind of flexibility. Indeed, one of the best reasons to strive to be the boss, if you can do it either before you have caregiving responsibilities or even during, is the much greater latitude you have to make sure meetings and work are in sync with your schedule rather than someone else's.

Real flexibility—the kind that gives you at least a measure of control over when and how you work in a week, a month, a year, and over the course of a career—is a critical part of the solution to the problem of how to fit work and care together. So why then is it only a half-truth? In most workplaces, flex policies—which range from telecommuting and variable workday schedules to more radical policies like part-time jobs, job sharing, prolonged sabbaticals, or shortened workweeks—exist largely on paper. It is often exceedingly difficult, if not impossible, for employees to avail themselves of them. Indeed, reading through the various studies on this point reminds me of reading through the constitutions of countries behind the Iron Curtain in the former Soviet Union and in dictatorships around the world: they all guaranteed a full panoply of rights and liberties, but only for show.

The HR department may roll out flex policies, but if you have an old-school manager, someone who came up never seeing his or her family, you are likely to face what academics drily call an "implementation gap." In other words, some managers simply refuse to let their employees take advantage of policies on the books, which explains why the National Study of Employers finds a virtual chasm between the percentage of companies that allow *some* workers to work at home occasionally (67 percent) and the percentage of companies that allow *all or most* workers to work at home occasionally (8 percent). The managers who resist change like the workplace culture the way it is—based on presence, and hence control, more than on performance. In the words of one human resources manager: when some managers "can't get someone right there at that particular moment it is actually an uneasy [feeling] for them."

Even when firms mean what they say and managers support flex policies, employees often don't ask. And for good reason. In a work culture in which commitment to your career is supposed to mean you never think about or do anything else, asking for flexibility to fit your work and your life together is tantamount to declaring that you do not care as much about your job as your co-workers do. Dame Fiona Woolf, a British solicitor and former lord mayor of London, puts it succinctly: "Girls don't ask for [flexible work] because they think it's career suicide."

Flexibility Stigma

IN 2013, THE *Journal of Social Issues* published a special issue on "flexibility stigma." It included several studies showing that workers who take advantage of company policies specifically designed to let them adjust their schedules to accommodate caregiving responsibilities may still receive wage penalties, lower performance evaluations, and fewer promotions.

A young woman who wrote to me, Kathryn Beaumont Murphy, was already a mother when she became a junior associate— a rarity at big law firms. She had a generous maternity leave and took advantage of their flextime policy when she returned after having her second child. She was allowed to work "part-time" for six months after her maternity leave ended, though it was still forty hours a week. "At the end of that six-month period," Murphy says, "I was told by the all-male leadership of my department that I could not continue on a flexible schedule as it would hurt my professional growth." She ended up leaving the firm entirely for a less prestigious job that pays much less, but where she has more control over her schedule. Her children are now five and eight, and after her experience she now believes that "flexibility is as valuable as compensation."

If anything, men who try to take advantage of flexible policies have it even worse. Joan Blades and Nanette Fondas, co-authors of *The Custom-Fit Workplace*, give the example of a law firm associate named Carlos who tried to arrange for paternity leave and was told that his company's parental leave policy was really meant just for women. But even if his firm had said yes, it's likely that he then would have paid an even bigger price in terms of his chances for advancement and overall mistreatment than his female colleagues did.

A Catalyst study showing that men and women tend to use flexibility policies differently underlines the dangers that men perceive. The men and women in their study were equally likely to use a variety of flextime arrangements, from flexible arrival and departure times to compressing work in various ways across the week. But women were 10 percent more likely than men to work from home and men were almost twice as likely as women to say that they had never telecommuted over the course of their careers. Patterns like these show that men are aware that if a certain kind of flexibility means a lot less face time at the office, they won't run the risk of being penalized for taking advantage of it.

To be stigmatized means to be singled out, shamed, and discriminated against for some trait or failing. Stigma based on race, creed, gender, or sexual orientation is sharply and explicitly disapproved of in contemporary American society. Why should stigma based on taking advantage of company policy to care for loved ones be any different? Workers who work from home or even take time off do not lose IQ points. Their choice to put family alongside or even ahead of career advancement does not necessarily affect the quality of their work, even if it reduces the quantity.

However effective flexibility policies may seem in theory, flexibility cannot be the solution to work-life issues as long as it is stigmatized. The question that young people should be asking their employers is not what kinds of family-friendly policies a particular firm has. Instead, they should ask, "How many employees take advantage of these policies? How many men? And how many women and men who have worked flexibly have advanced to top positions in the firm?"

DANGER: When Flexible Means Disposable

THUS FAR, I'VE BEEN WRITING primarily about the white-collar world. Yet as with most things in the workplace, even the limited flexibility that white-collar workers take for granted doesn't exist at all for low-income hourly workers. More than 70 percent of low-wage workers in the United States do not get paid sick days, which means that they risk losing their jobs when a childcare or health issue arises. In fact, nearly one-quarter of adults in the United States have been fired or threatened with job loss for taking time off to recover from illness or care for a sick loved one.

Consider the case of Rhiannon Broschat, who was fired from her job at Whole Foods during the frigid winter of 2014 because Chicago schools were closed due to inclement weather. Broschat, who is also a student at Northeastern Illinois University in Chicago, called her mother to see if she could watch her son, but her mother had to work too. Then she called several friends to babysit, but they too had to work. Broschat couldn't swap shifts with a co-worker, because at the time, Whole Foods policy required workers to swap shifts forty-eight hours in advance. She had no way out. Broschat's story—she is now a senior at Northeastern Illinois—is so emblematic of how low-wage women struggle to get childcare that she spoke on a panel called "Why Women's Economic Security Matters for All," with Hillary Clinton, Representative Nancy Pelosi, Senator Kirsten Gillibrand, and Representative Rosa DeLauro in September 2014.

Schedules that are too rigid to accommodate family needs on the one hand are often too flexible on the other. Many companies have begun to manufacture goods on flexible schedules keyed to changing demand in real time, rather than predicted demand. On the consumer side, they also now track customer flow more carefully and ask employees to adjust their schedules accordingly. In both cases, the ebb and flow of employee hours tracks the ebb and flow of customers and their desires. Walmart, Jamba Juice, Pier 1, Aeropostale, Target, and Abercrombie & Fitch are among the companies that employ a just-in-time workforce.

University of Chicago social services professor Susan J. Lambert points out that sales associates and restaurant servers only learn about their weekly schedules a few days in advance, and those schedules are always in flux. They may work seven hours one week and thirty-two the next. "Hotel housekeepers might work Tuesday, Wednesday and Friday one week, and then Sunday, Thursday and Saturday the following week," she says.

This kind of flexibility translates into radical unpredictability, which is a nightmare for caregivers. High-income lawyers, bankers, or consultants who work at the whim of a client's demand experience such stress all the time but typically buy their way out of it by having full-time or live-in childcare. The majority of workers without that luxury must face the drama of having to find child- or eldercare on a moment's notice, week after week. Workers who live with extended families can sometimes manage, but they are also the most likely to have eldercare as well as childcare responsibilities.

New York Times reporter Jodi Kantor brought this experience home to millions of readers in August 2014 with her heartbreaking front-page story about twenty-two-year-old Starbucks barista and single mom Jannette Navarro. Thanks to scheduling software, which allows chains to use customer data to inform its day-to-day staffing, Navarro rarely knew her schedule more than three days before the start of the workweek. This wrought havoc on her ability to find consistent childcare for her four-year-old son, which in turn put immense strain on her familial and romantic relationships. Her aunt became frustrated with having to pick up last-minute babysitting duties due to Navarro's erratic schedule; her boyfriend broke up with her because she was too worn out after work to keep her promises to him. She and her son lost two homes within six months, and her schedule—which some weeks required her to close the store one night at eleven P.M. and be back the next morning to open it up again at four A.M. the next day—left her so sleep-deprived she napped on the sidewalk outside the store.

The day after Kantor's article ran in the *Times*, Starbucks executives vowed to revise the scheduling software for their 130,000 employees, giving local managers more discretion and preventing employees from having to close up shop one night and then open it back up again in the predawn hours the next day. But individual fixes like this aren't a cure for the larger problems that retail and hourly workers all over the country have to deal with every day.

For millions of American workers, then, flexibility is not the solution but the problem. Women and men at the top cannot advocate for more flexibility without insisting that these policies be implemented in ways that help workers rather than hurt them. The kind of flexibility we need is about making room for care in all our lives, not an additional excuse to stop caring about the human impact of our policies.

HALF-TRUTH: "HE WHO WORKS LONGEST WORKS BEST"

"TIME MACHO," AS I LIKE to call it, is the relentless competition to work harder, stay later, pull more all-nighters, travel around the world and bill the extra hours the international dateline affords you. One of the paragons of time macho was Ronald Reagan's ferociously competitive budget director Dick Darman. According to one story, "Mr. Darman sometimes managed to convey the impression that he was the last one working in the Reagan White House by leaving his suit coat on his chair and his office light burning after he left for home." (Darman claimed that it was just easier to leave his suit jacket in the office so he could put it on again in the morning, but his record of successful bureaucratic warfare suggests otherwise.)

In my younger years, I was an active participant in this game. Gene Sperling, who rose to become director of the National Economic Council under President Obama, was a legendary workaholic. I used to meet him at two A.M. at the vending machines in the tunnels at Harvard Law School when we were both staying up all night working on cases for different professors. And indeed, when my parents came to visit for my law school graduation, they wanted to see the big armchair in my professor's office where, I joked, I had spent more nights than in my own bed.

My patterns continued when I worked for a big New York law firm in the summer. But even as I prided myself on my ability to stay at my desk round the clock, I was uncomfortably aware that one of my close friends who was a fellow associate with me always managed to leave by six or seven P.M. and did just as much work as I did. She was simply far more efficient, spending less time procrastinating, reading the paper, talking with the guys down the hall. She later made partner at a top New York firm and explained to me that when she saw a pile of work on her desk she immediately thought about what was the most efficient way to get it all done: what she could delegate to others and what she had to do herself. I was reminded of her work habits in the fall of 2014 when I heard Virginia Rometty, the first woman CEO of IBM, explain that the key to her efficiency was doing work "that only I can do" while leaving to others all the work that could be done by someone else.

That was the first inkling that perhaps my habits were evidence not of dedication but of inefficiency. My suspicions grew shortly after I turned forty. With an infant and a toddler at home, a full load of courses to teach, research to be done, and articles to be written constantly hanging over my head, I routinely tried to get by on five to six hours of sleep, which left me short-tempered and with a constant blurry feeling that Andy used to describe as "skin-crawlingly tired." I would call meetings with my research assistant at nine or ten P.M. at my house after the kids were in bed and not even be able to remember what it was we were supposed to be working on. One day I decided I had had enough, that life was too short to go through it in a haze of fatigue. I quickly discovered that when in fact I let myself get seven or eight hours of sleep I was happier, pleasanter, and unquestionably more productive.

That is the revelation that inspired Arianna Huffington's book *Thrive*, where she describes literally collapsing from exhaustion and cutting her eye and breaking her cheekbone as she fell. "I was lying on the floor of my home office in a pool of blood," Huffington writes, when she finally had a moment of clarity. Since then she has become a self-proclaimed "sleep evangelist," urging women and men alike to "sleep their way to the top!" She reports that more than 30 percent of people in the United States are not getting enough sleep. The cost of that massive sleeplessness is reduced cognitive functioning and lower levels of emotional intelligence, empathy, and impulse control.

Let's be clear. Many jobs have crises or deadlines where round-the-clock presence really is necessary to get the job done, where being there and doing your best really does matter more than some abstract measure of performance. I have had plenty of times in my life when I needed people working for me who would be willing to go the extra mile and do whatever it took to get the job done, including staying up all night. When I was in the State Department and was responsible for a massive review laying out a strategy for reorganization and reform, I and a team of six Policy Planning staff members essentially worked around the clock for the better part of a month to get it across the finish line. Secretary Clinton wanted it by December 15, and given the slow and obstacle-ridden interagency approvals process, as well as the inherent difficulty of getting something done when many people with differing views had to sign off on it, that is just what it took.

I also counsel many of my students and mentees that they should divide their work lives into those phases when they *can* travel anywhere, anytime, and work long hours and those when they will not be able to, either because of caregiving responsibilities or because they want to slow down and do other things that are important to them. Working really hard for something and someone you believe in is exhilarating and often necessary. But it can and should be punctuated with periods where you take far better care of yourself. Under normal circumstances, valuing face time over results—measured by the quality and promptness of work that actually needs to get done—is just bad management.

Less Can Be More

DURING THE 2014 SUPER BOWL, Cadillac ran an ad that was meant to be a celebration of American workaholism. It showed a clean-cut fifty-something white man with blazing blue eyes walking and talking his way through his mansion while extolling the virtues of the American work ethic. "Other countries, they work, they stroll home, they stop by the café, they take August off. *Off.* Why aren't you like that? Why aren't we like that? Because we're crazy, driven, hardworking believers," says the guy, who looks like a cartoon version of a one-percenter, to the camera. The moral of the ad: If you just work hard enough, avoiding vacation and "creating your own luck," anything, including the ownership of a $75,000 car, is possible.

The ad drove me crazy. The man was so smug and so completely out of touch with what I consider to be the real values that Americans have traditionally proclaimed and tried to pass down to their children. Yes, Europeans and others often criticize American culture for being materialistic, but when Thomas Jefferson described humankind's "unalienable rights" in the Declaration of Independence, he took English Enlightenment philosopher John Locke's "life, liberty, and estate" and substituted "life, liberty, and the pursuit of happiness." And as the behavioral psychologists tell us, happiness is more likely to be found in the pleasures of human connection and experience—a good meal, a play or movie or sporting event, a bouquet of flowers or a bottle of champagne—than it is in an endless catalogue of possessions.

I wasn't alone in my reaction. One reporter wrote, "You know what really needs attention? What working like crazy and taking no time off really gets us[?]" It gets Americans to the grave earlier, it's made us more anxious than people in other developed countries, and it's created a group of people more disengaged from their jobs than in countries with more leisure time.

In the end, it was *New Yorker* writer Jeffrey Toobin who made the most damning argument against the commercial. As we were talking about it, he pointed out that Cadillac was disparaging the vacation-loving Europeans in an effort to sell luxury cars to a wealthy U.S. audience who prefer *German* BMWs and Mercedes. Last I checked, German workers get a mandated minimum twenty days of vacation every year.

It's that simple. German workers work at least two weeks a year less than American workers do and yet produce better cars. Perhaps that is because German managers still subscribe to the empirical findings that led Henry Ford to establish an eight-hour workday in 1914. When Ford looked at in-house research, he realized that manual laborers were finished after eight hours of work a day. After he cut hours, errors went down, and productivity, employee satisfaction, and company profits went up.

We actually have a growing body of data in support of the proposition that working less means working better. According to much more recent research, people who work principally with their brains rather than their hands have an even shorter amount of real daily productivity than manual laborers. Microsoft employees, for instance, reported that they put in only twenty-eight productive hours in a forty-five-hour workweek—a little less than six hours a day. Futurist Sara Robinson found the same thing: knowledge workers have fewer than eight hours a day of hard mental labor in them before they start making mistakes.

This relationship between working better and working less holds particularly true in any job requiring creativity, the wellspring of innovation. Experts on creativity emphasize the value of nonlinear thinking and cultivated randomness, from long walks to looking at your environment in ways you never have before. Making time for play, as well as designated downtime, has also been found to boost creativity. Experts suggest we should change the rhythm of our workdays to include periods in which we are simply letting our minds run wherever they want to go. Without play, we might never be able to make the unexpected connections that are the essence of insight.

Understanding this relationship between time on and time off also requires us to rethink leisure. Timothy Keller, a Christian theologian, laments the Western obsession with work as a cultural phenomenon. Americans think about leisure as merely "work stoppage for bodily repair" rather than a time to "simply contemplate and enjoy the world."

The Declaration of Independence notwithstanding, the United States comes fifteenth in the *World Happiness Report*, an index published annually by three distinguished economists that measures happiness as both an emotional state and a measure of life satisfaction across the globe. Switzerland came in first in 2015, but Denmark took the top spot in 2013 and 2014 and came in third in 2015. Observing this phenomenon, Brigid Schulte set out to discover the secret of Danish happiness and found it in the concept of *hygge*, which essentially means being and thriving in the moment.

After Schulte's book *Overwhelmed* came out, New America sponsored an evening reception and panel in our New York offices. We invited the Danish consul general, thinking he could expand on why the Danes are so happy. He said, very simply, that the Danes think people who work all the time are boring. They don't have time to read a book, see a play, or engage in athletic or charitable activities. So why would you want to have a conversation or spend time with them?

Risky Business

FOCUSING ON HOW LONG YOU are at work rather than what you actually get done is part of a larger set of assumptions about what it takes to do a good job when you are on the job. Bankers and consultants describe their work, often with a note of pride, as "24/7," meaning that they are "always on." And ambitious professionals of all varieties are increasingly tethered to their iPhones, responding to emails at all hours of the day or night. We have just seen that switching off will mean you will shine that much brighter when you turn back on, but the 24/7 mantra is also meant to capture an attitude of complete and total devotion to the task at hand.

In April 2013, women in the financial world got a rude example of the discrimination they face due to this issue. Hedge fund billionaire Paul Tudor Jones told a symposium at the University of Virginia's McIntire School of Commerce that mothers will never rival men as traders because babies are a "focus killer." Speaking about one of his own previous associates, he added, to illustrate his point, "As soon as that baby's lips touched that girl's bosom, forget it."

Jones should not be seen as some kind of chauvinist dinosaur; during the firestorm generated by his remarks a number of women spoke up for his overall character and others said they were grateful that he put out in the open what they knew many of their male colleagues thought but would not say.

Moreover, Jones explained his reasoning in a way that encompasses some men and that is open to reasoned challenge. In his view, "macro trading requires a high degree of skill, focus, and repetition," which is why he also rules out "men going through a divorce," which he says will automatically reduce their trading results by 10 to 20 percent. Similarly, with respect to women, "The idea that you could think straight for sixty seconds and be able to make a rational decision is impossible, particularly when their kids are involved."

Here Jones is simply wrong; several studies demonstrate that over the long term women traders outperform their male peers. He is locked into the world of floor traders, who require quick reflexes and intense concentration to make snap decisions in a chaotic environment. That world requires a kind of focus that allows a trader to be hyper-rational, immune from emotional turbulence of any kind. That's why he equates women with babies with men going through a divorce. He wants to rule out any kind of emotion that might separate a human being from a machine: the perfectly rational creature we know as *Homo economicus*.

Another name for that kind of focus is tunnel vision, a decidedly bad thing for high-level decision makers. Indeed, in a book entitled *Scarcity: Why Having Too Little Means So Much*, Princeton psychologist Eldar Shafir and Harvard economist Sendhil Mullainathan have demonstrated how the scarcity of either money or time leads to decisions that are rational in the short term but irrational over the longer term. People under the stress of having to perform when they don't have enough time tend to focus intently on the problem right in front of them, in a way that allows them to meet their immediate deadline but gets them in trouble over the long term. Less stress, on the other hand, means broader vision and better long-term decisions.

People liberated from the stress tunnel may also have a different but equally profitable attitude toward risk. Financial expert and neuroscientist John Coates examined all the data he could find on men and women's trading patterns and identified a difference in the way that men and women trade. He finds that they are equally willing to take risks, but they take them in different ways. Men like to take them quickly, thrilling to the rapid-fire pace of the trading floor (think modern-day battlefield), whereas women prefer to take more time to analyze a security and then make the trade. Coates makes it clear that successful financial traders should be judged by "their call on the market and their understanding of risk once they put on a trade; and there is no reason to believe men are better at this than women. Importantly, the financial world desperately needs more long-term, strategic thinking, and the data indicate that women excel at this."

Coates then, as a man, is not afraid to identify and point out differences between the way men and women behave. For him, different does not mean inferior, it just means different, and quite possibly better. Assuming that the best way is the way things have always been done is hardly a prescription for success in a fast-changing economy. Men who are focused 24/7 on the present are likely to miss the future.

I started teaching law in 1990, when most law faculties still had very few women. One of the consequences was that even as an assistant professor I was asked to serve on the faculty hiring committee almost every year. That committee, like all faculty committees, needed diverse representation, and schools simply did not have enough women to go around.

Faculty hiring committees at law schools look at hundreds of résumés every year, asking a small number of people to make presentations and give interviews. The committee then deliberates about whether to hire the candidate. Early on in my career, when I served on the committee at the University of Chicago Law School, I recall one of my colleagues telling me after a particularly intense round of deliberations, "Everyone tries to hire himself."

What he meant was that each of us believes that we deserve to be on the faculty, so when we see candidates who have similar career paths to our own, we assume consciously or subconsciously that they deserve to be where we are. Faculty members who followed the traditional path of top grades, the presidency of the law review, and a Supreme Court clerkship not surprisingly look for those credentials as the minimum bar that a prospective candidate must meet. Faculty members who followed an unconventional path, as I did (mixed grades, no clerkship or law review, but a Ph.D. in another discipline and a demonstrated aptitude for scholarship), look for creative thinkers and unusual career profiles.

Hiring patterns like these are hardly restricted to law schools. Perhaps the best way to understand calcified work patterns is to recognize that the white men who got to the top by working around the clock and sacrificing their own time with their loved ones inevitably believe that the people below them who behave as they did must be the best candidates for advancement. They are thus highly suspicious, if not downright disbelieving, of data that show the benefits of working less, working differently, or even taking time out and not working at all for a while.

Joan Williams makes this point harshly but directly: "If you've lived a life where holidays are a nuisance, where you've missed your favorite uncle's funeral and your children's child-hoods, in a culture that conflates manly heroism with long hours, it's going to take more than a few regressions to convince you it wasn't really necessary, after all, for your work to devour you."

I'm not sure that it's necessary to look at the many men and far fewer women who have made it to the top and rub their noses in what they have missed. Better to acknowledge the sacrifices they have made as prisoners of their time and cultural norms while asking them to envision a different world for their children. Better still to understand that for the majority of men, working hard *was* exercising their family responsibilities as they under-stood them and that they developed their own ideas of being a good man accordingly. As the women's movement gained steam, we focused on being allowed to do that work ourselves, helping to make a fetish of income-generating work as a foundation of self-worth.

Now it's up to all of us, women and men alike, to make the next big push toward equality between men and women. We'll have to start by changing how we think.

Part II

Changing Lenses

MY FRIENDS SARAH AND EMILY ARE BOTH PSYCHIATRISTS WHO married seven years ago and now have four-year-old twins. Although they love being mothers, they also both love their work and have flourishing careers. Twins are a handful, of course, and even though Sarah and Emily can afford to hire a caregiver to help out, one or both of them needs a more flexible work schedule or part-time work to be there for sick days, school holidays, snow days, and emergencies great and small with either the children or any paid caregiver.

How should they divide responsibilities between caregiving and breadwinning? Who should throttle back and work less to have more time at home? Should they both rearrange their practices or change jobs to work more flexible schedules? Or should one of them stop working to be a full-time caregiver while the other is the full-time breadwinner?

What criteria should they use to decide? Which one of them earns the most, or which enjoys her work the most? Which one has the best prospects for promotion? Which one is more comfortable with a flexible work schedule and a slower career trajectory, or which one's workplace is the most flexible and accom-modating of caregiving responsibilities?

Sarah and Emily decided that they will both keep working, but Sarah, who is older and earns more, has continued to work full-time while Emily cut back her practice so that she works three days a week. Their situation is not unique. My male friends in same-sex marriages tell me that they face exactly the same questions sorting out roles, all because of the absence of default rules. Gender stereotypes, no matter how much we may try to transcend them, provide those defaults. The woman starts from her "natural" position as caregiver and the man from his "natural" position as breadwinner; they negotiate, implicitly or explicitly, from those baselines. But in a relationship of two men or two women, what are the starting points? Both are breadwinners; both are equally potential caregivers.

That is the lens that same-sex couples offer the rest of us. It is no longer possible to assume, even at the subconscious level, that one member of the couple will be better at raising children and running a household and the other will excel at earning income and climbing a career ladder. There is only negotiation between two people who have different talents, desires, and obligations and who love each other, their children, their parents, and other family members.

Considering these choices invites heterosexual couples to think about the division of labor in the same gender-neutral way that same-sex couples do. It also lays bare another fact and fissure in our society: the person in a couple who stays home will be val-ued less than the person who goes to the office. Again, when gen-der is removed from the equation, it's no longer possible to insist that discrimination against caregivers is just another way of de-scribing discrimination against women. The truth is that we value people of either gender who invest in themselves more than we value people who invest in others.

I said in the last chapter that the women's problem well-meaning executives want to solve is actually a care problem, a problem of not making it possible for workers with family responsibilities to work more flexibly and still stay on a leadership track. But the problem of care—or more precisely, of not valuing care—is much bigger and deeper than the challenges facing companies who want to promote women.

Fifty years ago middle-class women stayed home, cared for their families, and were manifestly unequal to their breadwinning husbands. To make them equal, we liberated women to be breadwinners too and fought for equality in the workplace. But along the way, we left caregiving behind, valuing it less and less as a meaningful and important human endeavor. Plenty of pathologies have resulted: mommy wars, distorted labor markets, shameful numbers of children in poverty, narrower options for men, and a continued advantage for all the male executives with a spouse at home.

The women's movement challenged women and men alike and changed our thinking profoundly. But we are only halfway home. These next chapters reveal the work left undone, outlining the intellectual and emotional challenges we still have to meet and conquer.

4

COMPETITION AND CARE

TODAY, MANY FEMINISTS FOCUS THEIR ATTENTION ON A SINGLE problem. It's not quite the glass ceiling, or even the "sticky floor," a term coined in the early 1990s by sociologist Catherine White Berheide to mean women who are trapped in low-wage jobs without much hope of professional advancement. Women have broken through the corporate ranks in most industries and professions; they have risen in politics, universities, foundations, and many other leadership roles. Instead, the problem is the Great Stall, the barely perceptible increase in the percentage of women leaders in all these institutions since the early 1990s. We seem to be stuck at 15 percent, rising to 20 percent in good industries and falling to 5 percent in bad ones.

This stall galvanizes many feminist scholars and public figures today. Fifty years after the second wave of the feminist movement roared into life, girls are raised to believe they can be anything they want to be. They pour out of top schools with great credentials and flood into the workforce. But the growing numbers of talented women who start out on professional career tracks just make it more frustrating to see how few actually make it to the top.

I too have been primarily focused on this problem for much

of my adult life, and indeed I wrote my *Atlantic* article to address this specific issue. Since then, however, I began to realize the ways in which focusing primarily on women at the top, while understandable from the perspective of wanting women to have access to the levers of economic, political, and social power, creates a distorted lens. It is as if we were to diagnose a disease by examining the symptoms in only one part of the body.

If the ultimate goal is the real equality of men and women in American society, then it's vital that we look at the situation of *all* women.

A COMMON PATTERN

Widening the lens beyond the ranks of women with professional careers reveals an unlovely symmetry. We see far too few women at the top, yes, but we also see far too many women at the bottom. The statistics are equally jarring in both directions. Women hold less than 15 percent of executive officer positions in Fortune 500 companies and 62 percent of minimum-wage jobs. As a result, one in three adult women is living in poverty or just on the edge of poverty. For single mothers, the picture is particularly bleak. Almost two-thirds of them are working in dead-end, poorly compensated jobs without flexibility or benefits.

When we broaden our definition of the problem in this way, the solutions offered to help advance women in recent years (including some of my own) are radically incomplete. It just isn't plausible that too many women are at the bottom of American society because they are not trying hard enough, are too perfectionist, or lack confidence. Those factors may well play an important role in holding back educated women with great initial career prospects, but they cannot explain why single mothers continue to fall through the cracks and end up in poverty.

It's possible, of course, that women at the top and at the bottom simply inhabit different spheres, with different explanations for what's holding them back or keeping them down. British economist Alison Wolf points out that for much of history women essentially shared the same fate. "Elite or poor, Irish or Indian, marriage and child-bearing were women's necessary aspirations. You married well, or badly. You bore living children to support you, or did not. On those realities, as a female, your whole life hinged," she writes in her book *The XX Factor*. Today, she argues, women's life experiences have diverged dramatically, such that "womanhood" is no longer a category that defines a common experience.

I don't challenge Wolf's data, but in looking at the stark facts of women at the top and at the bottom, a common pattern in their seemingly disparate experiences begins to emerge. Once we see it, it's like looking at an impressionist painting composed only of little dots of color that suddenly becomes comprehensible when we step back a bit. From the right vantage point, the dots fall into patterns that reveal a recognizable scene, a luncheon party or a field of flowers.

The key to that pattern lies in two complementary human drives: competition, the impulse to pursue our self-interest in a world in which others are pursuing theirs, and care, the impulse to put others first. These are the two great motivators of men and women alike. Anthropologists, sociologists, psychologists, and now neuroscientists study the ways in which different impulses in our brains and the resulting behaviors have allowed the human race to survive and progress. We fight with one another and strive to outdo one another in ways that push innovation and change, but we are also social animals who need relationships and human connection to thrive. Indeed, anthropologist Sarah Blaffer Hrdy observes that the capacity for caring about strangers is so unique to humans that "along with language and symbolic thought this capacity for compassion is quintessentially human." Indeed, it is "what . . . defines us as human."

Suppose then that what unites all women is the struggle to combine competition and care in a system that rewards one and penalizes the other? Yet if they are two equally valuable and necessary human drives, why should that be? It is no more justifiable to value the production of income over the provision of care than it is to value white over black, straight over gay, or men over women. Competition produces money. But care produces people.

Think about it. Countless women have described the ways that they became invisible the minute they left paid work to take care of their children or other family members. Sociologist Pamela Stone quotes Maeve, a 52-year-old former lawyer, on this point: "It was like all of a sudden I didn't exist. . . . You know, six months ago I was working in the U.S. Attorney's office doing all this hot stuff. My name was in *The New York Times*. . . . Now I'm nobody."

"Nobody." In other words, if all you do is care for other people, an activity just as if not more essential to the survival of the human race as earning an income, you lose your very identity as a person of value.

It is this devaluing of and discrimination against caregiving that provides the common thread linking the experiences of women at the top and at the bottom. If a young female lawyer or banker on a promising career track decides to leave early every day to be home with her kids for dinner, work part-time, or take time out for a while to be a full-time caregiver, she is quickly knocked out of the game—meaning the competition for the top.

And if she takes time out completely, her time spent caregiving is a black mark on her résumé going forward, a hole that she will vainly try to cover over or explain away when and if she tries to re-enter the job market.

Now consider the woman at the bottom. She is likely to be a single mother who has no choice but to be the sole breadwinner *and* caregiver for her family. Half of single moms in the United States make less than $25,000 a year. Compared to single parents in other high-income countries, American single parents have the highest poverty rate and the weakest income-support system.

Statistics like these provide an abstract summary of the lives of large numbers of people. But let's bring it home. Ranie Sherr is a single mom of two in South Scranton, Pennsylvania, who makes minimum wage. Because of childcare issues and a fall on the ice during the long winter of 2013, Sherr missed four days of work in a single week. "My next check is only going to be for 7.5 hours," Sherr told *The Times-Tribune* of Scranton. "I don't know how I'm going to make ends meet."

María, a single mom in Providence, Rhode Island, worked in a factory and earned $7.40 an hour. If she missed a shift because her son was sick, they would take her off work for two weeks, and then they'd give her fewer hours when they finally did let her return. She told researchers at the Urban Institute, "There was no flexibility even to go to the bathroom. You can't go to the bathroom more than twice a day, and they yell at you, 'Where were you?!' 'Move it!'—it's incredible. And they watch you when you go to the bathroom and they follow you to the bathroom. 'Move it! Move it!' 'Are you tired? You can't be tired here!'" She lost that job and, subsequently, her childcare arrangement for nine months. She found a new job, with better bosses, though she still had low pay and limited flexibility to care for her son.

As a society, we value Ranie's and María's breadwinning. Indeed, the entire reform of U.S. welfare programs under President Bill Clinton was designed to insist that the beneficiaries of what had been called Aid to Families with Dependent Children, which was overwhelmingly aid to single mothers, go to work in return for their benefits. Fair enough, if you believe, as I do, in the dignity and value of work. But why don't we believe in the equal dignity and value of caring for others? Particularly when those "others" are our own future citizens? President Clinton intended the new welfare work requirements to be coupled with investments in child care that would allow women to work. Yet today we don't provide affordable daycare, early-education, and after-school programs that take up the caregiving slack. We don't provide paid leave that any worker can use when a child is sick. The result is that a mother with dependent children must patch together an unstable and unreliable network of caregivers in ways that sharply hamper her ability to succeed at her job and climb out of poverty.

For middle-class families, the struggle to balance caregiving and breadwinning is a daily grind and often the tipping point that drives them into poverty and bankruptcy court. In *The Two Income-Trap*, Elizabeth Warren and Amelia Warren Tyagi describe how a divorce sent Gayle Pritchard, a college-educated HR professional, into bankruptcy. She couldn't afford to make mortgage payments on the family's modest home on her $46,000-a-year salary alone, and her ex-husband was not required to pay much in the way of child support. Pritchard's story is all too common; indeed, "Motherhood is now *the single best indicator* that an unmarried middle-class woman will end up bankrupt." (emphasis added) Those mothers continue to pay the price long after their children are grown. Ann Crittenden notes that because unpaid caregivers do not earn Social Security credits or have access to other parts of the social safety net, motherhood is "the single biggest risk factor for poverty in old age."

Privileged women who can afford to take time out or choose more flexible schedules to fit in caregiving may give up promotions and the shining aspirations that led them through college and professional school and into the workforce. Poor women who are both breadwinners and caregivers find themselves in far more serious straits, wondering how they are going to feed their families. They are often giving up on any hope of escaping the poverty they grew up in and creating better lives for their children. Without minimizing the differences in these women's lives, they all pay a price for having loved ones who need care.

Not valuing caregiving is the taproot, the deeper problem that gives rise to distortion and discrimination in multiple areas of American society. When we open our eyes and change our lenses to focus on competition and care rather than women and work, we can see new solutions and new coalitions that can open the door to progress and change. Care can provide a new political banner under which all women can unite.

REUNITING THE SISTERHOOD

THE EARLY DAYS OF THE women's movement, which we knew in the early 1970s as "women's lib," were part of the much larger social revolution of the 1960s and 1970s. The banner of the women's movement was "liberation," from stereotypes, restrictions, pedestals, boxes, discrimination, sexism, harassment, bras, and girdles—everything that confined women in predetermined roles. Young people wanted to be liberated from the establishment conformism of the 1950s—think the gray suits, perfect wives, and nonstop martinis of *Mad Men*. African Americans wanted to be liberated from the institutionalized legacies of slavery. The common thread was a revolution for equality, fairness, peace, and above all justice: equal rights under law.

Women came together in what felt like a genuine sisterhood. One of the earliest focuses of the movement was to define sexual harassment and then make it illegal; to tighten up on rape laws; and to fight to give women control over their bodies. Women may have been divided on the desirability of working outside the home, but women of every race, ethnicity, class, and creed could make common cause over being treated as sex objects.

Gloria Steinem, an icon of the new feminism who managed to combine miniskirts with media savvy and a gift for leadership, gave a commencement address at Vassar in the early summer of 1970 that became a manifesto for a much broader vision of what women were fighting for. She called the women's movement "a revolutionary bridge" "between black and white women" and between women and "the construction workers and the suburbanites, between Mr. Nixon's Silent Majority and the young people it fears." Women could provide the link between all those groups, she said, because they "are sisters; they have many of the same problems, and they can communicate with each other."

Steinem's vision still inspires, but she was assuming a lot even then. Many poor women, and certainly many women of color, never felt included. Less than a decade after Steinem spoke, for instance, Alice Walker coined the term "womanism" as a larger umbrella term that included feminism but focused more on the experiences of women of color and oppressed groups more generally.

Four decades later, even the sisterhood that was forged has frayed considerably. Wealthy, middle-income, working-class, and poor women live very different lives. African American women, Hispanic women, Asian women, lesbian women, married women, single women, Democratic women, Republican women, women in the workplace, and stay-at-home mothers—all have different life experiences and many are represented by advocacy or affinity groups that themselves pursue different agendas. But all, in different ways, have experienced the impact of discrimination against caregiving, as have women around the world.

Rich and Poor

I HAVE BEEN CRITICIZED FOR being a privileged, wealthy, liberal white woman who cannot imagine the lives of the vast majority of women across the United States. Feminist scholar Catherine Rottenberg, for instance, argues that the whole idea of "balance" is a privileged preserve. "From Private Woman through the New Woman and Superwoman," she writes, "it has finally become possible to speak about the Balanced Woman," a narrative "predicated on the erasure or exclusion of the vast majority of women." Rottenberg believes we place far too much emphasis on happiness and positive affect, and far too little emphasis on "equal rights, justice, or emancipation as the end goals for . . . feminism."

Susan Faludi, the Pulitzer Prize winner and author of feminist classics like *Backlash* and *Stiffed*, believes that books like *Lean In* and articles like my piece in *The Atlantic* are evidence that we've abandoned the collective struggle for women's liberation to focus on the individual advancement of the already privileged and that we've fully bought into a corrupt system. "It's been more than forty years since 'Dress for Success' and 'Having It All' (neither, by the way, coined by actual feminists) were enshrined in the liberatory lexicon and crowded out the authentic feminist dream of transforming human society," Faludi writes. "Four decades later, we are seeing the sad fruits of that failure of will. We have rede-fined feminism as women's right to be owned by the system, to be owned as much as men have been owned."

I am sympathetic to the view that contemporary feminism no longer unites women in its original quest for broader social trans-formation. I knew and acknowledged that I was writing my article for a relatively wealthy and educated audience. Yet many women who wrote to me from less privileged backgrounds told me that my experiences and perspectives spoke to them as well.

Tanya Sockol Harrington, who works with firefighters, was one example. She lamented that she could not get the college degree she needed to advance in her career. "As a mother to four, one of whom has medical issues, married to a man with a full-time career of his own there is simply no way I can attain this level of education," she wrote me. "I have my high school diploma and the classes I took for the fire service at our local community col-lege. While my husband is a nice person the reality is that the bulk of the home responsibilities fall on my shoulders."

The question of how to fit caregiving together with our goals for ourselves is common to both Tanya and me. To deny this unity of experience is to deny equality of purpose to women in lower income brackets. We all have aspirations in the realms of education and in our professional lives, but we want to be there for our loved ones as well. Catherine Rottenberg and others are right, however, to highlight the ways in which focusing on work-life balance speaks primarily to women with professional careers. "Balance" is a luxury. Equality is a necessity.

When we stop talking about work-life balance and start talk-ing about discrimination against care and caregiving, we see the world differently. We see a link between a post-maternity leave flextime mother who gets less interesting assignments for less important clients and an employer's refusal to provide sick days, personal days, or any flexibility to a working mother (or working father) in the first place. In both instances the workplace is discriminating in favor of workers who can outsource caregiving to someone else. And in both cases employers are assuming that it is impossible to be both a committed caregiver and a good worker. But why should that be? The least we can do is to force employers to justify that assumption.

Similarly, we see a common discriminatory assumption embedded in our view of a woman's caregiving years spent out of the paid workforce as a yawning gap on her résumé and our failure to include the hundred million–plus hours of unpaid care work done in households across the country every year in our national GDP. In both cases we assume that care work is not work that really matters, even though it is essential to the dignity and the well-being of the elderly and the sick and to the very brain formation and growth of the young. Nor do we assume that it can in any way benefit the caregiver in ways that are individually valuable and desirable in other contexts.

At the low end, the motherhood penalty becomes something much more dire: what economist Nancy Folbre called, back in 1985, the "the pauperization of motherhood." Three decades later, in a 2012 volume on care provision and policies in the United States published by the prestigious Russell Sage Foundation, Folbre and her co-authors note all the ways that low-income families are affected by the relatively sparse public subsidies for care provision. They typically have more children than higher-income families, meaning that they simultaneously have greater caregiving demands and a greater need for paid income. At the same time, "with low wages and little savings" they have a much harder time navigating the special demands of aging or ill family members. And while mothers are paid less up and down the income ladder, that difference has a far greater impact on families who have little to begin with.

In our new vocabulary, the motherhood penalty is a prime example of discrimination against caregiving, a bias that operates up and down the income scale. Though the consequences are far worse for poor women, still, in relative terms, the pauperization of motherhood at the bottom parallels the penalization of motherhood at the top. If we truly valued caregiving—thought that it was not only necessary but important and valuable and hard—we would make every effort to accommodate and support it and judge workers based not on our assumptions but on their results.

Caught in the Middle

THE LIVES OF MIDDLE-CLASS WOMEN in the United States are increasingly shaped by the tug-of-war between competition and care, but in two sharply different ways. On the one hand, the substitution of two breadwinners for one breadwinner and one caregiver has made those families far less resilient. Warren and Tyagi document the ravages of the "two-income trap" among American middle-class families, showing the ways in which women's entry into the workforce over the past four decades has meant losing the safety net that once allowed traditional single-breadwinner families to ride out financial reverses. "A stay-at-home mother served as the family's ultimate insurance against unemployment or disability": insurance because if Dad lost his job, Mom could still go to work and keep the family afloat. But with both parents working and the family depending on dual incomes as a baseline, the safety net of Mom getting a job if she has to disappears.

Warren and Tyagi's point is not to put mothers back in the

home: these mothers are working because it takes both parents to provide for their families. It is to highlight the ways in which a stay-at-home parent provides substantial economic value to a society, as insurer and also back-up caregiver, able to step into the breach when a family member falls sick or an elderly relative requires help driving to the doctor or balancing a checkbook. As a society, the ways in which we value breadwinning over caregiving have made us blind to these costs: we miss the ways in which more money cannot actually substitute for care.

In those middle-class families with two parents that are still surviving on a single wage, it's still more likely to be coming from Dad than from Mom. I asked Pew Research to crunch the numbers, and Richard Fry, a senior researcher, discovered that among middle-income couples where only one spouse was employed, 70 percent of those breadwinners were men. But those numbers are slowly shifting, as jobs in traditionally female sectors are expanding just as jobs in traditionally male sectors have contracted.

In communities across the country where manufacturing jobs for men have disappeared, the decent jobs that have remained are overwhelmingly in "eds and meds": education and healthcare. These are care jobs—work that involves the nurturing and support of the young, the sick, and the old. They are jobs that we have traditionally valued less and paid less than jobs in the competitive sector of the economy; indeed, most schools and hospitals are not-for-profit, taking the competition out of the sector. They are women's jobs.

That pattern is set to continue. As I noted in chapter 2, books such as Hanna Rosin's *The End of Men* and Liza Mundy's *The Richer Sex* document the ways in which the economic shift from industry toward service and information is advantaging traditionally "feminine" skills such as social intelligence, open communication, and even the ability to sit still. Rosin examines the thirty professions projected to add the most jobs over the next decade and concludes that "women dominate twenty, including nursing, accounting, home health assistance, childcare, and food preparation."

I had a personal experience with this phenomenon several summers ago, when Andy suddenly fell sick in London and he checked into a central London hospital. As he was moved onto the ward, I looked at the nursing chart and thought to myself that it looked exactly like a corporate board chart in reverse. Of some twenty-five nurses, all were women except for three or four men (and none of them appeared to be British-born). My recent encounters with the U.S. healthcare system have revealed similar patterns. Only about 9 percent of nurses in the United States are men, which works out to about 330,000 male nurses compared to 3.2 million female nurses. Yet we have a chronic nursing shortage.

These statistics make it all too clear that the middle-class map has been redrawn by women leaving their traditional caregiving roles due to the economic necessity of having two breadwinners to support a middle-class family, and men losing their traditional breadwinning jobs and being unprepared, unwilling, or unable to take on work in the caring sectors of the economy. Valuing care—and paying for it—could make care jobs more attractive to men and help bolster the middle class.

Women of Every Color

Focusing on care as equal to competition also holds out the possibility that white women, particularly upper-class white women, will hear the voices of many women of color differently. For generations of African American women, caregiving and breadwinning have been the same thing; they have earned their living and supported or helped support their own families by caring for other people's families. As Lonnae O'Neal Parker writes, "There has never been a national effort to keep black women at home, caring sweetly for their children. They have always worked, and their work has never been a separate thing from their mothering."

No single African American thinker or writer can speak for African American women as a whole, of course, but Taigi Smith, a writer and network news producer, offers a powerful critique that further emphasizes Alison Wolf's claim that feminism for elite women has deepened "gender segregation" for women as a whole:

> I declared myself a womanist when I realized that white women's feminism really didn't speak to my needs as the daughter of a black, single, domestic worker. I felt that, historically, white women were working hard to liberate themselves from housework and childcare, while women of color got stuck cleaning their kitchens and raising their babies. When I realized that feminism largely liberated white women at the economic and social expense of women of color, I knew I was fundamentally unable to call myself a feminist.

From this perspective, being able to stay home and raise your own children is a different kind of liberation. Indeed, the writings of many African American feminists offer a strong, positive, affirming vision of motherhood. They describe motherhood as a source of power, not penalty, providing a way to push back against negative stereotypes rather than to confirm them. Black women writers like Gwendolyn Brooks, Marita Golden, and Alice Walker all describe the ways that a child connects the mother "to some power in herself, some power to speak, to be heard, to articulate feelings."

Walker makes this point in her driving and rhythmic prose:

> It is not my child who tells me: I have no femaleness white women must affirm. Not my child who says: I have no rights black men must respect. It is not my child who has purged my face from history and herstory, and left mystory just that, a mystery; my child loves my face and would have it on every page, if she could, as I have loved my own parents' faces above all others. . . . We are together, my child and I. Mother and child, yes, but sisters really, against whatever denies us all that we are.

Caring here is a source of power, growth, and personal fulfillment for the caregiver as well as the person being cared for. The child gives the parent dignity and purpose; the parent gives the child hopes of a better future.

I certainly cannot claim to speak for women of color; I can only try to hear them. Many come from cultures that emphasize the bonds of family far more than white Anglo-Saxon Protestant culture does. As the United States becomes plurality Hispanic, for instance, the care networks of extended families that are a strong part of Hispanic culture should become a much more evident part of American culture. African American culture has also long placed a greater emphasis on caring for all relatives, not just members of the nuclear family, than white culture does.

Starting from the perspective of care would place a much higher value on the work that women of color have traditionally done and open the door to many new conversations. They will not be uniform, of course. But at the very least, they help us escape the assumption that the experience of white well-off women in the United States is the feminist benchmark.

CARE BEYOND FAMILIES

SINGLE PEOPLE NEED BALANCE TOO. As Kate Bolick, author of *Spinster: Making a Life of One's Own*, noted on *The Atlantic*'s website, when you work in an office, regardless of marital or parental status or gender, "You get home way too late, you don't exercise enough, you blow too much money on mediocre lunch options, you die a slow death in each long, pointless meeting." Another former student of mine who is single and in the Foreign Service observed that his married counterparts fought tooth and nail not to get assigned to hardship, dangerous, or unaccompanied posts. "Granted, single people don't have the demands of a family, but it doesn't mean that we make any less of a sacrifice or that we enjoy such posts either," he wrote to me.

The story of care and the single person has several strands. First is the resentment that many singles or members of childless couples feel at being ignored or talked over in work-family debates, an omission that often translates into the implicit assumption that care is only for parents. We love and care for many different people in our lives, in our nuclear, extended, and constructed families. Taking time to spend with a friend living through or dying of cancer, for instance, should rank certainly as high or higher on the care meter as watching a child's soccer game.

A second strand is the assumption that people who do not have family members to go home to have no reason to want to go home. Even viewed purely from the performance standpoint as competitors, they will perform far better if they rest and recharge. Care also has many faces. Caring for members of your community—your church, temple, mosque, YMCA, local food bank, Little League, Big Brothers and Sisters organization, and so many more—occupies a different but no less important part of the care spectrum as family responsibilities.

The third and final strand, perhaps least well understood, is the importance of self-care. The millennials who are now insisting, well before they have families, that they "want a life" are smart enough to know that caring for themselves, for their bodies through regular exercise and for their minds and souls through activities that stretch and sustain them beyond their work, is essential to their health and happiness over a lifetime. They may have been forced into this discovery due to the sharply limited work options they have confronted since the Great Recession, but they appear to have made a virtue of necessity. They are investing in themselves more intelligently than their older colleagues who stay chained to their desks in response to the outmoded and inefficient dictates of a twentieth-century workplace.

PAID CARE

THE EASIEST WAY TO MEASURE the value we place on care is to see how little we are willing to pay for it. Caregivers are among the lowest-paid American workers. Moreover, "low-income African American and immigrant women are heavily overrepresented in the most poorly paid care jobs." That's the trifecta of low value: woman, color, and care.

A remarkable young Chinese American woman named Ai-jen

Poo has fought an important and courageous campaign to improve the incomes and living conditions of paid careworkers. She has been organizing immigrant women workers for almost two decades; her work led to the Domestic Workers' Bill of Rights in New York, which gives nannies and housekeepers the right to overtime pay, a day of rest for every seven days worked, three paid days off each year, and explicit protection under New York State human rights laws. Writing about that campaign in her book *The Age of Dignity*, she describes a "winning coalition that crossed lines of race, class, gender, and age": union members, farmworkers, "racial justice groups, immigrant groups, women's organizations, faith-based groups, students, celebrities." She also links the importance of the work these women do to the "elder boom" in America, which is already upon us as the baby boomers age, pointing out that in care work, the boss cannot be the enemy. The employers of home-care workers are often the very people they care for, or those people's parents or children.

The point here is that the economic, social, and human dimensions of care intersect so many lives in ways that cannot be captured by traditional economic, social, and political divides. Atul Gawande, a surgeon and a writer who describes his experiences with elder patients and his own father in his book *Being Mortal*, reminds us that even if we are not giving care ourselves now, we cannot avoid needing it later. "Your chances of avoiding the nursing home," he writes, "are directly related to the number of children you have, and, according to what little research has been done, having at least one daughter seems to be crucial to the amount of help you will receive." All of us, then, have a stake in ensuring that when we get to that stage of life, our children or other younger relatives have the ability to help care for us. Valuing care now is in our own self-interest.

A COALITION FOR CARE

CARE IS THE CRUCIBLE THAT can help reforge the sisterhood of the early feminist movement and expand and shape it into a much broader human coalition. Care can unite women up and down the income scale and across races and ethnicities. It can unite the experiences of heterosexual and same-sex couples, older generations and younger ones. It can provide a common metric for the quality of single and married life, for couples and communities of different kinds.

Valuing care also offers a compass to a new set of workplace and national policies. Challenging employers, politicians, and ordinary citizens to explain why, exactly, it is more important and valuable to compete with one another than to care for one another forces a hard and searching look at what we say but do not do, what we assume but won't admit.

5

IS MANAGING MONEY REALLY HARDER
THAN MANAGING KIDS?

During the course of writing this book, I gave a lecture called "Having a Life" to Princeton's graduating seniors in which I argued that they should value breadwinning and caregiving equally over the course of their lifetimes. I asked a number of my volunteer student researchers to canvass their male friends in particular for their reactions, and one young man, an economics major, offered a careful response. From his perspective, the problem is "that people internalize the judgments of the market on caregivers and breadwinners." It's much easier to value the contribution of breadwinners, because their performance is compensated in the common metric of money. Moreover, consider the laws of supply and demand. "There is a more limited supply of able breadwinners than there is of caregivers. This means that socially, the worth of caregivers is 'priced' lower than that of breadwinners." To illustrate the point more fully, he outlined a thought experiment.

> Suppose we decide that the value of janitors and computer scientists to our society is the same. We clearly need both for our society to function the way we want it to. However, it's

unlikely a janitor will get as much social respect as a computer scientist, because many people can be janitors (just as many people can be good caregivers), but few can be good computer scientists (as relatively few can be successful breadwinners). So, while it is perfectly valid for us to argue that breadwinners and caregivers should be valued equally in theory, it will be nearly as difficult to achieve social equality for breadwinners and caregivers in reality as it will be for janitors and computer scientists.

I was grateful for his honesty. He was willing to bring out into the open a deep assumption about the nature of caregiving: that it is something many people can do with little training. Although he doesn't quite go this far, to him caregiving is nearly analogous to being a janitor. Janitors clean floors; caregivers bathe children or aging parents. Software developers or, for example, money managers do important work that requires high-level training.

But is managing money really harder than managing kids? This chapter will challenge that assumption head-on. Not by trying to lower our estimation of the difficulty and value of money management, but by raising our estimation of the value and importance of caregiving and the skills we need to do it well. In economic terms, caregiving is investment in human capital, our most precious asset as a society.

It may seem obvious, but let's be clear about the meanings of "breadwinning" and "caregiving." In any society that has a system of exchange beyond barter, adults have to earn income—to pay the rent or the mortgage; buy food, clothing, and furniture; pay for transportation, heat, electricity, health insurance, and a phone. Breadwinning.

One or both members of a couple must also do the work that turns that income into goods and services necessary for survival and flourishing: shopping, cooking, cleaning, washing, driving, repairing, organizing, and outsourcing. And that is just the physical dimension of care, the taking care of another human being in the same way that a caretaker looks after a house or property. "Caregiving," the term we typically use when we mean taking care of other people, includes the additional emotional component of love and nurture, the transformation of an income stream into the lifeblood of human connection.

This broader understanding of caregiving also includes teaching, discipline (holding the line even in the face of tears, threats, and curses), coaching, encouraging, problem solving, character building, and role modeling. Often caregiving is about reliability: simply being there when being there is important to your child, your parent, or your spouse. And it's about support: focusing on someone else's needs and figuring out how to meet them, whether finding a lost sock, book, or cellphone or offering a genuinely attentive ear.

Care is the complement to competition in whatever we do. Good caregivers, including managers and leaders, certainly know how to use competition to sharpen incentives to succeed. But good competitors equally understand the value of care.

CAREGIVING

IN *THE PRICE OF MOTHERHOOD*, Ann Crittenden tells a story about being in the home of a family-care provider and watching her serve lunch to a group of kids ranging in age from eighteen months to five years.

> When a four-year-old tipped over a glass of milk, she calmly said, "Uh-oh, that's why we have plastic over the table." She

fetched a cloth and wiped up most of the spill, then handed it to the boy to finish the job. Within a minute he was happy again, unaware of all that had gone into the incident: the preparation of a child-friendly, accident-proof environment; the everyone-makes-mistakes acceptance of a small child's natural clumsiness; the avoidance of blame; the efficient, can-do solving of a problem; the child's assumption that he was part of the solution, expected to clean up a mess and presumed to have the competence to do it.

Wow. I certainly never managed to communicate all of that to my kids when they spilled something. Indeed, I flinch a bit as I think back to breakfast time when they were under five and we had to get them out the door to daycare at the same time that Andy and I were trying to read early morning email, prepare for class, or meet some writing deadline, all while trying to get out the door ourselves. As one colleague of mine said about such mornings, "The question was not whether there was yelling, it was just about when the yelling started." But even with more time and less stress, I don't think I would have figured out how to handle a spill in a way that teaches important life lessons, at least not without a lot of time and reading.

Perhaps, then, we can bump caregiving a couple of notches higher than cleaning. According to Megan Gunnar, a Regents Professor at the University of Minnesota who works at the intersection of developmental psychology and neuroscience, a good early-childhood caregiver needs the analytical skills of a physicist, the adaptive abilities of a crisis manager, the emotional insight of a psychologist, and the range of general knowledge of a *Jeopardy!* champion. As she puts it, caring for young children "requires this capacity to analyze what's happening in the moment, figure out what concept the child could be learning. Which physics concept should I be teaching here? Which numerical concept is this appropriate for? What language arts can I do? [Responding] in the moment, dynamically, really takes analytic skills, executive function, ordering and sequencing, and knowing a lot of information."

What difference does that kind of care make? Today we have neuroscientific evidence for the proposition that the kind of care you receive from birth to age five can set you up or keep you down for life. Over a decade ago the National Academy of Sciences published the book *Neurons to Neighborhoods: The Science of Early Childhood Development*. The book opens with a simple proposition: "From the time of conception to the first day of kindergarten, development proceeds at a pace exceeding that of any subsequent stage of life." Moreover, that development "is shaped by a dynamic and continuous interaction between biology and experience."

A more recent study tallied the results of a North Carolina social experiment that first began in the early 1970s. The Carolina Abecedarian Project compared two sets of disadvantaged children: one set received high-quality, stimulating care and excellent nutrition eight hours a day from birth to age five; the other set was the control group, which received no external intervention. Four decades later, the adults who received great care as children were over four times more likely to have a college degree, and they were also physically healthier than the adults who were in the control group as children. Think about the implications of this study. It means that we are baking in the achievement gap between disadvantaged citizens and their privileged peers in the first five years of life. But it also means that if we want to, we can level the playing field.

If we value human capital as a society, we should value the array of jobs involved in caring for and educating young children—from birth through age eight—every bit as much as we value money managers or computer scientists. We should be looking for people of intelligence, creativity, education, and experience who see their jobs as cultivating the neural development, discipline, character, independence, curiosity, and creativity in children that will determine their life chances. They are, quite literally, growing the next generation of citizens, ensuring that they have an equal shot at fulfilling their individual potential and that we have the talent, creativity, and resilience we need as a nation.

When I think back to my childhood, so many of my memories are of my parents and grandparents taking me to libraries, museums, and historic sites; of them reading to me and answering my questions once I was old enough to read myself. My Belgian grandfather, Grandpère, had a wonderful collection of small objects on his desk, each with a story that opened the door to a history lesson or a reflection on human nature. I particularly remember a small framed picture showing three scenes of two donkeys tied together by a rope. In the first scene they are pulling at cross-purposes, each straining to get at a separate pile of hay. The second and third scenes show them working together to eat first one pile and then the other. The caption is "Cooperation." How often, during the many years of my life that I have spent studying conflict and cooperation between states, have I remembered that picture and our discussions of it.

At the other end of life, educated caregivers can expand the length and the quality of life for the generation that is leaving the stage. The central message of Atul Gawande's *Being Mortal* is that we treat elders the way we treat preschoolers, focusing more on their safety than their autonomy. Imagine how difficult it must be to lose your independence at the end of your life—being forced to return to a world in which your mealtimes, bedtimes, and activities are completely regulated by someone else. Good eldercare-givers, who are trained to understand the physiology and psychology of aging, can make almost as much difference in how we end our lives as childcare-givers make in how we live them.

Keren Brown Wilson, one of the originators of the concept of assisted living, points out that supporting people to do what they want to do, from dressing themselves to eating to reading, is a lot harder than just doing it for them—as every parent of a toddler knows! Anyone may be able to do the physical work of taking care of people. But again, actually *giving* care, enabling the person being cared for to flourish and make the most of his or her capabilities at a particular stage of life, requires knowledge and experience.

CARE-GETTING

THE CONVENTIONAL WISDOM IS THAT caregiving is just that, *giving*, an activity about others, while competing is about *winning*, advancing the self. That is a cramped and narrow view, however. In fact, caring is about exploring and developing the side of yourself that flourishes in connection to other human beings, rather than in competition with them. Caring has its own personal rewards, just as competition does, but of a different kind. When you give, you get—in so many ways.

Allison Stevens, a Washington, D.C.–based journalist, wrote a comment on how Betty Friedan experienced the obligations of child rearing as an endless cycle of ennui and mopping and tooth-brushing. In Stevens's experience, however, mothering has included plenty of hard work and boredom, "but it's also been laughter, sunshine, swing sets and wonder. Some of the best stuff life has to offer." The "wonder" part, as Alison Gopnik puts it in

The Philosophical Baby, is the ability children have "to explore both the actual world and all the possible worlds," an attribute we also associate with genius.

Even with all the frustrations of trying to haul teenage boys out of bed in the morning, get decent food into them at some point in the day, and convince them to use just a little judgment, seeing my older son go off to college this year left a hard lump in my throat. Hanging out late at night after he convinced me to bring up a milkshake, against all household rules about eating in his bedroom and after he'd already eaten a huge dinner, talking about nothing in particular but then suddenly something important—those are the moments I treasure and know will never come again in quite the same way. Listening to my younger son and my husband argue over piano practice night after night can be tiresome, but then suddenly the piece comes right and I simply marvel at the idea that anyone in the house, much less a child of mine, can make such beautiful music.

Sunday dinners have provided another small but pleasing ritual. Over the past few years, given the boys' teenage schedules and my own commute to Washington, D.C., a couple of days a week, it has been very hard to have a regular dinner schedule. But I usually manage to cook on Sundays and the kids know not to make other plans. I am hardly a domestic goddess; on the contrary, I adamantly refused to learn to cook, sew, or iron growing up. And yet planning and making a nice meal, or organizing a holiday and hosting our extended family, satisfies something deep in my soul.

Equally valuable is the opportunity as a parent to release all your inhibitions. I remember one family dinner years ago when Andy got up to get something out of the refrigerator. He opened the fridge door and then shut it again quickly, with a wide-eyed look on his face. Turning to the boys, who were probably four and six at the time, he said dramatically, "There's a tiger in there!" much to their delight. That's my hyper-rational professor husband I'm talking about, being wonderfully goofy, showing a side of himself that most of the world never gets to see. Jennifer Senior puts it best: the joys of being crazy with kids "give us a reprieve from etiquette, let us shelve our inhibitions, make it possible for our self-conscious, rule-observing self to be tucked away. For a few blessed moments, we're streaming, uncorked ids."

Beyond the silly and satisfying moments are far deeper benefits. Wharton School professor and sociologist Adam Grant has drawn on extensive empirical psychological research to explode myths about leadership for men and women. In his book *Give and Take*, Grant starts out by asking which category of people are most likely to be at the bottom of the work hierarchy: "givers," "takers," or "matchers." Almost everyone presented with this question answers "givers." Sadly, they are right.

Grant then asks the same question with regard to the personality type of people most likely to be at the top of corporate hierarchies. After thinking for a second, most people answer "takers," although some may guess "matchers." They are wrong. The answer, once again, is "givers."

Givers are great successes not just in fields like education, where doing things for others might fit in better with the core mission, but also in business and even politics, which are not generally seen as warm and fuzzy fields. That's because being a giver doesn't mean you're a doormat, and it doesn't even mean that you're necessarily nice. It just means you continuously do things without expecting anything in return.

Grant describes how Abraham Lincoln's political career was built on giving. When Lincoln first ran for the U.S. Senate in Illinois, he ended up withdrawing so that he could help Lyman Trumbull win—that's because Lincoln and Trumbull shared a commitment to abolishing slavery, and that goal was more important to Lincoln than being a senator. Though Trumbull lost, Lincoln's behavior built goodwill and trust, and it helped him establish a reputation that would eventually land him in the White House.

It's worth noting that Lincoln's supportive actions didn't pay off right away. His behavior over time led to networks of supporters who ultimately helped him along the road to the White House. Working parents are especially well equipped to bring that same kind of giver sensibility into the office, and taking the long view is important for them, as they may have moments when they need to step back from work. We need to stop thinking of that giving, caring personality as a roadblock to success or leadership and start thinking of it as a new, authentic way forward.

CARE GROWING

ANDY COMES FROM A LONG line of professors, including his father, his aunt and uncle on his father's side, and his father's father, a great Hungarian professor of Byzantine history. His aunt Edu, a retired professor of linguistics at the University of Wisconsin, is beloved by all the family. A few years ago, Edu sent me a small book entitled *On Caring*, by a now little-known philosopher named Milton Mayeroff. It was first published back in 1971 as part of a series of forty-five books called World Perspectives, an effort by some of the most distinguished scholars, politicians, and artists of the time to help make sense of the world "in a new era of evolutionary history, one in which rapid change is a dominant consequence." Sounds familiar!

This slim volume was a revelation to me, like a secret that had been hiding in plain sight. A man wrote it. A man who was writing not for an audience of women who want "work-life balance" but for entrepreneurs, leaders, and managers, as well as men and women of all types trying to figure out what a well-lived life might look like. After reading *On Caring*, I felt like I finally had the missing piece of a complicated puzzle; everything finally fit together. Suddenly, I saw how all the aspects of a caring personality, though commonly derided as "soft," are actually just as vital—at home *and* in the workplace—as any of the "hard" aspects of a competitive personality.

The book's central message is that the essence of caring is to help another person grow and realize his or her potential—the exact opposite of simply using that person for one's own ends. Caring requires us not to put ourselves aside but to put others *first* in ways that allow them to flourish as independent people. "In caring as helping the other grow," Mayeroff writes, "I experience what I care for (a person, an ideal, an idea) as an extension of myself and at the same time as something separate from me that I respect in its own right."

Any parent, grandparent, older sibling (sometimes!), teacher, or mentor of a younger person will recognize this sentiment—the process of nurturing and teaching means that you are pouring your own experience, values, and views into the other person while at the same time, if you are doing it right, giving her space to be herself. What is particularly striking, though, is that Mayeroff does not distinguish between caring for a person and caring for "an ideal or an idea"—anything that you create or are committed to.

Think about how great artists describe their process of creation. Sculptors talk about having an idea for a sculpture but then having to follow the grain of the wood or the fissures of the stone. As they age and gain experience and confidence, painters typically become freer and more abstract with their brushstrokes, letting the paint guide their hands rather than the other way around. I think of my mother, who became a full-time artist after we left home, showing me the work in her studio and often saying that a canvas I think is perfect "still needs something," almost as if the painting is talking to her.

In writing, many novelists, including Henry James, Marcel Proust, E. M. Forster, Alice Walker, and J. K. Rowling, have described how their characters can sometimes "take over" and dictate the course of their novels. At some point in the writing process, as the characters develop and start seeming to have their own independent lives, the author stops struggling to invent new dialogue and plot and instead just thinks about what a character might say or do in a certain situation and then writes it down. Sometimes, a character might even change an author's original idea, taking the story in a whole new direction.

A talented artist knows how to allow his or her creation to develop its own integrity, to let it shape itself in a way that requires his guidance but is not entirely within his control. This is exactly like being a parent. A good parent is deeply connected to the child but also knows when to let that child form his or her own path and understands how to raise an independent, autonomous person, not just some sort of "mini me."

This vision of care is as demanding and rewarding as any other field of human endeavor. Indeed, Mayeroff lists a number of elements necessary to be a good caregiver, attributes that are just as necessary to be a good employee or manager. His roster includes knowledge, patience, adaptability to different rhythms, honesty, courage, trust, humility, and hope.

Each of these elements links to a specific dimension of caring. Knowledge, because "to care for someone . . . I must know who the other is, what his powers and limitations are, and what is conducive to his growth."

Patience will be obvious to anyone who has ever dealt with a young child or an elderly adult. But as Mayeroff explains, the patience involved in caring is not just about time but also about space: by listening to someone who is upset, we are present in a way that gives that person space to express his emotions and to identify their source. That same ability is the essence of good management, as opposed to overly controlling bosses who micromanage and immediately insist on taking over when a problem or a conflict arises.

True patience also "includes tolerance of a certain amount of confusion and floundering" on the part of others who are figuring things out for themselves. That attitude, according to Mayeroff, leads to an acceptance of time that may appear to be wasted but in fact is part of the "free play" necessary to growth. Google could not have said it better, with its insistence on Lego bricks, ping-pong tables, scooters, and toys everywhere.

Patience is also involved in what Mayeroff calls embracing "alternating rhythms." Caring for a person or for an artistic endeavor means trying to express yourself in a way that attains the result you want—teaching a child a concept or writing a paragraph on a page—and then stopping and assessing whether you have been successful. If not, you try again. Caring is thus a continual process of adapting to figure out what works, moving between your own needs and the needs of another, between the needs of the moment and needs over time. Interestingly, this process is exactly what entrepreneurs like Eric Ries, author of *The Lean Startup*, say about how to take an idea and make it a successful business. "Nobody has a great idea the first time out of the gate. Nobody, ever. You have to iterate, and change and pivot" in response to what you learn in the marketplace.

Honesty, in Mayeroff's catalogue, is seeing the person—or the idea or painting or music—as it truly is, not as you want it to be "or feel it must be." It is also looking at yourself clearly enough to see whether your actions help or hinder the growth of the person or idea you care for. That kind of honesty takes courage, the courage to accept things that you may not like or want to see, as well as the courage to go "into the unknown." In my experience, courage is one of most essential attributes of leadership. Having to face my own limitations as a parent, finding the courage to acknowledge what I don't know and apologize when I have made a mistake, has certainly made me a better leader.

Mayeroff's catalogue of caring attributes are all bound together. If honesty requires courage, courage requires trust. That trust is certainly leavened by humility and hope, the humility of accepting your own limitations. I think about this dimension of caring often in my frequent conversations with my sons about procrastination. My father is a procrastinator; he always used to laugh and tell me, "Don't do as I do, do as I say," when he would urge me to get to work and I would point out that he was still reading the paper. Now the shoe is on the other foot, as I urge my sons to start earlier and not leave their projects until the last minute, while knowing full well that I have looming deadlines all over the place!

Humility also means accepting that you have done the best you can, however imperfectly, combined with the hope that inspires us to believe we can always do a little better today than we did yesterday and that if we just keep trying, things will come right. How often, as a parent, have I felt that I am at wit's end, that I have tried and tried to get my children to understand why it is important that they study or focus or be nice to each other! How often have I thought to myself that I just have to hope and have faith; that if I keep trying, keep repeating, keep insisting, somehow it will sink in.

More generally, the virtues that caring for others teaches and builds are part of what *New York Times* columnist David Brooks would call "the cultivation of character." I believe deeply in character, that hard-to-pin-down combination of integrity, morals, self-direction, strength, and courage that I see in the people I admire most. It is what I have dug deep for at critical junctures of my own career: when I decided not to work for a big law firm but instead to try my hand on the teaching market to see if I could become a law professor, even though I looked like a very unusual candidate; when I accepted Hillary Clinton's offer to be her director of policy planning, even though I had never served in government; and when I chose to leave the academy, the wonderful secure world of tenure and long summers to work in any way you like, for the much more uncertain life of running a young organization.

My competitive side certainly played a role in those decisions, but as I reflect on Mayeroff's writing, I can see a strong link between caring about the people I love most in the world and caring about ideas and ideals in ways that have shaped many of my professional decisions. I can also say, without reservation, that I would hire anyone who has all or even most of the attributes Mayeroff lists as essential to caring in a heartbeat. Furthermore, any boss who *doesn't* have at least some of those attributes isn't tougher or stronger or better, just a bad boss.

WE GET WHAT WE PAY FOR

HERE IN THE UNITED STATES, we pay a great deal for managing money. We pay far less for doing anything with kids. Megan Gunnar, the psychologist who specializes in early education, points out that Americans pay early-childhood workers, those stimulators of young brains, the same wages we pay those who "park our cars, walk our dogs, flip our burgers, and mix our drinks."

We "pay" people in the sense of not only money but also social prestige. Conduct your own experiment. Go to a cocktail party and tell half the people you meet that you are an investor. Tell the other half that you are a teacher, and measure how long it takes for your newest acquaintance to turn away or look over your shoulder for someone more important to talk to.

And we do indeed get what we pay for: third-rate public education, near the bottom of the league tables among advanced industrial countries. Look at what happens at the tops of those tables. In Finland, a country that ranks high on all international educational measures, teaching is a prestigious profession. To become a teacher in Finland, you must be accepted to one of eight teacher training colleges, which are about as difficult to get into as MIT. If you want to teach language arts, for example, you must take a difficult literature exam. Finnish teachers make an amount comparable to other college graduates in their country. By contrast, in the United States, many teachers' colleges have no admissions requirements, and so our country produces two and a half times the teachers we need each year and then pays them less than what other college grads make.

Just to drive home the point, the most successful effort by far to raise the social prestige of teaching has been Wendy Kopp's Teach for America. She did it by creating a highly selective competition, such that in some years it has become almost as hard to become a Teach for America fellow as it is to get into some Ivy League schools. Human nature works in the United States just as in Finland: higher standards lead to more prestige. But that aura of selectivity and success does not extend to career teachers.

So why *don't* we value teachers? Or coaches, therapists,

nurses, nannies, primary care physicians, gerontologists, elder-care specialists—essentially any profession centered on helping others flourish rather than winning ourselves? I can think of a number of reasons for this distortion in our value structure. The most obvious, at least to most women, is that we are talking about men's traditional work versus women's traditional work, and we have traditionally valued men more than women.

Another possibility is that the professions that involve competition more than care have much more measurable outcomes; it is easy to figure out who won—the deal, the lawsuit, the sales contract, the race to invent a new product—and to compensate the winner accordingly. It is much harder, as teachers and education reformers both know, to measure learning outcomes. You can reduce those outcomes to multiple-choice tests, but real learning often suffers in the process. Parents know the drill: it often takes years to find out that a particular conversation or life experience with a child planted a valuable seed that actually flowered.

I first started thinking about these questions when I watched an elementary school class shortly after becoming a law professor at the University of Chicago. My beloved friend and college roommate Nora Elish was teaching first grade in New York. As I sat in the back and watched her guide a group of six-year-old boys through various reading exercises, carefully calibrating her interaction with each one, I kept thinking: *If I fail in my task of teaching civil procedure or international law, my students may do less well on their exams or go through their legal careers disliking those subjects. If Nora fails, however, her students' lives could be blighted forever. Learning to read is the foundation for almost everything else they will do in life.*

In terms of both prestige and compensation, that is not exactly how the world sees it. I don't mean to diminish my own accomplishments in passing through the narrow needle that is the law school teaching market. But that's just it. The prestige and high salary that accompanies a teaching position at Chicago or Harvard law schools is a reward for winning out over many others on a fast and difficult track. It reflects the expectation that the professor will advance the frontiers of knowledge through his or her research; students who are admitted to those schools then have the opportunity to study with leading scholars. But at no point are we measuring the value of teachers in terms of what students actually *learn*.

I have had to re-educate myself to, when I meet a teacher, therapist, or coach next to a banker or businessperson, push back against the reflexive assumption that because the banker is richer and more powerful, he or she is thus somehow smarter, more interesting, and more *valuable*. I think to myself that the teacher has the harder and ultimately more important job, one with the potential of altering a life for good or ill. When I had minor but scary surgery right under my left eye, the nurse whose calm and experienced presence made such a difference told me she had left a career in advertising. At that moment, I was very glad she had chosen to apply her intellect and emotional intelligence to a caring profession rather than a commercial one. Teachers and nurses also have the courage and character not to respond to the dominant measures of value in our society.

It may be a constant in human history that having money is valued; even under communism humans found a way to become far richer than their fellows and wielded power as a result. But what we consider cool and attractive has changed continually across time and cultures, from men in wigs and elegant hose to jocks to geeks, from Rubenesque figures to social X-rays. What we value is ultimately up to us.

THE COMPETITIVE MYSTIQUE

So is managing money more valuable than managing kids? It should be clear by now that I think the answer is emphatically no.

In theory, at least, the rest of the world agrees with me. Ann Crittenden opens *The Price of Motherhood* with the observation that it is a commonplace to say that being a mother is the most important job in the world. "In the United States, motherhood is as American as apple pie. No institution is more sacrosanct; no figure is praised more fulsomely." A video circulated in the spring of 2014 that purported to show people being interviewed for a position called "director of operations." It involved working all the time, with no breaks for holidays, lunch, or even sleep, and required "excellent negotiation and interpersonal skills." The position was unpaid. The candidates responded to the job description by balking. "That's inhumane!" they cried, "That's insane!" Then, at the end of the video, the interviewer told them that someone actually holds this job already—in fact, billions of people. "Moms," he tells the job seekers, who laugh and thank their mothers.

But behind this public approbation of motherhood lies a deep well of insincerity. I was reminded of a letter from a young woman who was at the time a first lieutenant in the Air Force Reserve. She wrote to tell me that when she accepted an offer for a tenure-track faculty position, the guy she was dating broke up with her because it was apparent that she would not be putting his nascent career first. At the same time, she reported, "My commanding officer had a chat with me about my priorities. When was I going to stop working so much and start a family? He proceeded to show me a picture of his wife with their 5 children and told me that is what life is about."

If that's what life is about, why don't these men stop working, or scale back their careers, and spend more time caring for their families? There's the hypocrisy. If caring for those we love is just as important and valuable as competing in the marketplace or the military, then we should put our money where our mouth is by finding a range of ways to compensate both paid and unpaid care-givers, with prestige if not with cash.

And yet we don't, because there remains a hidden bias in American society, even among those of us who believe that men and women are equally talented human beings. I've called this the "competition bias": the reflexive way in which we value competition over care. But perhaps, following Betty Friedan, this bias is better understood as a mystique—an ineffable something that we are drawn to and strive to imitate without fully understanding why.

So let us call it "the competitive mystique." It is a mystique that is equally attractive to men and women—the sense that they are succeeding in setting and achieving their individual goals and winning out over others. More generally, it is a mystique that has steadily grown as the world itself has become more competitive over the past few decades, largely through the twin forces of glo-balization and technology. More people are continually compet-ing in more ways.

Overcoming the competitive mystique means dismantling its aura of mystery and power. Bluntly, it means asking ourselves why we think people who have made more money than anyone else or risen to the top of a particular hierarchy by beating out others are automatically role models. What about their values? How do they treat other people? What was the cost to their families—the peo-ple who brought them into the world, people they married, peo-ple they were responsible for bringing into the world? How can that part of the story not be relevant to who they are and how we should think about them?

Overcoming the competitive mystique also means rethinking

our assessment of the relative difficulty of different professions. In the title of this chapter, I deliberately asked whether managing money is *harder* than managing kids to challenge us all. Many of us, deep down, agree with the claim made by the economics student we heard from earlier: that the work we do as professionals is "harder," in the sense that it takes more skill and education, than the work we do as parents or caregivers.

I certainly understand and respect paying for expertise, but over the past three years, I've come to think that although much of the work I do in foreign policy and nonprofit management is intellectually harder than being a mother, parenting is emotionally harder and often far more perplexing. I have also come to believe that we should think about paid care work, from home health service to therapy to teaching, the same way we think about any other profession, including money management. You can do it at a basic level and at a highly advanced level. Your compensation should depend on a combination of your education, experience, and the value we place on the activity as a society.

Don't get me wrong. I'm plenty competitive. I'm the granddaughter of an all-American football player recruited by the NFL; I got none of his athletic ability but I can still remember being in the second-best reading group in first grade and being determined to make it into the first reading group. Competition, with myself as well as with others, has helped drive many of the best things I have done in my life. But loving and caring for my family and friends, teaching and mentoring my students, helping and watching staff members grow into and then out of their jobs is every bit as rewarding. In each of those cases I get as much as I give. Indeed, I often feel that even if my work dies with me, enabling and empowering others will live on in ways I cannot predict.

Overall then, I am not proposing to *devalue* competition; I am proposing to *revalue* care, to elevate it to its proper place as an essential human instinct, drive, and activity. If we can actually teach ourselves to value competition and care equally, to think that managing money and managing a household full of other human beings are equally valid and valuable occupations, we will be on the way to real equality between men and women. We will no longer see work and family as a woman's issue but as a parent's issue, a son's or daughter's issue, a spouse's or sibling's issue, a devoted friend's issue. An issue for anyone who works and who also loves and cares for someone else.

It won't be easy. My generation of feminists was raised to think that the competitive work our fathers did was much more important than the caring work our mothers did. We were socialized to believe that work that leads to winning, to individual achievement and success, is much more important than work that leads to giving, to empowering others to succeed. The generations after us have gotten that message ever more strongly, as girls have been raised to believe that of course they can combine their careers with caregiving, that that is what being a successful woman means. Moreover, for younger generations the competition—for everything—has steadily become more intense. Simply consider how much harder it is to get into a good college and get a decent job with decent wages and opportunities for promotion in 2014 than it was in 1974, 1984, or 1994.

I do not question the importance of equipping girls and boys with equal education, encouraging them to have equal aspirations and to gain sufficient independence that they can support themselves financially. From that perspective, the message we send our children about the importance of competition is absolutely right. But the message that a woman's traditional work of caregiving—anchoring the family by tending to material needs and nourishing minds and souls—is somehow less important than a man's traditional work of earning an income to support that family and advance his own career is false and harmful. It is the result of a historical bias, an outdated prejudice, a cognitive distortion that is skewing our society and hurting us all.

In the long quest for gender equality, women first had to gain power and independence by emulating men. But as we attain that power and independence, we must not automatically accept the traditional man's view—which is really the view of only a minority of men—about what matters in the world.

A Princeton alumna of the class of 2010, Cale Salih, wrote me a powerful letter shortly after my article came out. She began with the reflection, "I have often wondered why I should feel guilty for simply daring to say yes to a momentous personal opportunity." She continued:

> For the past two years, I have been consistently congratulated for making career choices that reflected great ambition, but often came at the expense of personal relationships. Now, I am considering moving to be closer to my long-distance boyfriend. In conversations with people in my own cohort, I find myself making up pretexts to hide the real reason for my move. On occasions that I do reveal the most important motivation behind my move, I am often met with subtle but noticeable eye rolls or, worse, patronizing lectures: "You're too young to make life-altering choices for a boy." While making life-altering choices for a relationship is seen as weak or naive, making similar sacrifices for a job is often seen as a sign of strength and independence.
>
> No more do I want to be unemployed than do I want to be the power woman who goes home after work to eat moo shoo pork alone in her apartment. Why, then, should I be

proud of investing in one goal, and be embarrassed of investing in the other?

The social pressures that Cale is responding to are very real. In January 2013, Princeton senior Margaret Fortney published a reflection in the campus newspaper describing her friend "Molly," who, toward the end of a conversation in which the two young women were contemplating their futures, "leaned in closer to me" and whispered: "I don't want to go to grad school. I don't even know if I want a career. I want to get married, stay at home and raise my kids." Distraught after this admission, Molly said, "What's wrong with me?"

When I was a Princeton student in the late 1970s I certainly would have said that an Ivy League alumna who did not pursue a career was letting down our side. That was still an era in which many men questioned Princeton's decision to go coed at the beginning of the decade, precisely on the grounds that women would just "waste their education" by dropping out of the workforce and having kids. Indeed, if I am truly honest with myself, I would have to admit that a good part of me still questioned the value of being a stay-at-home mom right up until the set of experiences that led to my writing my *Atlantic* article.

But no longer. I would advise all students fortunate enough to attend a top college or university to ensure that they will be able to use their education over the course of their lives to be able to support themselves *and* to enrich their lives and the lives of others, certainly including children. I continue to believe as an article of faith that the vast majority of people want *both:* to advance their own goals and create an identity through rewarding work, and to be able to care for their loved ones.

I believe that individual women and men land in different places on the spectrum between extremely caring and extremely competitive. My aunt Mary falls way over on the competitive end. She was a tennis champion in the 1950s; was the first woman to win a varsity letter at the University of Virginia, *on the men's team*; and is still winning happily at golf and bridge at eighty. My hairdresser, Aziz, is highly entrepreneurial, but he is also a born nurturer. Caring for others is what makes him happy.

Moreover, the best competitors are often players who think about others enough to be able to play well on a team, subjugating their own ego to be able to make the pass that will allow another teammate to score. Similarly, the best caregivers are those who can take enough time for themselves to avoid burnout; the best managers, those who know how to get their team's competitive juices flowing but also to look out for the needs of individual team members. Valuing care can mean understanding the many ways that care and competition complement each other.

If we succeed in freeing ourselves from the competitive mystique, understanding that competition is a valuable human drive but no more valuable than care, we will no longer see the liberation of women as freedom only to compete. On the flip side, if we truly believe that care is just as valuable as competition, then we will realize that men who are only breadwinners are missing out on something deeply satisfying and self-improving. And if both men and women traded off caring and competition in more equal measure, then it would become much easier to customize both workplaces and careers to allow time for both.

Such a vision may sound utopian, but it could happen tomorrow. It just needs one thing . . .

6

THE NEXT PHASE OF THE WOMEN'S MOVEMENT IS A MEN'S MOVEMENT

THERE'S AN ALL-TOO-COMMON STORY OF GENDER DISCRIMINATION in America today, one that's now as iconic as the old tales of women entering the workforce and being asked to serve coffee. It's the story of what happens when a fully competent dad meets a well-intentioned but clueless woman at the park or the grocery store. In an article titled "I Hate Being Called a Good Dad" posted on the *New York Times* blog *Motherlode*, Matt Vilano writes:

> It started the way all of our twice-monthly trips to Target do—the 1-year-old in a backpack on my back, the 3-year-old leading the charge, yanking my hand like a sled dog with a view of the open trail.
>
> We charged through the automatic doors, waving at ourselves on the video screen as always. We grabbed a shopping cart. We stopped at the complimentary sanitary wipes. Then I engaged in what my Big Girl calls "the wipedown": A comprehensive (read: wildly neurotic) disinfecting of any part of the cart she possibly might touch.
>
> About halfway through the ritual—let's estimate nine wipes in—I noticed a middle-aged woman watching us, smiling.

"You're a good dad," she remarked, in a tone that implied she had just seen a Sasquatch.

For Vilano, this incident reflects a "heinous double standard," where he is praised for behavior that in a mother would be regarded as absolutely routine. Andrew Romano, author of a *Newsweek* cover story on masculinity, calls it the "soft bigotry of low expectations."

Just for a moment, flip it and imagine that as a woman you're praised for writing a good report at work, a completely routine action for a man, and praised in a way that makes clear that the person who is complimenting you didn't actually expect you could do it so well. For years when Andy and I first knew each other, I would say something and he would respond, "That's really smart," in a tone that made it clear he was slightly surprised. I would blow up, of course. But Vilano concludes on exactly this point: "The act of labeling someone 'a good dad' suggests that most dads are, by our very nature as fathers, somehow less than 'good.'"

To counter these assumptions and carefully prescribed roles, men need a movement of their own. Most of the pervasive gender inequalities in our society—for both men and women—cannot be fixed unless men have the same range of choices with respect to mixing caregiving and breadwinning that women do. To make those choices real, however, men will have to be respected and rewarded for making them: for choosing to be a lead parent; to defer a promotion or work part-time to spend more time with their children, their parents, or other loved ones; to take paternity leave or to ask for flexible work hours; to reject a culture of workaholism and relentless face time.

Men need to hear this message not as admonition so much as permission: not what they should do, but what they can do. They are free to be caregivers too, and they can be just as competent in these roles as the women in their lives. Women need to hear this message as encouragement to rethink how we imagine and value the men in our lives.

Real equality for men and women needs a men's movement to sweep away the gender roles that we continue to impose on men even as we struggle to remove them from women. To ensure that we socialize boys to believe that they can be anything they want to be, from full-time father to elementary school teacher to investment banker, on an equally valued continuum. To make providing for a family about time as much as about money. To make caregiving cool. To make being a family man just as masculine as being a he-man.

Moreover, they will have to be respected and rewarded *as men*. In a column entitled "How Brad Pitt Brings Out the Best in Dads," *Financial Times* columnist Simon Kuper discusses the value of seeing an undoubtedly masculine movie star "with a toddler strapped to his chest." Pitt and his fellow baby-toting movie star dads are not actually spending their days chasing children, of course—most have an army of paid help. But the subconscious role modeling helps, Kuper argues. The images have the same impact on men that pictures of women CEOs have on women. Men are free to be caregivers too; they can be just as competent in these roles as the women in their lives; and yes, women will still be attracted to them.

For all the skeptics who shake their heads and think I'm challenging nature itself, consider just how certain men have been for centuries that the highest and best role for women was as wives and mothers, daughters and sisters, nurturing and caring for others. My eyes were opened on this score by a letter from a young man who identified himself as "an African American male with a degree from a top 10 university and a salary of near 100k." I'll call him Charles. He took issue with my statement in *The Atlantic* that when choices have to be made, women seem to feel a deeper imperative to trade off work in favor of family than men do. He asked, "Couldn't you write a 'Why Men Can't Have it All' article with the exact same statistics arguing that social pressures on men force them to put work over family and women are better off because they more often get the family part?"

Anticipating my skepticism, Charles went on: "One response might be that because we haven't really heard that from men they likely don't feel this way. However that would be to deny the larger implications of social pressures on men to be manly in general." But of course, deep down, as a woman who has been surrounded by men all her life, I think I know what men think and want, whether I admit it or not. Charles was one step ahead of me here too. "When it was the norm that women were dutiful silent wives," he wrote, "I'm sure many men believed women didn't want careers. As a man, I may choose a high-powered career over child rearing, and be deeply saddened by it, but I won't cry, or complain, or let on at all publicly. Instead, it remains the norm for me to have to suck it up and take it like a man."

Check and checkmate. None of us are free from the biases we grow up with, imbibing them from the nursery on. Indeed, even in the process of writing this book, I realized that I never ask my teenage sons to clean up the kitchen the way I did as a girl, but instead to do more "boy" chores like taking out the trash, the kinds of chores my brothers did. They set the table and bus their plates, but I think that if I had daughters, I would have asked them to rinse those plates, load the dishwasher, wash the pots, and wipe down the counters long since. So we all have plenty of work to do. As men often discovered in the first couple of decades of the women's movement, it's tough to retrain yourself after years of knee-jerk thinking.

The majority of American women have demanded over the last half century that society reject and revise traditional norms about what women want and what they can do. It is time to do the same for men.

WHAT MEN WANT

About six months after my *Atlantic* article came out, I had dinner with a group of Princeton undergraduates. We talked about a number of things that were on their minds: politics in general, the presidential debates, work and family. A number of students asked foreign policy questions, and then several young women asked me about the responses I received to the article. After about ten minutes of that conversation, I saw that the men in the room—roughly 50 percent of the attendees—had gone completely silent. When I commented on the suddenly one-sided nature of the conversation, one young man volunteered that he "had been raised in a strong feminist household" and considered himself to be fully supportive of male-female equality, but he was reluctant to say anything for fear he would be misunderstood. A number of the other guys around the table nodded in agreement.

That male silence is widespread, at least in public. But it is changing. Roughly 15 to 20 percent of the responses to my article that I have personally received have been from men—the same percentage of men that I find in my audiences when I give speeches. And more and more men are taking to the blogosphere and the pages of periodicals to insist that the debate about relations between men and women not be conducted almost entirely among women. They want to be heard and they have very clear ideas about what they want to say.

A Supreme Court Clerk Stays Home

IN THE FALL OF 2014, *The Atlantic* published another article that sparked widespread debate among men and women. This one was called "What Ruth Bader Ginsburg Taught Me About Being a Stay-at-Home Dad," by a hotshot young lawyer—a former clerk for Justice Ginsburg—named Ryan Park. Ginsburg is famous for her own battles on behalf of women's equality as a lawyer in the 1970s and as a woman navigating her own difficulties fitting her family and career together. She told her clerks, "If you have a caring life partner, you help the other person when that person needs it." In that spirit, Park decided to support his wife, who is a doctor, by spending a year as the primary caregiver for their toddler daughter, Caitlyn.

Park writes that the time at home with his daughter reminded him "of the time I'd spent living in a foreign country. There was the same perpetual novelty, that intense awareness that elevates even the most ordinary moments." He asks himself,

> Did I miss the thrill and challenge of debating knotty legal
> questions with a Supreme Court justice? Well, let's just say
> that most of the books I was reading now came with pictures
> of panda bears and barn animals. But every night, even after
> the most pedestrian of days, I sat and reflected on the beauty
> of the moments that had passed.

Park is also refreshingly candid about society's prejudices regarding men. He describes the "good-natured skepticism" that people often express when he discusses what he calls his "struggle to manage my competing commitments to family and career." He encounters an "underlying assumption that women and men have different visions of what matters in life—or, to be blunt about it, that men don't find child-rearing all that rewarding, whereas women regard it as integral to the human experience."

I could not have said it better. As a woman, I object to the presumption that I am somehow more domestic and nurturing than my male colleagues are. That may be true in any individual case, but it should not be assumed because I am a woman. But why then should we impose the opposite stereotype on men, assuming that they automatically want to invest more in work than in their relationships with their families? Park says, "I do not think this assumption is true, generally speaking. I am certain it is not true for me."

Change Is Coming

RYAN PARK IS NOT ALONE. Evidence of a profound shift in the ways men are thinking about themselves and their lives is glimmering on the horizon. Wharton School professor Stewart Friedman reports that for the first time ever, one of his eighteen-year-old male students, when asked what he wanted to do after college, replied that he planned to be a "stay-at-home dad." Kunal Modi, then co-president of the Harvard Business School Student Association, wrote an article in which he urged his fellow male students to "man up" for economic and egalitarian reasons. "Raising children and running a household are not 'women's' roles," he wrote, and "treating them as such is counterproductive to your own family's economic well-being." And at Harvard Law School, Dean Martha Minow says that the one change she has observed over thirty years of teaching law is that today the questions about how on earth these prospective lawyers are going to manage work and life are coming from young men as well as young women.

Even professional athletes, who are under so much pressure

to be seen as traditionally masculine, are now bragging about their infant-wrangling skills. The Mets' second baseman Daniel Murphy was criticized for taking three days of paternity leave; he responded not by buckling to the flack, but by telling reporters about changing his son's diaper in the middle of the night.

One of the best indicators of changing norms is, as always, Madison Avenue. The ad men (and women) learned quickly what not to do. In 2012 Kimberly-Clark, manufacturer of Huggies, created a series of ads filled with fathers watching their babies at home, which they thought would be cute and appealing to parents of both genders. The ads included a female voiceover saying, almost condescendingly, "To prove Huggies diapers and wipes can handle anything, we put them to the toughest test imaginable: dads, alone with their babies, in one house, for five days, while we gave moms some well-deserved time off. How did Huggies products hold up to daddyhood?"

Many fathers reacted furiously to the message of presumed paternal incompetence. A stay-at-home father from Oregon named Chris Routly started a Change.org petition called "We're Dads, Huggies. Not Dummies." It got more than 1,300 signatures. Huggies eventually pulled the ad and apologized, repeatedly, and in person, at a dad blogger convention called Dad 2.0.

It hasn't taken the advertising industry long to learn from its mistakes. In the 2013 World Series, Chevrolet aired an ad for its Malibu sedan that had a gentle male voice talking about the importance of family over material wealth. "We don't jump at the sound of the opening bell, because we're trying to make the school bell," the voiceover intones, as a dad corrals his son into the car, adding, "Corner booth beats corner office any day." The 2015 Super Bowl ads continued the trend, featuring an ad for Dove Men+Care that depicted children, young and old, calling out to their fathers from a highchair all the way to the dance floor at a wedding reception. In case viewers missed the connection, the tagline asked, "What makes a man stronger?" Answer: "Showing that he cares."

The companies making these commercials spend millions of dollars on consumer research. They are plugging into something their customers want before they fully understand that they want it. The statistics tell the tale. The 2013 Pew Research study that found roughly equal stress levels among mothers and fathers was subtitled "Roles of Moms and Dads Converge as They Balance Work and Family." Mothers are still spending more time with their children than fathers are, but almost half the fathers surveyed would like to be spending *more* time with their kids, as opposed to just over a fifth of mothers.

EXPANDING CHOICES FOR ALL MEN

So far, so good. Nothing particularly jaw-dropping about the idea that fathers who are equal caregivers with mothers should have the same options as those mothers and should merit an equal presumption of competence. But dads are only the beginning. Men—*all* men—need and deserve the same revolution in their lives and circumstances that the majority of women in the United States and many other parts of the world have experienced since the late 1950s.

Here again, it is not hard to find signs of change. Writer and co-founder of the Fatherhood Institute Jack O'Sullivan wrote in 2013 that though the debate about men is oftentimes "overwhelmingly negative," men are actually on the brink of an "extraordinary transformation." Like women, men "are belatedly escaping what we now recognise to be the confines of our gender. Many of us are enjoying a massively increased engagement with children. . . . We are changing our relationships with women and with each other." Organizations like the Good Men Project, a media company and social platform that describes itself as "a glimpse of what enlightened masculinity might look like in the 21st century," are encouraging a new conversation.

The most poetic description of the changing definition of manhood I have seen comes from a Dartmouth alumna, Betsy Bury '87, who canvassed her classmates and wrote up her impressions for their twenty-fifth reunion book. Dartmouth men, she wrote, are "starting to feel this pull of multiple directions; quietly they have started being promised more too. Came a little later for them maybe, but it is no longer just whispers that they do not need to feel consigned exclusively to grey flannel suits, the emotional range of John Wayne or parenthood dominated by only a few tossed balls or late arrivals at school plays."

I came to the realization that men need more choices not in my professional life, nor in the course of trying to think through how to advance women in the world, but as the mother of two sons. It dawned on me that the majority of American mothers in the twenty-first century are raising our daughters with more life paths open to them than are open to our sons.

For at least two decades we have been telling girls, "You can do anything boys can do, as well as what girls have traditionally done. You can be a mother, a daughter, a sister, and a wife, *and* you can be anything you want to be professionally. Indeed, you are part of a historic cause, with plenty of glass ceilings left to break."

Raise children with a mission, a sense of their own destiny, and watch them thrive. Immigrant children, for instance, often grow up with a mission to fulfill their parents' hopes for them in a new country that offers opportunities and possibilities that would have been denied them in the old. Girls and young women are still immigrants on the shores of a world led and dominated by men. They have a world to conquer, and judging by the ways they are outpacing boys in elementary school, high school, and college, they are out to succeed.

Contrast the messages we send to our sons. Upper-middle-class white parents may expect our sons to become successful professionals but see no special achievement in it the way we still do for girls. They will not be making history, just repeating it—hardly inspiring or motivating. On top of that, boys still get very traditional messages of what is masculine and what is not. As one of the men I work with at New America puts it, "My daughter can go to the park in jeans, roll around in the mud, drop-kick another kid . . . and no one bats an eye. My son comes to school with his nails painted . . . and his class erupts."

Because of our unspoken but still very real view that caregiving is unmanly, we are reinforcing a much narrower set of choices for our sons. We are still telling them, fundamentally, that they have to be breadwinners. Their wives can also be breadwinners, but I am fairly confident in saying that few mothers out there, and probably fewer fathers, are really giving their sons the message that being a full-time or part-time father or caregiver is just as much an option as it is for our daughters.

At the same time, at least among white upper-middle-class parents, expectations for boys versus girls have shifted sharply. Many feminists who are mothers of sons are living in a split universe. In our professional lives we still very often live in a largely male world, certainly in the higher reaches. We mentor younger women to lean in, sit at the table, speak up, and put themselves forward. But at home we face a different gender balance: the steady rise of girls, or, as many parenting books and articles describe it, "the boy crisis." Michael Kimmel, author of *Manhood in America*, summarizes the problem: "Girls are surpassing boys in college attendance (about 60 percent of entering first-year students [in 2013] are female); achievement (girls have caught up in science and math, and far outpace boys in English and language); and behaviors (boys are far more likely to be retained, suspended, diagnosed with ADHD and get into fights)."

The academic and popular literature on why we see these patterns and what we should do about our boys is vast and growing, as is awareness among parents. In Princeton we have a parent group for mothers of boys. And I've had countless conversations with other parents in which someone will say, "My kids get themselves up in the morning" or "My child has taken on fifteen extracurricular activities and organizes them all," and another parent will respond, "You have girls, right?" Indeed, we women who fight so furiously to avoid any discussion of essentialist differences with respect to men and women openly debate them with respect to boys and girls.

I often tell the story of my bemusement and mild consternation when my oldest son, then in elementary school, offered, matter-of-factly, "Girls are smarter than boys" as a reason why he should not be expected to be at the top of his class. The feminist in me applauded the progress we have made from an era in which girls just assumed that boys were smarter than they were; the mother in me said no way!

Still, it's easy to overdramatize here. Sociologists Claudia Buchmann and Thomas DiPrete point out that girls have actually done better than boys in school grades for more than a century, but that for most of that time women felt pressured to choose between getting an education or having a family, or else getting an education to be able to be a better mother. Only in the last forty years or so have girls been able to see a clear link between how well they do in school and how well they will do in life, so that instead of hiding their smarts, they have every incentive to embrace their intelligence and achievements. Moreover, upper-middle-class boys are still doing fine relative to the rest of the population of Americans, men and women.

The real crisis in the United States is among poorer boys from minority communities. Of the four major demographic groups in the United States (whites, Asians, Hispanics, and African Americans), blacks and Hispanics have the lowest rates of graduation, and black males are one of the only subgroups whose graduation rate decreased between 2007 and 2009. It's not just getting African American boys to the finish line in their caps and gowns; the problems are far more systemic and begin in elementary school. A report called *A Call for Change* from the Council of the Great City Schools explains that "only 12 percent of Black fourth-grade boys in large city schools are proficient in reading, compared with 38 percent of White boys in the nation, and only 12 percent of Black eighth-grade boys in large city schools are proficient in math, compared with 44 percent of White boys in the nation."

As Michael Kimmel again points out, drawing on ethnographic work by psychologist Wayne Martino, in middle and early high school even boys in well-educated communities get the message "It's not cool for guys to do well in school." And although Buchmann and DiPrete found that girls have long outperformed boys in school, they nevertheless agree that many boys are studying and engaging less and denigrating the importance of good grades. Particularly for working-class boys, if their schools, parents, or peers have a dominant male culture that "opposes academic achievement" and emphasizes narrow masculine ideals, it can exacerbate the gender gap. Boys' success depends on what answer they are hearing, consciously or subconsciously, to the question "What makes a good man?"

Suppose we were to tell our boys that they have the opportunity in their lifetimes to expand the social and economic roles for men in the same way their mothers and sisters expanded the roles for women? That they could take the definition of masculinity into their own hands and bend it in whatever direction they chose? The biggest unconquered world open to men is the world of caring for others. If we tell boys that they can break down centuries-old barriers and be pioneers of social change, suddenly they have a mission, an inspiration, and a new kind of role model to emulate—a new definition of a good man.

BEATING BIOLOGY

ABOUT TEN YEARS AGO I taught a seminar with a terrific group of secondary school history and social studies teachers assembled by the Gilder Lehrman Institute of American History. One of the participants, a middle-aged man from South Carolina whom I will call Jim has stayed in touch with me on foreign policy and, more recently, work and family issues. He wrote to me after my *Atlantic* article came out to say that my account of juggling work and family captured his wife's experience as she worked her way up the corporate ladder of a large global medical equipment company while also raising their daughter.

Jim went on to talk about his own experience, pointing out that the husbands of women in corporate or professional careers inevitably face challenges of their own. "To begin," Jim writes, "there is something subtly if not overtly that our society attaches to a husband whose wife's income is obviously much greater than his." He says that he has "enjoyed a wonderful professional career as a high school teacher and coach," a choice he has never regretted, and that he has brought in extra income in a number of ways. Still, his wife is a businesswoman whose salary "naturally exceeds that of an educator."

In Jim's view, even with the best will in the world, "It is far too idealistic to pretend that there are times when this is not a difficult position for a married man to find himself in. In social settings, it is politely ignored, but I think it fair to say that it is something that a married man knows others are thinking about." Jim went on to wonder whether his feelings were "an archaic standard of a past that no longer fits, or an instinctual, primal urge."

I received a similar email after I gave a commencement address at Tufts advising the young men in the graduating class to think about how they were going to fit work and family together—the kind of advice speakers usually give young women. A parent in the audience wrote to say he had been married for twenty years to a woman he loved and with whom he had two wonderful children. When his wife received a great business opportunity he decided to move for her, but his own career suffered as a result, even as hers surged. The resulting conflict led to divorce. He was honest enough to say that the "resentment towards my wife ran deeper than jealousy and existed in spite of the conscious knowledge that I made the right pragmatic decision; rather it was a very deep feeling of failure to be a real father."

Whereas Jim wondered about his "primal urge," my Tufts correspondent believes that our ape ancestors evolved into monogamous relationships in which the mother and child are vulnerable for long periods of time, leading "to very high level of positive selection for males that protected and provided for their mates and offspring. I believe this is one of the core components of why men love. If a man cannot protect or provide, he probably will not or cannot love."

In fact, anthropologists like Sarah Blaffer Hrdy point out that in early human groupings both men and women looked after the offspring collectively. In the book *Sex at Dawn*, a psychologist and a psychiatrist look deep into the evolutionary, anthropological, and sociological research and find that hunter-gatherers lived in entirely egalitarian societies, where childcare was generalized, food was shared, and sex was nonmonogamous, not because they were utopian romantics, but because "it works on the most practical levels."

Economist Paul Seabright looks at men's and women's differing sexual strategies back to the Pleistocene era, starting from the abundance of sperm and the scarcity of eggs. That basic asymmetry means that "women's sexual psychology has been shaped by the need to be selective in their reactions to men, just as men's has been shaped by the need to be persistent in their approaches to women." But this biologically dictated dance of cooperation and conflict is consistent with a wide range of sexual behaviors that fly in the face of what we so often consider "natural."

In short, we have *lots* of primal urges, men and women alike. Which ones come out on top has just as much to do with economics and society as biology. And, as any of the world's top biologists will tell you, we still have much to discover about the history of our species' male-female relationships and interactions. Our body of knowledge, at this point, is far from complete, so anyone who claims to know what is "natural" is simply revealing his or her own biases.

Who knows what we might find if we look a little harder and cast aside our preconceptions?

MUST MONEY STILL MAKE THE MAN?

A COUPLE OF YEARS AGO, I had breakfast with a very successful banker and philanthropist, a woman ten to fifteen years older than I who is divorced. She was blunt about the ways in which men cannot handle their partner's success but argued that they simply will not own up publicly to the way they feel about their wives outearning them because the truth is not politically correct.

In the mid-1980s, journalist Bebe Moore Campbell conducted more than one hundred interviews with men and women in two-career couples in which the wife's career had taken off, as well as with many therapists counseling couples in similar situations. The result was a book entitled *Successful Women, Angry Men*. She found plenty of husbands of successful career women who were outwardly very supportive of their wive's careers but were inwardly anxious about the shifting power dynamics in their marriage. One vice president for a multinational energy company summed up the fears of many: "If my wife didn't need me for my money, she didn't need me."

Ah, but that was thirty years ago! Sadly, not much has changed. According to a 2011 study, "Men's breadwinning is still so culturally mandated that when it is absent, both men and women are more likely to find that the marital partnership does not deserve to continue." Andy and I know many professional couples, a number of whom we met in grad school when both the men and the women had equal career prospects. Today we know only a handful in which the wife outearns the husband. Moreover, Andy says that if he makes a comment about how I outearn him, many people—especially women—will shift uneasily and almost try to correct him, as if he had made a self-deprecating remark.

Perhaps it is just the discomfort of talking about what any of us earn, a subject that, at least when I grew up in Virginia, was as taboo as religion or politics. But both Andy and I think it's more than that. His acknowledgment of what should be an obvious fact, given that I was a dean when he was a professor and am now the president of an organization, makes his listeners uncomfortable in ways that simply would not happen if I made a comment about how my husband was the principal breadwinner in the family. He's not shy about it; in his view he got lucky! But as a society we still have a long way to go.

Sara Blakely, the billionaire founder of Spanx, took the stage at the Women in the World Summit in New York in 2013 and told the story of how several of her boyfriends ended up being scared off by her financial success. She went on to explain that it took her a long time to tell the man who is now her husband about her fortune, waiting until shortly before their wedding date, and concluded by saying how relieved she was when he took it in stride.

Blakely's story confirms the point I am making, which is that money and masculinity are still deeply intertwined. In the end, however, she obviously did find her man—a man secure enough to marry her. Marrying a billionaire may not seem like a particularly brave thing to do, but the men who are willing to break the barriers of traditional masculine roles have the same kind of courage that pioneering feminists did when they pushed their way into the all-male preserves of business and law.

THE COURAGE TO CARE

RYAN PARK WRITES, "DURING MY time as a stay-at-home dad, I was dismayed by the novelty of my choice." He reports that as he took his daughter to libraries, parks, and playgrounds, he could "go weeks without seeing another man between the ages of 5 and 70 during the weekday working hours." Worse, the mothers he encountered assumed that he must not actually be home with his daughter by choice; rather, it had to be the result of not being able to find a job. Over time, this assumption that he must "be a professional failure" got to him, no matter how hard he tried to resist it. It is in fact true that more than half of American stay-at-home dads either have a disability or couldn't find a job, which means that the men who *do* choose this path voluntarily are all the more admirable.

As in every other kind of behavior change, it turns out that the social network makes a huge difference here. Andy was strongly influenced by his dissertation supervisor, Robert Keohane, who is one of the leading political scientists of his generation and a close friend. Bob left Stanford to go to Brandeis when his wife, Nannerl Keohane, became president of Wellesley and later left Harvard to go to Duke when she became the first woman president of Duke. It is impossible to know Bob without seeing his enormous pride in Nan's big jobs shine through. Bob has been a role model for Andy in the same way that Nan has been a role model for me.

The chain continues. One of Andy's cousins is an actor, musician, and artist in Los Angeles who took on the primary caregiver role for his two children while his wife brought in most of the income. When I asked him whether he felt comfortable with that decision, he acknowledged that the social pressures could be tough, but he noted that he had always looked up to Andy and so figured that if Andy was cool in that role, he could be too.

In short, men need role models to be comfortable making the choice to put their families first, particularly role models who are willing to use their alpha male status to change the definition of an alpha male. Mohamed El-Erian resigned as CEO of PIMCO, an investment management firm, in large part because he felt as if he was missing his daughter's many milestones. He took on several advisory positions instead to give him the flexibility "to experience with my daughter more of those big and little moments that make up each day." Similarly, Max Schireson, the former

CEO of MongoDB, a database company, announced he was quitting his job because he wanted to be more present for his three kids. His resignation was accompanied by a blog post, in which he wrote:

> I recognize that by writing this I may be disqualifying myself from some future CEO role. Will that cost me tens of millions of dollars someday? Maybe. Life is about choices. Right now, I choose to spend more time with my family and am confident that I can continue to have a meaningful and rewarding work life while doing so.

These men are in rarefied positions, but, like Hollywood fathers, they can have a wide impact. Men somewhat further down the economic ladder are looking at their options and making similar decisions—decisions that women have been making for decades. Rob Boland, who was a senior VP at Fidelity Investments, and his wife, Beth, who was a partner at the law firm Mintz Levin, realized something had to give with two big careers and three small kids. So Rob took a less demanding job, and then two years later became a stay-at-home dad. According to *The Boston Globe*, Boland's son told his pediatrician, "The happiest day of my life . . . was when my dad came home from work and told me that he was going to stay home and take care of us from then on."

If men whom other men respect can handle a high-powered wife who brings in a larger salary or can step back from their own big jobs to spend more time with their families, those other men will follow suit. Men who are strong enough to take risks, break the mold, and prove themselves in new roles can define a new frontier. After all, the "man's world" that American women still experience is actually a world shaped by and for a relatively small number of privileged, educated, heterosexual, white alpha males, a group less and less reflective of American men as a whole. It's up to other men to make that world their own.

LIFE LESSONS

BRONNIE WARE, AN AUSTRALIAN BLOGGER who has worked in palliative care for years and written a book entitled *The Top Five Regrets of the Dying*, writes that the regret she heard most often, from men and women, was "I wish I'd had the courage to live a life true to myself, not the life others expected of me." The second was: "I wish I didn't work so hard," which she said "came from every male patient that I nursed. They missed their children's youth and their partner's companionship."

Old age reveals important truths. But why is this so hard? Why is it that so many men only realize what they have missed at the end of their lives?

Ryan Park gets it as a young man. Writing about his choice to spend as much time as possible with his daughter while he could, he says, "My deepest fear is that, decades from now, I will look back at the heart of my life and realize I made the wrong choices in favor of work." One of his friends, a surgeon, sees the fragility of life every day. As he told Park, "I've seen too many 30- or 40-something fathers rushed into the O.R. after a car crash and never get the chance to say goodbye to their young children. . . . You have to focus on what is important while you can."

President Obama, for one, agrees. In his words,

> Everything else is unfulfilled if we fail at family, if we fail at
> that responsibility. I know that when I am on my deathbed
> someday, I will not be thinking about any particular legisla-

tion I passed; I will not be thinking about a policy I promoted; I will not be thinking about the speech I gave, I will not be thinking about the Nobel Prize I received. I will be thinking about that walk I took with my daughters. I'll be thinking about a lazy afternoon with my wife. I'll be thinking about sitting around the dinner table and seeing them happy and healthy and knowing that they were loved. And I'll be thinking about whether I did right by all of them.

That's man enough for me.

LET IT GO

LIKE MANY PEOPLE, I LOVED THE MOVIE *Frozen*. MY BOYS ARE A little old for it, however, so I have to admit that during one of my many long plane flights I watched it happily on my own. When I got to the theme song "Let It Go," sung by one of the movie's two heroines, who has decided to let go of all the suffocating expectations about how a princess should behave and finally use her long-suppressed magic powers, I wanted to cheer.

This chapter embraces that song's message of liberation—with a twist. Women not only have to let go of society's traditional expectations about who a woman should be and what she should do. We also have to let go of our *own* expectations about who a man should be and what he is and is not good at.

TURNING THE SPOTLIGHT ON OURSELVES

VIRTUALLY ALL THE WOMEN I know and most of the women in my audiences have deeply embedded stereotypes about men in the home. I certainly indulge them myself. I often laugh with other women about "male looking": that phenomenon when a man opens a cabinet in the kitchen, stares blankly straight ahead, and then yells, "Where's the peanut butter?" Typically it's right in front of him. I've also often said that "my husband believes in Santa Claus," because as far as he's concerned Christmas just magically appears, stockings and all. With an audience of women, this line never fails to get a knowing chuckle.

A certain amount of gender teasing is completely fine and funny. Given that our household is three men and me, we all indulge in plenty of eye rolling about male and female differences. I truly don't get a lot of humor that both my husband and sons find hilarious, almost invariably involving bodily functions. And they are often bewildered by female behavior that seems perfectly obvious to me. Overall, I am happy to acknowledge and embrace gender differences.

But I'm not talking about difference here. I'm talking about presumed superiority: the ways in which a majority of American women actually think we are better than men in the entire domestic realm, from kids to kitchens. About the things we don't actually want to give up. And about the roles many of us want men to play and the roles we are willing to let them play.

Consider the following scenario. You walk into your office on your first day of work and your boss, a man, says, "I have evolved biologically to do this job better than you can, but I'm going to let you try. To be sure it's done right, however, I will leave you detailed instructions for every individual task. And when I travel, I will call in every couple of hours to make sure you are following those instructions to the letter."

Most women in such a situation would complain immediately to human resources and perhaps start considering a lawsuit. But when I describe this hypothetical scene to audiences of women, the laughter of recognition begins to ripple along the rows by the time I get to "I will leave you detailed instructions." They know exactly what I'm talking about. This is precisely the way the majority of us treat our husbands or male partners when we leave them in charge of the children. For every woman who remains frustrated by her husband's description of an evening with the kids when she is out as "babysitting," another would not dream of leaving the house without prepared meals in the fridge and long lists of what Dad needs to do. When I point out our own double standards in this regard, double standards we have long ago fiercely rejected in the workplace, I see a number of women looking slightly shamefaced. But inevitably at least one woman in the audience will raise her hand and say what many others are thinking:

"But they really *don't* know how to do it."

"Do you have any idea what the house would look like if I weren't there?"

"My husband would feed them pizza every night."

I laugh and agree. But then I point out that I have spent many years in my career wondering why men seem to think that their way of getting work done is the best or only way. The cult of face time; the endless sports metaphors; the assumption that bigger is (almost) always better. I often have a different way of doing things, and who are my male colleagues to say I'm wrong, as long as the work gets done and done well? The first round of pioneering feminists had to accept the roles and routines of office work on male terms; increased equality today means that women are increasingly free to do it our way. Why shouldn't men have that same liberty and equality at home?

Men are certainly aware of a widespread female presumption that we really do know better when it comes to home and kids. In an article in *New York* magazine, therapist Barbara Kass calls many of us out on this account: "So many women want to control their husbands' parenting. 'Oh, do you have the this? Did you do the that? Don't forget that she needs this. And make sure she naps.' Sexism is internalized." On *Huffington Post*, dad blogger Aaron Gouveia notes it's mostly the moms "who claim to be over-worked and desperate for dads to do more" who also criticize dads for not doing things right when they do step up. "And by right, I mean their way. I've seen dads criticized and made fun of for how they dress the baby [and] for how they feed the baby."

Still, for the sake of argument, let's assume for the moment that the average woman you know *is* better at managing all the household tasks and childcare than the average man. Now ask yourself why that might be so. Both practice and confidence come to mind.

Think about the household division of duties in areas where gender stereotypes don't necessarily operate. Doing the taxes, for instance. Did your mom or your dad do them? In my household my dad did them, but I did them the first time Andy and I filed a joint return because I had a bigger salary and had been doing mine before we were married. I did them once, then became the person who knew what to do, a competence that inevitably grew over the years such that it would make no sense for him to take it over now. Similarly, he is the trip planner. His father always planned every detail of his family's trips, so he planned our first vacation and every vacation since. But it could quite easily have worked out the other way. The point is that if you gather the knowledge to do it once, you become the designee for that task, a status that only expands the more knowledge you gain and more expert you become.

Now transpose that pattern to children. In families with bio-logical children, the mother bears the child and typically breast-feeds. That means she instantly begins gaining competence, even if at first she's having a whole new experience. Babies don't come with instruction manuals. Confidence—or lack of confidence—are self-fulfilling prophecies, as we know from social psychologist Claude Steele's work on priming. Steele and his disciples have shown over and over again that reinforcing positive stereotypes a fraction of a second before challenging a student to do a task produces better outcomes, while reinforcing negative stereotypes leads to lower performance.

In Steele's book, *Whistling Vivaldi*, he discusses how stereotypes can be both cultural and situational. For example, women, blacks, and Latinos are told they are bad at math, and so they don't do as well in math overall as Asians and men. But Steele showed that "stereotype threat" can be situational, too. He did a study where researchers told one group of white male Stanford students with high math ability that they were taking a difficult eighteen-question test on which "Asians tend to do better than whites." A control group of white male students was told nothing. The results were stark. The white men who were told that Asians do better on the test performed three questions worse than the students who were told nothing at all, the difference between an A and a B grade.

If women assume they can do whatever needs to be done in the domestic space better and faster than men can, they are likely to be better. Conversely, as Rutgers professor Stuart Shapiro puts it, "If a man is told repeatedly he is not good at child care (or cooking dinner), or that the family is better off if the woman does more of it, he will probably start believing it (as he is probably predisposed to anyway)." Writer and co-founder of the Fatherhood Institute Jack O'Sullivan agrees, arguing that one reason men are so silent in debates about work and family is that "even the most senior male chief executive often lacks confidence in areas that might be defined as personal, private or family."

Just think about how we all continually reinforce this stereo-type: when a child starts to fuss and a man is holding him, many women in my generation, at least, will immediately reach for him with the assumption that they know how to handle a baby better. And almost all the men of my father's generation and a fair number in mine are likely to look around for a mother, grandmother, or aunt.

Once again, biology rears its controversial head here. Women produce big doses of the "love hormone," oxytocin, during labor, which plays a part in that magic moment when you look into your baby's face and your world shifts under your feet. Men don't. Women breast-feed. Men don't. In nature only 5 percent of male mammals are engaged fathers; the other 95 percent inseminate and depart. Surely then, even if we feminists deny it with our dying breaths, women are "naturally" customized for child rearing.

But not so fast. It is true that women get that dose of oxytocin and that they breast-feed. Neuroscientists Kelly Lambert and Craig Kinsley have shown that motherhood makes rats smarter, more emotionally resilient, and physically agile. It turns out, however, that similar changes, and the same hormones, are found in the brains of male California deer mice, one of the species in which both males and females care for the pups. And deer mice are not the only species in which the male is affected by parent-ing. Endocrine systems and neural circuitry are altered in a man-ner "strikingly similar to that in mothers" in male marmosets, owl monkeys, and, of course, human beings.

More recent neuroimaging research on new fathers has in-deed shown structural changes in their brains—not just increased activity at the sight of their infants but longer-term changes in the parts of the brain associated both with nurturing and with anxiety.

This work is at a tentative and early stage, but one new father of twins, writing about this research, says, "When you become a dad, it's like a plate has been set spinning in your brain (or two in my case)—suddenly, no matter where you are, or what you're doing, you have this restless vigilance for your fragile offspring. And then there's the time spent playing and feeding, when you're alert to every flicker of emotion on their little face, every tiny hiccup or cry." Sounds just like a mother to me!

I don't know that Andy ever thought very much about having children before we were married; he certainly didn't think about the details of caring for them. But because he was a professor, he could be around as much as I was in those early days of parenthood. I was ten when my younger brother Bryan was born and I had taken care of him plenty, so the habits of rocking, burping, and diaper changing quickly came back. Mostly, though, we had to figure out *this* baby with the equipment of this era. Andy was much more likely to read parenting books and research various products. Even when I breast-fed, Andy would take the last feeding of the day with a bottle. He was in charge, testing and discarding multiple methods of trying to fill Edward up as much as possible to buy us an extra hour or two of sleep. They bonded early and fast.

We are entering a vast new age of knowledge about our brains, our bodies, our biology. What we should assume above all right now is how much we *don't* know about what men and women can do and about what we are programmed and conditioned to do by both nature and nurture. Are we different? Of course. But different in ways that constrain our abilities and possibilities as either breadwinners or caregivers? We have no idea.

It's worth remembering Kelly Lambert's words of wisdom: "If nature teaches anything, it's that those species flexible enough to adapt to changing environments are the ones that survive."

WE DON'T WANT TO GIVE IT UP

I VIVIDLY REMEMBER THE FIRST time one of our sons woke up in the night and called for Daddy instead of Mommy. My first reaction, to put it politely, was deep dismay. I'm his *mother*. Kids are supposed to call for their *mother*. If he's not calling for me, then I must not be a good mom.

All this is racing through my head while my husband is sleeping soundly next to me; I, after all, was the one who woke up when our son called out. (Andy swears that he wakes up when I'm not there; I'll never know! But our sons have never complained of crying out and no one coming when I'm away.)

On that particular occasion, I got up and comforted my son, telling him Mommy was here and that Daddy was sleeping downstairs; all was right with the world. Over the years, on the many other occasions when our sons turned first to Andy rather than to me—for homework help or advice on subjects ranging from music to girls—I have had some tough conversations with myself. Even if, as my mother would say, I have always wanted to have my cake and eat it too, I simply cannot have all the rewards and satisfactions of my career and expect to be the person my sons call for first.

I have also reflected on my emotion that night. Was it guilt? That ideal of the good mother as the person who is always there when her kids need her? In the United States, at least, we've beaten that subject to death in recent years, asking ourselves repeatedly why the standards of mothering have become so exacting and all-consuming. I have often wondered what happened to the mantra of "benign neglect," which my mother used to quote as the best guide to child rearing. As one of my friends put it, nowadays "benign neglect would result in someone calling social services."

In her 2014 bestseller *All Joy and No Fun: The Paradox of Modern Parenthood*, Jennifer Senior points to the confluence of several factors—Americans having fewer children, women having more control over their reproductive lives thanks to widely available contraception, and parents having children later than they did in my mother's day—as reasons why benign neglect went out of style. From 1970 to 2006, the proportion of women having their first child after the age of thirty-five increased nearly eightfold. "Because so many of us are now avid volunteers for a project in which we were all once dutiful conscripts," Senior writes, "we have heightened expectations of what children will do for us, regarding them as sources of existential fulfillment rather than as ordinary parts of our lives."

If I am honest with myself, the hardest emotion to work through when I heard our son call for Andy rather than for me was not guilt but envy. Even with all the rewards of my career, I would still like for them to call for me first. As the psychiatrist Andras Angyal writes, "We ourselves want to be needed. We do not only have needs, we are also strongly motivated by *neededness*." Mothers have gotten that special rush for years when a child reaches for us and says no one else will do; the question is whether we really want or are willing to share that role with others.

Katrin Bennhold is a young journalist whom I met over a decade ago. I was immediately impressed with her intelligence and drive; I then followed her columns in the *International Herald Tribune* and agreed to occasional interviews on foreign policy issues. Over the years she married and had two daughters. A year after I published my *Atlantic* article I was delighted but not surprised to read her reflections on exactly the question of who gets to be the most needed parent.

Bennhold won a Nieman fellowship at Harvard, one of journalism's most prestigious honors, which allows the recipient to spend nine months in Cambridge. Nieman fellows include a wide roster of the world's top journalists in their ranks; traditionally a male journalist would pack up his wife and children, if he had them, and head for Harvard's ivy-covered halls. In Bennhold's case, however, her husband had a job in London that he could not leave, nor could she manage to care for their two daughters on her own in Cambridge. So she did what I did when I went to Washington: she moved for her job and left her husband as primary caregiver back in London.

On her trips back home, she found that her husband understood the challenges of parenting in a new way, including the "leaden fatigue" of staying up all night with a child and then going to work the next day. "But he also gets the power of being The One—of being the ultimate source of comfort for a child." She, in turn, now knows "the sting of rejection when a child strains to be soothed by the other parent."

Bennhold also knows, as I do, the power of being liberated to pursue your career goals full-time, "the freedom of not being responsible on a day-to-day basis, of being the scarce parent, the fun-time parent rather than the one in charge of brushing teeth or disciplining." She is honest enough to admit that she used to think "that because I gave birth, the bond with my children was something my husband—always a very involved father—could not quite match." She has now concluded that "responsibility and time, not gender, determine the depth of the bond with a child." In addition, she and her husband "have become more equal" by each "slipping into the opposite gender's role."

I would agree on both counts. It is still unquestionably important to me that our sons turn to me first on some things; I specialize in emotional issues and moral dilemmas. My personal balance between competition and care meant that I came home from D.C. so that I could still be part of our sons' lives enough to know when and how I could help. That's simply part of what makes me whole, just as it is important to me to be there for my own parents, my siblings, and my close friends.

Overall, however, I have to accept that if I'm going to travel as much as my career often demands, then Andy is going to be the anchor parent at home. I remind myself that my father was often gone when I was growing up, yet he and I are very close. But I also tell myself that our sons are lucky to have close relationships with both of us and that I am privileged to have both a career and a family I love.

My experience, like Katrin Bennhold's, can't be said to reflect a universal truth. But being needed *is* a universal desire and the traditional coin in which mothers have been compensated. If we accept that trade-offs are necessary for women if they want to reach the top of their careers, even if they have money and choices, and if we're prepared to let men be equal caregivers just as we insist on being equal competitors, then we have to be very honest about our deepest needs and desires. It is one thing to let go of the housekeeping. Quite another to relinquish being the center of your children's universe.

FIFTY SHADES OF CONFUSION

SHORTLY AFTER MY ARTICLE IN *The Atlantic* came out, I met a young woman outside the CNN studios in New York who recognized me and thanked me for launching a conversation about work and family. We talked briefly about the importance of having an equal partner, but she then wrinkled her nose at the idea of a "house husband, a man doing the dishes." Her reaction cuts to the heart of the continuing inequality between men and women.

A woman can drop out of the workforce and remain an attractive partner. For men, that is still a risky choice. Though we may be more welcoming to stay-at-home dads than we used to be, we're certainly not at full equality yet. In 2010, when Pew Research asked respondents if it's very important for a man to be a good provider, 64 percent of women said yes; when they asked the same question about women, only 39 percent of women said yes.

Young men are keenly aware of the gap between what many women say they want and what they choose. In *The End of Men*, Hanna Rosin quotes David, a twenty-nine-year-old with a master's degree, talking about the idea of a stay-at-home dad: "Yeah, he haunts me. It doesn't matter how Brooklyn-progressive we (urban, educated men born after 1980) are, we still think he's pitifully emasculated. I'm progressive and enlightened, and on an ideological political level I believe in that guy. I want that guy to exist. I just don't want to *be* that guy."

Guy Raz, the host of NPR's *TED Radio Hour*, who doesn't work the normal Monday to Friday nine to five, notes that he is often shut down by moms at the playground, where he is usually the only dad among mothers and nannies. "Even in the most open-minded communities, there's always the snickering and the 'Mr. Mom' jokes," Raz writes.

Women define the nature of masculinity as much as other men do. If *they* are going to change, *we* have to find and embrace an image of a man who can care for children; earn less than we do; have his own ideas about how to organize kitchens, lessons, and trips; and still be fully sexy and attractive as a man.

For the moment, however, we are sending mixed messages at best. While almost 3 million people went to the *Atlantic* website to read all or part of my article and more than 2 million people have bought *Lean In* as of March 2015, more than 100 million readers have bought at least one of the books in the Fifty Shades trilogy, a fantasy about a handsome billionaire who plays all sports effortlessly and owns houses, planes, cars, closets full of expensive clothing, and a playroom where he can dominate his girlfriends. He takes care of everything; the entire storyline of these books is about how the woman who will ultimately become his wife and the mother of his children pushes back, but only enough to be able to pursue a modest career of her own, to turn his lust into love, and to ensure that he's kinky enough to arouse but not really hurt her. The media certainly presumes that the readership of the trilogy and the audiences for the movie are overwhelmingly female, but the men in their lives would have had to be hermits to miss the splash it created.

As I see it, *all* of us, men and women, want to be cared for at various times; I have always said that one of the hardest things about being a mom is that when I get sick no one is there to tell me to stay in bed, to put a cooling hand on my forehead. I also certainly love the protective side of the men in my life and am more than willing to let them take charge at times. But the fantasy of a man with all the money in the world who can fix every problem and make everything all right is just that: a fantasy.

It is not surprising that we are confused, just as many men are confused. But we can at least be honest about that confusion. As much as we say we want fully equal partners at home and at work, many of us resist the obvious: if the vast majority of male CEOs with families have wives or partners who are either at home full-time during the caregiving years or whose work flexibility allows them to be the lead parent, then women CEOs are going to need the same thing. We want our own careers. We want families. We want mates who are equal (or perhaps even slightly better) than us in every way. Something has to give.

LEAVE SUPERWOMAN BEHIND

THE FIRST THING WE HAVE to let go of is our insane expectations of ourselves. University of Chicago economist Marianne Bertrand and her colleagues Emir Kamenica and Jessica Pan show in a time-use study that women who outearn their husbands do more housework than women who do not. This sounds crazy until we consider the psychological factors. In *Power Through Partnership: How Women Lead Better Together*, Betsy Polk and Maggie Ellis Chotas write:

> Consider the women you know. How many are struggling to squeeze even more into already packed lives? How many are saying yes too often and no all too rarely? How many are trying to convince themselves that perfection is just beyond the horizon? All they have to do is work harder, sleep less, push more, smile wider, be tougher, and, then, maybe, they will get there, somehow, someday.

These women—and Polk and Chotas count their past selves among them—"are striving to be superwomen, summoning up all their energy to reach a mirage of perfection, trying to scale mountains of exalted expectations (their own and those of others) as they struggle to lean in deeper and deeper."

It is this same superwoman perfectionism that led Debora Spar to write *Wonder Women*. She says, forthrightly, that her generation of women "made a mistake." (Spar is only seven years younger than I am, but that means I came of age in the 1970s and she came of age in the 1980s, a crucial difference in terms of the feminist trajectory.) "We took the struggles and victories of feminism and interpreted them somehow as a pathway to personal perfection." Her entire book makes a powerful and often witty case for letting go of an entire "force field of highly unrealistic expectations" to be model mother and star employee, to "save the world and look forever like a seventeen-year-old model."

Spar and I disagree a bit on whether men will ever be able to step up and take the reins domestically as equal or primary care-givers. And I have to say that I personally am simply not a perfectionist; I'm comfortable with the fact that I don't fit the image of the ideal mother because I always valued the side of *my* mother that painted extraordinary paintings far more than the baker of cupcakes. But to women who continually up the ante on themselves, believing that if they just got up earlier or used their time better or tried harder they would somehow be able to make it all work, I say, *Stop.* Let it go.

LET THEM DO IT . . . THEIR WAY

IN OUR STYLIZED ACCOUNTS OF the past, women were homemakers, confident and capable in their own sphere. Men owned the world of work, confident in theirs. Now women are rising fast at work, glorying in their ability to be all the things men used to be and to be just as good or better. A woman who manages to both "bring home the bacon and fry it up," all while managing a calendar on the fridge that looks like an air traffic control chart, is a superwoman. She may be completely exhausted and less happy than she was forty years ago, but at least she has that.

We need to step off our new self-created pedestals. When we are feeling overwhelmed, we need to let go and ask for help. It often takes much more strength on our part to acknowledge weakness than to pretend infinite competence.

Some readers who have already abandoned superwoman aspirations are probably thinking at this point: *Of course! That's exactly what we have been asking for. We want the men in our lives to pick up the slack, to be equal partners as caregivers so that we can be equal partners as breadwinners.*

But that's exactly the final place we have to let go. We have been asking for "help." That means we decide what needs to be done and we ask the men in our lives to help us do it. It's not going to work that way. Real equality means equality at home just as much as at work. It means a whole new domestic order.

Gro Harlem Brundtland was the first woman prime minister of Norway. As she tells the story, when she was first asked to join the government as the environment minister in 1974, she was thirty-five with four children under thirteen. Her husband encouraged her to take the offer and said he would take care of the kids, on one condition: he would do it *his* way. She knew what he meant; they had both shared various domestic responsibilities, but she had taken the dominant role in the household. Now he was saying he would do it, but not with her telling him what to do. She recalls one of his innovations: when their kids learned to iron, they did it in pairs. He set up two ironing boards so that the kids could talk to each other as they did it, thereby making it a much less onerous task. He also put up a sign that he found in a Virginia airport: A HOUSE MUST BE CLEAN ENOUGH TO BE HEALTHY AND DIRTY ENOUGH TO BE HAPPY.

It has taken Andy and me a long time to get to the same place. For years, I got upset with Andy about why everything domestic seemed to be my responsibility. Although he did lots of stuff, it was almost always when I told him what needed to be done, and he never seemed to feel the urgency or necessity of getting it done himself. He didn't really get it until we realized how much the shoe is on the other foot when we travel. He does all the trip planning: the flights, cars, connections, hotels, itinerary. And he is always chivvying the rest of us to get up or hurry up or pack up. The boys and I do what he says but rarely as quickly or efficiently as he wants us to. We have the blissful sense that someone else is in charge, so we don't really need to take responsibility to check the schedules, foresee possible contingencies, or worry about what's coming next.

When I pointed out to Andy that his frustration at our willingness to take instruction but not responsibility when we travel was the flip side of the way I so often felt at home, it made sense to him. But I also realized something else: for a long time I wasn't really willing to let him take responsibility. I did feel, deep down, that I knew what I was doing in terms of running our household better than he did. I didn't really trust him to be able to do it on his own, or certainly not to do it the way I would.

As our sons would be quick to point out, that's sexism, plain and simple. I was assuming, like almost all the women I know, that he wouldn't be able to take care of the kids or run a household as well as I could because he's a man. But of course if a man were to assume that I really can't practice law or medicine or business or any other profession or job as well as he can because I'm a woman, I would hit the roof.

So why won't we let go? At least part of the reason why women assume that we are superior in the home, and that our way of parenting or decorating or homemaking generally is the right way, is the oft-cited mantra that women are better than men at multitasking.

In her controversial article "The Retro Wife," journalist Lisa Miller writes, "Among my friends, many women behave as though the evolutionary imperative extends not just to birthing and breast-feeding but to administrative household tasks as well, as if only they can properly plan birthday parties, make doctors' appointments, wrap presents, communicate with the teacher, buy the new school shoes." She goes on to cite a 2010 British study showing that "men lack the same mental bandwidth for multitasking as women. Male and female subjects were asked how they'd find a lost key, while also being given a number of unrelated chores to do—talk on the phone, read a map, complete a math problem. The women universally approached the hunt more efficiently."

Okay. For the sake of argument, let's assume that women are better at doing multiple things at once. So what? It was not so long ago that we looked at people (women) who did multiple things at once as "scattered" or "jack of all trades, master of none." Since when did being able to do multiple things at once become the one and only measure of success and ability?

Andy and I agree that I am certainly better at multitasking than he is. I can remember various appointments while making a list for dinner while emailing the kids' teachers. But just as he can put a tastier dinner on the table faster than I can, so can he also sit next to our younger son for hours on end working through the nuances and mistakes of his piano practice. He is also a much better disciplinarian. Many of these attributes come precisely from his ability to tune out competing priorities and put in sustained effort over a long period of time.

No matter which partner is better at focusing or multitasking, homework monitoring or organizing playdates, if we women truly want equal partners in the home, then we can't ask our husbands to be "equal" on our terms. Andy's view of how to run a household definitely differs from mine, just as his taste in everything from furniture to how to organize a kitchen differs. But why is my way the right way?

It's true that some homes run by some dads might look more like sports camps than the photo spreads in *Good Housekeeping*. I might even go out on a limb and say that on average homes run by dads will be more cluttered than homes run by moms. The dishes and the laundry may take second place to a game of catch after dinner or, as in my household when I was away in D.C., a game of poker *during* dinner. Your spouse might also be, as Jennifer Senior argues in *All Joy and No Fun*, less emotionally attuned to how your children are feeling at any given moment and more practically attuned to meeting their physical and intellectual needs. That may be just fine: an immediate emotional response may be exactly what is needed for soothing a skinned knee but less useful for sleep training a baby. We may find that more typical "dad" ways of parenting are no better or worse than typical "mom" ways.

Even if every stereotype holds, however, and our worst female fears of living rooms turning into man caves are realized, are we really so sure that our kids will come out worse? While single fathers may not be nearly as plentiful as single mothers, they have managed to raise plenty of successful kids. So have families with two dads or two moms. Alternatively, if women let go and let the men in our lives be genuinely equal or primary caregivers, we may just find that all these stereotypes of male/female parenting differences are socialized as well.

There is only one way to find out.

BACK TO THE FUTURE

EVERY GENERATION ASSUMES THAT THE way it does things is the way things are. Notions of who should be caregiving and who should be working, for instance, are as historically contingent as notions of who should be allowed to marry each other. Interracial marriage was illegal in many states until 1967; modern British royalty were not allowed to marry commoners until Prince

Charles married Diana, or previously divorced spouses until he married Camilla; and the struggle for same-sex marriage in the United States is still in full swing. What was once unthinkable in one age becomes normal in another.

With regard to caregiving, historian Mary Frances Berry pointed out in a *New York Times* op-ed back in 1993 that the "traditional idealized family" of a mother caregiver and a father working outside the home is a modern invention. (Berry's op-ed was in response to Kimba Woods and Zoë Baird both withdrawing from consideration for attorney general over childcare issues, but sadly, it feels as fresh today as it did twenty years ago.) Before the 1950s, Berry points out, white families relied on African Americans to take care of their children. Even working-class families had black maids. If we go back further, to the seventeenth and eighteenth centuries in the United States, many fathers actually were primary caretakers after the children were done nursing:

> [Fathers] not only directed their children's education and religious worship but often played with them, decided what they would eat and hushed them to sleep when they awakened in the night. Today's trend toward increased parenting by the father to relieve mothers from the stress of balancing jobs and child rearing may be seen as a return to the patterns of old.

In the days when childhood was short to nonexistent, children essentially "apprenticed" with the parent of the same sex, boys going to work with their fathers and girls with their mothers as soon as they were old enough to learn and help. Infant and toddler care was women's work, or, in richer establishments, the work of nurses, but nurture was certainly as much a father's job as a mother's.

Home economics has long dictated the changing roles of different family members; in the agrarian era families all worked together on the farm, while in the early industrial age children from poor families worked in the factories to free up their parents to work the fields. Children were only pushed out of the Western labor market in the first half of the twentieth century because of declining demand for unskilled labor; more families could also afford to keep them in school. As sociologist Viviana Zelizer describes it, "The useful labor of the nineteenth-century child was replaced by educational work for the useless child."

In her book *Stiffed: The Betrayal of the American Man*, Susan Faludi makes the valuable point that a sense of "manhood flowed out of [men's] utility in a society, not the other way around." Masculinity is not a detachable thing that you can take off like sunglasses or armor. "The men who worked at the Long Beach Naval Shipyard didn't come there and learn their crafts as riggers, welders, and boilermakers to *be* masculine; they were seeking something worthwhile to do," Faludi explains. In other words, if male caregiving becomes valuable economically and emotionally, we will redefine our concept of masculinity to include caregiving attributes. As the nature and place of paid work change, which is happening rapidly, we will change our values. If history is any guide, men should be able to take on a full range of caring and nurturing roles, from teacher to entrepreneur. But they will redefine all those functions *their way*. It's up to women to let them.

A NEW ERA

ENGLISH PROFESSOR ABIGAIL RINE WROTE a wonderful post on her blog, *Mama Unabridged*, in which she described her bearded, tattooed husband as "a cloth-diapering wizard, an amazing cook, a master gardener" and explained that he has established a "seamless rhythm" with their son "that is simply beautiful to witness." Rine realized that if her son wore mismatched socks or pajamas all day, that didn't mean her husband wasn't doing a bang-up job of childcare. She points out that the real revolution for this century "would be to stop seeing the home as a gendered space" but rather as both a male and female domain, just as we now see the workplace.

Close your eyes and just imagine letting it all go—the expectations you imagine others have of you and that you have of yourself, your mate, and your house. Imagine that if your children call for your husband or partner or any other loving adult in their lives, then you have the security of knowing that many different people can be there for them. Imagine that your mate takes charge of an equal set of domestic responsibilities and tells *you* what to do to help out and fill in.

If we can let go of the mountain of assumptions, biases, expectations, double standards, and doubts that so many of us carry around, then a new world of possibilities awaits. We may lose our status as superwomen, but we have everything to gain.

Part III

Getting to Equal

Justice Ruth Bader Ginsburg has fought the feminist fight for a very long time, winning seminal victories for women's rights as a lawyer in the 1970s and continuing to speak up in both opinions and dissents after she was appointed to the Supreme Court by President Clinton in 1993.

Ginsburg once gave an interview to a newsletter for Supreme Court employees in which she explained that she had given one of her clerks, David Post, a flexible schedule to allow him to take care of his two young children during the days while his wife worked as an economist. Ginsburg noted, "This is my dream of the way the world should be. When fathers take equal responsibility for the care of their children, that's when women will truly be liberated."

Note that she did not say "when fathers pull their weight at home" or "when fathers do their share of household chores." She said "when fathers *take equal responsibility for the care of their children.*" The difference between taking responsibility and "helping" is an ocean of logistics and worry, not to mention contingency planning. Women have to let it go; men have to take it up.

But can we actually make change of that magnitude? In the

summer of 2013 I gave a talk at TEDGlobal in which I exhorted the audience to think about the need to "resocialize men" in just the ways I have described here. I could feel the waves of skepticism rolling off the audience. "You may think it can't happen," I said. "But I grew up in a society where my mother set out little vases of cigarettes on the table at dinner parties, where blacks and whites had to use different bathrooms, and in which everyone claimed to be heterosexual. Today, not so much."

That got a rueful laugh. My point was to remind audience members just how much our world *has* changed over the past fifty years, vastly for the better from the point of view of African Americans, the LGBT community, and families who have lost loved ones to lung cancer. Given the magnitude of that change, think about how much change we can still make—in ways that might seem unimaginable today.

These last four chapters are about the concrete steps we must take to get to equal between women and men, to finish the great business of the women's movement. They include simple changes we can make in how we talk, changes in our career trajectories, changes in the workplace, and changes in our political system.

In 2012 my younger son and I were watching the Democratic National Convention. Then-senator John Kerry was speaking, and my son asked who he was. I replied that he was a senator, he had run for president in 2004, and that if President Obama were re-elected he was quite likely to become secretary of state. My son looked surprised and said, without missing a beat, "You mean a *man* can be secretary of state?" Born in 1999, my son was only five when Secretary of State Colin Powell was succeeded by Condoleezza Rice, who in turn handed over the keys of office to Secretary Clinton. Looking at him, I remembered how jubilant I felt the day the *first* woman secretary of state, Madeleine Albright, was sworn in in 1997, after more than two centuries of men.

Change often takes a long time to build, but then can happen very fast, like a torrent of rushing water finally breaking through a dam. My lifetime has been a period of revolutionary change for women, but the pace of that change has slowed and stalled. It's time for the next great wave, for women and for men.

8

CHANGE THE WAY YOU TALK

BACK IN THE EARLY 1980S, AS I BEGAN MY FIRST YEAR OF LAW school, I remember being startled by the way my professors talked. A handful of young male faculty members at Harvard (the roughly seventy-person department included only a few women at that point) were deliberately trying to change the gender messages they sent. So when, for example, my torts professor mentioned a judge, a doctor, a lawyer, an engineer, or any other profession, he would deliberately use the pronoun "she." I jumped every time he did it. It just sounded so strange. I didn't know a single woman doctor, judge, or engineer. As I used to tell my students, I'm not that old, but as recently as the early 1980s a shift in pronoun opened up my world.

A decade earlier, the honorific "Ms." (pronounced "Miz"), as opposed to "Miss" or "Mrs.," had come into use. It may be hard to believe now, but the introduction of "Ms." into the lexicon was a huge rallying cry for early feminists, led by the iconoclastic (and now iconic) magazine of the same name. "Miss" or "Mrs." immediately identified a woman as married or unmarried, on the assumption that her status in that regard was the single most important piece of information anyone would want to know about her. "Ms." gave women their own identities, regardless of marital status. A seemingly small change in language had enormous symbolic significance.

I tell you these stories to show that how we talk matters. A lot. The words we choose reflect and reinforce deep assumptions about what is normal and what is not, what is approved and what is not, what is valued and what is not. While changing the way we speak may seem subtle, it can send a very powerful message of inclusion and alter the default assumptions of those we talk to. Back in law school, hearing the pronoun "she" applied to professions and positions that I had only seen men hold shifted my conceptions about what was possible.

In the 1980s it was important to modify our language simply to include women—half the human race. Forty years later we are still expanding that linguistic circle. In 2014, Facebook changed its gender identity options. Before, you could only choose male or female when you built your profile. This made some gender nonconforming people feel as if their identities were being erased. Today on Facebook, you can choose from a long list of customized gender options, including transgender male, transsexual female, gender nonconforming, and androgynous. As GLAAD president Sarah Kate Ellis put it, "This new feature is a step forward in recognizing transgender people and allows them to tell their authentic story in their own words." Language is one of the principal ways that we make the invisible visible and the silent heard.

Think about how often married mothers are asked, "Oh, is your husband babysitting tonight?" during a night out. Can you imagine a married man in the same situation being asked whether his wife is "babysitting"? And why don't we describe a male employee with children as a working father? On the flip side, why do we call a man who is a primary caregiver "Mr. Mom"? These linguistic distinctions may seem subtle or insignificant, but an entire structure of assumed responsibility and approved behavior patterns hangs in the balance.

THE TROUBLE WITH EUPHEMISMS

When I left the State Department to return to my full-time position as a tenured professor, I was hardly leaving the ranks of career women. Yet many of the responses to my *Atlantic* article framed the debate as just another mommy problem. One commenter said that I was "backing away from [my] State Department job over mom-guilt." Another put my story squarely in the genre of women "dropping out, ramping down or finding they just can't combine career and family."

In the immortal language of Calvin and Hobbes, *Arrrrgh!* What was particularly frustrating is that I had anticipated such characterizations and had deliberately tried to counter them in the article itself. I knew all along that if I had kept my mouth shut about my kids and simply said that I was returning to academia at the end of my two-year public service leave like countless others before me, no one would have blinked an eye. The news—to the extent it made news—would have been: "Anne-Marie Slaughter resigned at the end of her leave to return to her position at Princeton."

But no. My brother Hoke, an investment banker who's always been hugely supportive of me and my career, faced his own frustrations trying to tell people he encountered in the financial world that I had hardly "dropped out." As he wrote to me in the wake of the reactions, the clear message in the media was that I am "someone who bailed because trying to be both a mother and a high foreign policy professional was 'too tough.'" I was, in effect, painted as someone who just couldn't cut it or couldn't manage the juggle of work and family, when in fact I was still teaching a full load, writing regular columns on foreign policy, giving thirty to forty speeches per year, and working on a new book. All I had really done was shift from inflexible intensive work to flexible intensive work that I could schedule myself and thereby spend more time with my family, and yet I was being described with a word we typically apply to students who fail to finish high school or college.

No wonder so many women and men, after making a choice to work at anything less than full tilt—whether part-time, in a less demanding job, or not at all—feel like failures. None of my critics were willing to say outright that I was a wimp, but that was certainly the message. Euphemisms like "opting out," or certainly "dropping out," send a deep cultural message about how we define success and failure, while also obfuscating that message in ways that make it very hard to challenge. Using coded language allows employers, journalists, and social critics to claim to be progressive while still marginalizing work-family conflicts as women's issues rather than work issues—and weak women's issues at that.

In Washington it's simply accepted that "leaving to spend time with your family" is a euphemism for being fired. This understanding is so ingrained that when Pentagon undersecretary for policy Michèle Flournoy announced in December 2011 that she would be stepping down after three years to spend time with her three children, ages fourteen, twelve, and nine, *The New York Times* covered her decision as follows: "Ms. Flournoy's announcement surprised friends and a number of Pentagon officials, but all said they took her reason for resignation at face value and not as a standard Washington excuse for an official who has in reality been forced out."

The Pentagon itself was so concerned about this perception that they addressed it publicly. "'I can absolutely and unequivocally state that her decision to step down has nothing to do with anything other than her commitment to her family,' said Doug Wilson, a top Pentagon spokesman. 'She has loved this job and people here love her.'"

Consider what this standard Washington excuse implies: it's so unthinkable that an official would actually step down to spend time with his or her family that it must be a cover for something else. Anyone who willingly chooses family over career, even for a short time, must not be able to cut it in the workforce, for lack of either ability or motivation. That's simply ridiculous. It's also a sign of deeply distorted values. So a first step that we can all take toward creating a world of real equality is to stop using this kind of undermining language when we talk about the choices women and men make about their work.

DISSOLVING DOUBLE STANDARDS

IF YOU'RE A WORKING MOTHER, think about how often you're asked about how you manage to juggle your work with your family. Now ask your husband how often he's asked that same question. Or if you're a woman who doesn't have kids yet but you are contemplating them, or maybe you're just at an age where other people *assume* you're contemplating them, consider how often you're offered advice on how to balance work and family. Now compare notes with male friends your age about how often they've had similar conversations. I'm sure you'll find that your male counterparts are not having these conversations nearly as frequently, if at all!

If you're a young woman who has recently been through a job interview, did your interviewer bring up family-friendly policies? (It's illegal for an interviewer to ask whether you're planning to have children.) Do you have any male friends who interviewed at the same firm? Ask them whether anyone raised such policies with them.

One of my mentees, who wrote her undergraduate thesis on family-friendly policies in law firms and is now a talented young lawyer herself, reports that "law firms trip all over themselves in an effort to showcase their 'family-friendly policies' (which almost universally means permitting a few associates to work from home or to work part-time and allowing slightly longer maternity leaves than other places). When I interviewed with firms, without my saying anything, I met numerous part-time associates and, at more than one firm, every female litigation partner with children." Her husband, however, is also a lawyer and had an almost identical résumé at the time, yet when he interviewed at many of the same firms he "met not a single woman," nor did he hear a word about family-friendly policies in his interviews.

Whether you are a woman or a man, be really honest and ask yourself if you've ever talked to a younger man about how he's going to manage having kids and a career simultaneously. I have long had the kids conversation with my female students, but I have to come clean and admit that although I've been mentoring and advising students for over twenty years, I too have been guilty of this glaring double standard. Only in my last two years at Princeton, after thinking very hard about what needs to change, did I start talking to my male students about whether and when they are planning on having kids.

Another telling double standard is what I call the "halo dad syndrome." Every mother I know with a caregiving husband has witnessed this phenomenon, the same one Matt Vilano noted when he was called "a good dad." Fathers do what is routinely expected of mothers and are treated as if they are extraordinary.

I ran into this phenomenon repeatedly when I was a young dean and Andy, who had a far more flexible schedule than I did, would show up for school events. I heard constantly from teachers and other mothers about what a fabulous father Andy was. In their eyes, his halo shined brighter just for working and taking care of his sons, behavior that was expected as a matter of course from me. As I've made clear, Andy has been indispensable as a father and I am deeply grateful. But the halo dad syndrome is an all-too-common example of double standards—holding men to a different standard of behavior for praise or censure than women. We need to stop overpraising dads for simply showing up—something working moms have been doing forever. What that praise really says is that we don't expect dads to behave in ways that are routine for moms, thereby reinforcing the very assumptions about traditional gender roles that we seek to change.

On the flip side, I have often, in a corporate setting, heard a woman introduced as a talented director, manager, marketer, or what have you. And then, after talking about her qualifications, the introducer will add something like, "And she has teenage twins on top of it all, so she is a master of work-life balance." It is indeed important to make clear in the workplace that we have lives outside of work. But the problem is that the same presenter will then introduce a man and never mention whether he has a family, once again reinforcing the assumption that caregiving is the woman's responsibility.

The first generation of working mothers understood that in order to succeed they had to act like the men they worked with, so they never mentioned their children. And many senior women today still play this game, saying that they have a doctor's appointment, or just an "appointment," rather than revealing that they are missing work for a child. But as one small yet powerful step toward creating a world in which breadwinning and caregiving are equal, let's be honest about our caregiving commitments when we are at work. This doesn't mean insisting that your colleagues spend time cooing over the pictures of your baby or listening to tales of your kindergartner's prodigious accomplishments. It does mean that if you can't make an early morning meeting because it's your turn to drive the kids to school, you're honest about it.

I propose too that when a man announces to his colleagues that he and his partner are expecting a child, we show the same concern and ask the same questions about his work-life issues that we ask women. We could just stop asking at all, but that would deny what we all know is true: that caring for kids is important and time-consuming. It's right to acknowledge that; what's wrong is to assume that it's all a woman's responsibility. Changing the conversation to include men is another important step in the right direction.

Recently I was invited to give a foreign policy speech at a big annual forum for the top management of PIMCO, one of the world's largest investment management firms. The organizer asked if I could give a second speech on work and family. I agreed and was pleasantly surprised to find myself talking not to a group called "PIMCO Women," but to "PIMCO Parents." The audience of more than fifty people was at least one-third men. The name change may seem small, but it is a big step in the direction of ensuring that family responsibilities are the province of all family members.

Mark Weinberger, CEO of EY (formerly Ernst & Young), has a great catchphrase for this shift. In his words, "Women don't want to be singled out; men don't want to be left out." Exactly.

A NEW VOCABULARY OF REAL EQUALITY

THE GREAT THING ABOUT LANGUAGE is that it is within the individual control of all of us. Each one of us can commit to talking differently, to talking as if care and competition are genuinely equal and equally valued for both men and women; as if we hold men and women equally responsible not only for creating children but also for raising them; and as if the people we respect and value most have full lives in which the people and things they love are just as important as their work. Here are a few more steps we can take to make that happen:

- The next time someone tells you how many hours she worked last week, or talks only about work at a party, ask her what interesting books she's read lately, or if she's seen any good movies. In other words, refuse to play the competitive game. Find out what people care about *other* than work.

- When you meet someone, try not to ask, "What do you do?" within the first five minutes. Ask him what he's interested in, what his hobbies are, what he's passionate about in life. Signal by the way you talk that you value more than how people earn an income.

- When you talk about men who are in the workforce and have children, try describing them as "working fathers" or "working parents." And if they are taking care of their parents or other family members, think about calling them "working caregivers."

- When you talk about a woman or a man who is home full-time with children, avoid using the term "stay-at-home mom" or "stay-at-home dad," a phrase that implies that the office is the norm and thus someone at home needs a qualifier. Try using the descriptors "lead parent," "anchor parent," or "full-time parent."

- When you're talking to a young man at your workplace who expects to have a family, try asking him, "How are you planning to fit your career together with your family?" If that man becomes the father of a child, ask him something like "How are you and your partner planning to divide responsibilities and what changes in your work life will help you manage?" It may seem a little intrusive and patronizing (though women are asked these questions all the time), but it's vital that we acknowledge the importance of caregiving when we're in the office.

- When one of your work colleagues or someone you supervise must leave early, come in late, or work from home because of caregiving responsibilities, try to avoid asking things like "How do you plan to get your work done?" even if the question is not accusatory and is spoken in a friendly tone. Questions like these reinforce the assumption that if you are committed to your family you are less committed to your work.

- If you have to come in late, leave early, or work from home because of caregiving responsibilities, make it clear that you're attending to something that is every bit as important as your work. And if you want to organize a group at your workplace to focus on fitting work and caregiving responsibilities together, call it a "parents' group" a "caregivers' group," or, best of all, a "how to work better group."

- If someone you thought was on leadership track slows down to work part-time or on a more flexible schedule due to caregiving responsibilities, assume that his or her ambitions have not changed. Initiate a conversation to find out. Talk about this period as an "investment interval" valuable for family reasons and for acquiring different skills and experiences. Plan together for ramping back up when she or he is ready.

- If an employee decides that even part-time or flexible work is too much, whether out of desire or family necessity, discuss the possibility of taking courses, volunteering, or working in ways that will be professionally useful down the road. And talk about these employees as alumni or alumnae of your workplace; if you're smart, you'll want to hire them again someday.

- Before you talk about someone you admire, first ask yourself if she is admirable all the way through—as much in the caring parts of her life as in the competitive parts. Talk about people in a way that indicates you value them in the round, for their successes in raising their children or caring for other relatives or their communities as much as their career accomplishments.

Lastly, it's worth mentioning that many of the common terms for describing the trade-offs we make between caregiving and breadwinning are still somewhat problematic. We've already discussed the pitfalls of the phrase "having it all," but others, even some of the seemingly innocuous ones, have their own difficulties. One of my close friends gets particularly incensed at the term "juggling career and family." As she points out, a juggler treats each of the balls or pins he is juggling equally; it's not the same with work and family. If your child or parent is in danger of falling, nothing else matters—the juggling stops. Other friends hate the term "balance," on the grounds that life never actually balances at some miraculous mechanical middle point between work and loved ones. Most of us are not balancing; we're running to keep up.

I use both "juggling" and "balance," but I prefer the idea of striving toward a good "work/life fit," a phrase I first discovered through Cali Williams Yost, a pioneering expert on workplace flexibility. "Fit" is a useful word because it implies customized policies for individual workers. Joan Blades and Nanette Fondas describe a "custom-fit workplace" as one that adapts to a worker's changing needs over the course of a week, a month, a year, or a chunk of a career. As the term suggests, fitting the demands of work and caregiving together differs day to day, and the only way to do it is to have the flexibility to adapt to continually changing circumstances, like a tightrope walker or a pilot in difficult wind conditions.

Talk alone will not change everything. But talk can change the way we think, which can then change the way we act. If we want to better our world and improve the way we value people and the choices they make, we can start by making our language reflect the change we'd like to see.

9

PLANNING YOUR CAREER (EVEN THOUGH IT RARELY WORKS OUT AS PLANNED)

IF YOU WANT A LIFE IN WHICH YOU CAN EXPERIENCE THE JOYS AND rewards of both a successful career and a loving family, you must plan ahead. As early as possible, you should try to anticipate the times in your future when you'll want to focus intensively on your job and the ones when you'll want to focus more on caregiving responsibilities. To the extent you can, tailor your professional choices accordingly.

I'm guessing, however, that if you are not yet married or you're not focused on having children and your parents and other family members are healthy and strong, you're probably thinking this advice doesn't apply to you. Part of being young is secretly believing that you're invincible—that even though you know many, many other people have struggled with these issues, some-how you will muddle your way through and everything will work out. I certainly hope that's true in your case; I do indeed know women—at least a few—who have managed to raise families and pursue their careers without ever having to make a major com-promise on either side. But as we say in foreign policy, hope is not a strategy; neither is counting on luck. The odds are that a day will come when you will have to confront these issues—either with or without a partner.

You should be prepared. Without even a basic plan, you are much more likely to end up making rash decisions you'll later regret. What's more, even *with* the best plan in the world, you will encounter plenty of obstacles. Whether you are a woman or a man, holding down two full-time jobs, which is what earning an income and taking primary responsibility for caring for others entails, is *hard*. Don't give up, but start thinking through different possibilities and planning for them, preferably together with your family, friends, colleagues, and superiors. Remember Dwight Eisenhower's memorable phrase about the army: "Plans are worthless, but planning is everything."

THE NEW CAREER SPAN

THE SINGLE MOST IMPORTANT THING to remember if you're a young man or a young woman planning a career in the United States or most other developed countries is that you have considerably more time ahead of you than your parents did. If you're an American woman born in 1990 or later, your life expectancy, according to the Social Security Administration, is about 86 years. That means that 10 percent of women will live to nearly 95, and 0.001 percent of women will live to 113. If you are an average American man of the same age, your life expectancy is 82, lower than women but still a decade longer than your grandfather's. The numbers vary by factors like education and race; due to the epidemic of obesity that is highest among the poorest Americans, in some categories life expectancy is actually, disgracefully, going down. Still, women who are educated and paid enough to be able to plan a career can expect to live much longer than their mothers and grandmothers.

As lives lengthen and women gain more options and control over our lives, caring for others need no longer be our principal occupation, even if we spend substantial chunks of our lives (preferably alongside partners) raising children or tending the needs of aging parents. These periods are *phases:* intervals of putting others first in a long life of both love and work.

Athletes have long understood that the best way to get into peak condition is to engage in interval training. You go all-out for a period of minutes, then slow down for a certain number of minutes before going at it again. Any StairMaster or stationary bike has an interval program: a baseline of steady activity punctuated by repeated periods of intense effort. Going at 100 percent all the time never gives your body a chance to recover; you have to be strategic about when and how you ramp up and ramp down.

Life, and careers, can be approached the same way.

Rather than picking a single professional ladder to climb as your parents and grandparents did, over the course of a forty- or even fifty-year career you'll encounter many hierarchies in various different jobs. Depending on your career goals, you'll want to put in the intense effort to climb at least some of those ladders, to do everything you can to make it to a certain level or even to the top. But between these periods of push, you'll also be able to plan intervals of less intensive and more flexible work, work that is much more compatible with caregiving.

Even better, if you take charge of your own professional development and think about your career in terms of a series of different jobs and life experiences, you can choose your intervals accordingly. While specific intervals cannot always be planned for, the idea of intervals certainly can.

U.S. demographics are already pushing in this direction. Millennials beginning their careers are treating their first decade out of school differently than their elders did. London Business

School professors Lynda Gratton and Andrew Scott predict the rise of a new "explorer phase," in which "people in their twenties keep their options open and experiment with different roles and skills to better understand what they are good at and what they enjoy." They'll take risks that they cannot afford to take later, either physical or entrepreneurial, and invest in building networks and new experiences.

At the other end of life, as baby boomers "retire" from whatever job they're in, many will be looking at several decades of energy and health ahead of them. The vast majority will also discover that they can ill afford to stop working completely. Some will opt for care intervals—spending the time with their grandchildren that they did not have for their children, often becoming invaluable extra caregivers helping their sons and daughters rise in their own careers. Others will become teachers, volunteer for the Peace Corps, run for office, work in small businesses, distill their wisdom and experience as consultants, gain new credentials, and create new businesses with spouses and friends.

Along the way, as they ease out of their current jobs or arrange deals with employers to continue working on different terms, they will be asking for flexible hours, part-time work, project-based work, and other arrangements that millennials and all workers juggling caregiving responsibilities will be only too happy to support.

THE CAREER PORTFOLIO

IN THIS NEW KIND OF career planning, we have to begin by rethinking what a career is. The first time I heard the term "portfolio career" was from Bridget Kendall, an award-winning British journalist who has been a BBC diplomatic correspondent since

1998. As we talked about different ways to fit work and family together, she mentioned that in Britain the idea of portfolio careers was taking off: making a career by working at a "portfolio" of part-time jobs, all of which together add up to a full-time job and each of which allows you to express a different part of your identity. The huge difference between Britain and the United States, of course, is that health and pension benefits are provided by the government rather than by individual employers. And yet, it is still possible to adapt versions of the idea to American circumstances.

As I thought about it, it occurred to me that I've developed a different kind of portfolio career over the years—a sequential one—although without ever thinking of it in those terms. I'm a lawyer, scholar, writer, teacher, public speaker, media commentator, manager, entrepreneur, and foreign policy expert. I have invested in developing different parts of that portfolio over the years in different full-time jobs, sometimes deliberately choosing new challenges in order to learn and add new skills and other times taking on new roles as a function of the circumstances in which I found myself. In either case, I believe that those roles have provided me with both versatility and security, a safety net of possibilities should any one of them not work out.

You can think about a portfolio career in either form— holding multiple part-time jobs at once or looking for a series of full-time jobs—each challenging you in a different way. Having different jobs, hobbies, and passions will give you a portfolio of diverse skills and experiences that will help you learn and advance in all the different stages of your life. Pick a dream job that you would like to hold someday and analyze all the different kinds of abilities and experience it requires: fund-raising, say, or strategy, management experience, profit and loss responsibility, writing ability, or public-speaking experience. Instead of gaining those skills by moving up through a preordained series of rungs on a corporate ladder, think about the many ways you could acquire them by doing different jobs at different times.

Many notable women have blazed this trail, including former Texas Republican senator Kay Bailey Hutchison and current Massachusetts Democratic senator Elizabeth Warren. Hutchison graduated from the University of Texas School of Law in 1967, only to discover that Houston law firms were not hiring women. She became a TV news correspondent, ran for and won a position in the state legislature, and later worked as a lawyer, banker, businesswoman, and mother before entering national politics. Elizabeth Warren had a brief spell as a full-time mom in her early twenties, attended law school as a young mother, did part-time work for a bit after she had her second child, and then became a full-time law professor in her late twenties. After a few government appointments in middle age, she began her first campaign for elected office at age sixty-two.

It's important to look at the different phases of your life, or at least what you hope your life will be. If you want to have children, you are likely to need more flexibility and control over your working hours at key times in their lives. The same is true if you want to be an important part of your parents' lives as they age. If you expect to be a single parent, you're even more likely to need that flexibility and control at various points.

Even if you don't want kids, and have a longer period of time to devote yourself single-mindedly to your career, you may want to immerse yourself in your community in some way, write a novel, learn a foreign language and live abroad, build a social enterprise, or devote yourself full-time to a hobby you are passionate about. These broader life ambitions are just as important as your career ambitions; it's up to you to figure out how to combine them.

As you look forward, try also to imagine what it will be like looking back at the end of your life and what it is you will most wish you had done. David Brooks contrasts "résumé virtues" with "eulogy virtues," noting that while résumés list the "skills that you bring to the job market and that contribute to external success," the "eulogy virtues are deeper." They're "the ones that exist at the core of your being—whether you are kind, brave, honest or faithful; what kind of relationships you formed." They're the ones, in the end, that matter most.

DON'T DROP OUT, DEFER

IF YOUR WORKING LIFE REALLY is likely to extend roughly from age twenty-five until seventy-five or even later, with periods of education, caregiving, and—if you are fortunate—life enrichment built in, then it makes sense to take some time when your children are younger and your parents are older to care for them and savor those moments. Planning your career as if you were going to peak in your mid-fifties and then retire by sixty-five is the equivalent of cramming a seven-course meal into the first three or four courses.

If you have any choice at all during these periods, don't drop out. *Defer.* Far too many women who have left the workforce planning to come back at some point, confident in their education and professional credentials, find that it's much more difficult than they expected to get back in. In 2003, Lisa Belkin published "The Opt-Out Revolution" in *The New York Times Magazine*, interviewing ten Princeton graduates who were all in the same Atlanta book club. Half of those women had quit work entirely to be full-time moms, one worked part-time, one had a business with her husband, two freelanced, and one had a full-time job and no kids.

Ten years later, Judith Warner interviewed a number of women who had made the same choice as Belkin's subjects to see how they were faring. Almost to a woman, they wanted back into the workforce, although they generally were looking for different kinds of work than the jobs they had left. Roughly a third of these women were able to transition back into paid jobs with relative ease, largely because they kept up their contacts, had the most prestigious educations possible, and volunteered strategically. As Warner puts it, "Fund-raising for a Manhattan private school could be a nice segue back into banking; running bake sales for the suburban swim team tended not to be a career-enhancer." But many had a hard time finding any work at all and have a much more sober view of their original decision to leave, although none regret the time they have been able to spend with their children. They chose to leave their jobs without realizing that they were also choosing economic and social disempowerment.

So if at all possible, stay in the game. *Plan* for leaning back as well as leaning in; make deliberate rather than unintended choices. If you're strategic about it, you can find ways to keep your networks fresh and your skills sharp even as you slow down, move laterally or even backward for a while.

One hard and fast rule will help you plan. I borrow this one from my brother Hoke, an investment banker for twenty-five years who has watched many of his colleagues come and go. *Never* make a decision about leaving your job when you're in crisis. Anticipate the crises, the times when you feel like you are both the worst caregiver and the worst professional in the world. Know that they will come, but know also that they are the worst possible time to make a life decision. Build a support network, at work and at home, to help you get through them, and make sure you nurture the relationships in that network. They are not a distraction from work but something that will help you work better and stronger over the long haul.

PHASE THREE

A FEW YEARS AGO, AS I waited in line at a coffee shop near my house, I overheard a snippet of conversation that has stayed with me. A woman who looked to be in her late fifties was saying to a friend that her last child was leaving for college and she was "beginning to think about phase three." Not retirement, not some part-time volunteering, but the next active phase of her life.

In every job, every profession, some workers will choose to be hares, ready to put in longer hours, take more trips, be available 24/7. And they will be promoted faster and reach various peaks earlier than those of us who choose a different rhythm.

That's only fair. People who choose to marry their work or who manage, one way or another, never to have to make a trade-off between competition and care—either by having a full-time caregiver at home and accepting the price of rarely seeing their loved ones or through some combination of money, a farsighted choice of jobs, and good fortune—will be able to advance faster to top jobs. Others may be perfectly content to stay in the middle, knowing that they are valued as managers and team players. The point is not to ensure that everyone who competes reaches the finish line at the same time, but to ensure that those who choose a slower path will still have an opportunity to compete on equal terms if they want to, whenever they're ready.

And why not? If Hillary Clinton wins the presidency, she'll be a healthy, smart, and experienced sixty-nine when she's elected.

For all the excitement about her potentially being the first woman president, I think it's equally inspiring that she would be the first grandmother president. She has had many phases in her career, even though it appeared that she had subordinated a successful early career as a children's rights lawyer to her husband's political ambitions. She ran for senator after her husband finished his presidency and, equally important, after Chelsea went to college. After losing a presidential campaign, she took on a job she never expected to hold, as secretary of state.

Clinton was following in Madeleine Albright's and Condoleezza Rice's footsteps as secretary of state. Albright was named the first woman secretary of state at age fifty-nine; she had already made careers for herself as a professor and a congressional staffer while she was still raising her daughters as a single mother (she and her husband divorced). Since leaving office in 2001, she has become an author, entrepreneur, and businesswoman. Condoleezza Rice has already had multiple careers as well, beginning as a professor, taking a position as a staffer at the National Security Council, becoming a provost at Stanford, then national security advisor and secretary of state, and now principal in her own strategic consulting group, while often being touted as the next NFL commissioner.

Clinton, Rice, and Albright lead very high-profile lives. But any of us could think about sequencing intervals of competition and care much more strategically. If you are married, consider Hanna Rosin's vision of "seesaw marriages," where couples take turns being lead caregiver or lead breadwinner. If you have children, plan for the day they leave home. We often talk about empty-nesters as if they are sad mother birds flapping forlornly around the nest, wondering what on earth to do now. I prefer thinking about phase three as a second surge, a time of renewed energy, focus, and commitment to a professional goal.

Who knows? Some of us, and certainly our children, may be thinking about phases four and five.

TOURS OF DUTY

FARSIGHTED EMPLOYERS ARE ALREADY BEGINNING to incorporate the interval training concept, albeit under a different name and without the same focus on the needs of caregivers. In *The Alliance: Managing Talent in the Networked Age*, co-founder and chairman of LinkedIn Reid Hoffman and his co-authors Ben Casnocha and Chris Yeh describe a new model of employer-employee relations that is sweeping Silicon Valley. The book starts from the premise that the lifetime employment model and the employee loyalty that it generated is dead. Millennial workers understand very well that they will hold many jobs over the course of their careers, leading them to limit their investment in their employers just as their employers have little incentive to invest in them. *The Alliance* proposes a very different model in which both sides, as the name suggests, ally to advance their mutual interests.

Hoffman, Casnocha, and Yeh discuss how the old model of work broke down in the 1970s and 1980s. The pressure to compete globally created a scenario in which workers were treated as disposable. As they put it, companies insist that "'employees are our most valuable resource.' But when Wall Street wants spending cuts, their 'most valuable resource' suddenly morphs into their 'most fungible resource.'" This attitude bred an understandable distrust among employees.

The way to regain mutual trust is to create a framework in which job contracts aren't seen as open-ended commitments; they're seen as tours of duty that have clearly defined goals and finite time spans. After your tour is up, you might go on to another tour within the same company or go to another company entirely. But neither party feels used or abused in this scenario. The employees feel like they are learning new things and they're not at the mercy of an unfeeling market; the employer feels like its investment is worthwhile.

The authors are careful to note that even though this approach was engineered in the flexible wonderland of Silicon Valley, its main lesson will work in any environment in which "talent really is the most valuable resource, and employees are treated accordingly." Companies like GE and the global nonprofit Endeavor already use a tour of duty framework. The most distinctive feature of this approach is that it allows jobs to be customized for each person and his or her specific relationship to an organization at a specific time in his or her life. Though lower-level workers with less bargaining power and desired skills still need government protection to make sure that they are not being exploited, the tour of duty notion looks like it is a possible new way forward.

The tour of duty concept fits perfectly with the idea of planning your career in terms of intervals of different intensity: these tours will only work if you can either get back in or ramp back up after a down interval. I see an enormous talent pool of women in their late forties through their late fifties coming out of just such a down interval, ready and waiting to throw themselves into full-time work again as their kids leave the house. Men will increasingly need and want those options as well.

My sister-in-law Laurie is a great example. She was a magna cum laude graduate and thesis prize winner at Princeton who made senior vice president at a major auction house by her early thirties. When she and my brother Hoke had children, one of whom has moderate special needs, they felt that it was critical for one of them to be at home full-time. Given the travel necessary for Hoke's job and the income it generates, the responsibility fell to her. In the conventional narrative, Laurie "sacrificed her career for her family." In fact, she's a woman in her early fifties who has combined an impressive professional track record early in her career with logistical abilities, management skills, and personal resilience, all strengthened by her work as a mother. She's ready for her next tour of duty.

The military—where the term and concept of tour of duty originates—is itself finding ways to let its members step out and step back in, precisely because they spend an enormous amount of time, effort, and expense in training their employees and thus suffer enormously if they cannot retain them. Beginning in 2009, the U.S. Navy launched a program called the Career Intermission Pilot Program (CIPP) to determine, in navy speak, "if retention in critical skills sets can be enhanced by permitting temporary inactivation from active duty and providing greater flexibility in career paths of service members." The program provides for a onetime temporary transition from active duty to the reserves for a period of up to three years, with a means for "seamless return to active duty."

The air force is planning to launch its own CIPP in 2015, hoping that with their program they'll be able to retain more female airmen. "Some women leave the Air Force because they want to start a family," air force personnel chief Lt. Gen. Samuel Cox told the *Air Force Times*. "So why don't we have a program that allows them, in some cases, to be able to separate from the Air Force for a short period of time, get their family started, and then come back in?" Exactly.

In the civilian sector, McKinsey has a program that allows its consultants to take up to ten weeks per year away from the office between projects. It's called Take Time, and employees have used it to travel, take care of family, and embrace hobbies. These programs are just a few years old, so it's hard to know what the long-term effects are going to be. However, McKinsey has reported that in the near term, Take Time has helped with employee retention and recruitment. Take Time participants report that they return to work feeling refreshed and engaged, instead of burnt out and bitter. These are baby steps in terms of the enormous need for greater career customization on the part of millions of American workers, but they are steps in the right direction.

It's still up to *you*, however, to start thinking now about what might happen later. A frequent comment from young women I meet goes something like this: "When I read your *Atlantic* article I thought it was interesting but not really relevant to my life. But I just got married [or 'we just had our first child'], and suddenly I get it. I'm trying to figure out what to do and it's a lot harder than I expected."

I sympathize, believe me. But don't wait. Assume that if you are expecting to have a family, or if your parents are sick or aging, you will face times when it will be very hard to focus intensely on your work. Start imagining the kinds of trade-offs you may need to plan for. Here are a few hypotheticals to help you anticipate what life likely has in store, compiled from actual situations a wonderful mother I know has faced:

- Your child has a fever of 101 for the third day in a row. The doctor says it will run its course, but daycare won't take him back until his fever has been below 100 for twenty-four hours. You have used up all your sick time for other childhood illnesses and doctor appointments and have no family in the area to help. Your partner has a major work presentation and can't stay home either. What do you do?
- The school play this year takes place during school hours and conflicts with a meeting you have been told you are

required to attend. Your partner is going to be out of town. If you don't go, your child will likely be the only kid with no parent there. What do you do?

- You haven't slept more than one or two hours a night for the past three months due to your colicky newborn. How will you/can you still handle the demands of your job?

- You have to leave at four P.M. to pick up your child from daycare on time. Everyone else in the office works at least till six P.M and resents you because they feel you are a slacker they have to cover for. You fear you will be let go, or at least never promoted. At best, it is not at all a collegial work environment. You work in an unusual field, and jobs are scarce. What will you do?

- To cover the school summer vacation between kindergarten and first grade, you have enrolled your daughter in a highly regarded summer day camp. However, she is unable to handle such a big transition and is acting out. The camp director has told you she is too disruptive and cannot stay. At this point, all the other quality camps are full and you are not sure she could handle them anyway. What will you do?

HAVE THAT CONVERSATION WITH YOUR PARTNER

AFTER I GAVE A SPEECH to a roomful of eight hundred women and men—mostly women—at a conference hosted by the Women's Leadership Center in northern Virginia, a young woman asked me about my claim that women who wanted to be at the top of their professions while also having a family would likely need a supportive spouse on the home front in the same way that male leaders do. She asked what to do if she and her boyfriend *both* wanted high-flying careers. As I began to answer, her boyfriend came over, saying that he certainly wanted to listen as well. I said that they might both be able to reach the top of their chosen professions and have a family, but not at the same time; that they would have to recognize that trade-offs and indeed sacrifices would be likely at various points; and that they should discuss how they would plan to make those choices up front. I could tell it was not a message that either of them particularly wanted to hear, but you can't run away from it.

In the past far too many couples simply never had that conversation. They put off planning before marriage or having a child, and then, when the time came, as it so often did, that they realized their children—or their aging parents—were going to make it impossible for both of them to travel and work with the intensity their careers demanded, it was already too late. It may be hard for young men and women to believe, but many of the couples even of my generation, coming out of school in the 1980s, pledged themselves to full equality. We were determined to create different gender patterns than the ones we grew up with. But once children arrived, most of us discovered that we had to make choices; the choices we ended up making systematically disadvantaged the women's careers.

Now it's your turn. You are a young woman in a relationship. He says he fully supports your career, and he was raised by a working mother, so of course he believes in full equality. What more do you need? (This hypothetical applies equally if you're a young man in a relationship with another young man or a young woman in a relationship with another woman, although lesbian couples seem to have a somewhat easier time with the division of labor.)

As it turns out, you need to get much more specific—less

about the little things than the big ones. In 1970, the feminist writer Alix Kates Shulman wrote a now-famous essay called "The Marriage Agreement," which stipulated that all household and childcare tasks should be shared between Shulman and her husband equally. It listed all the details of their shared responsibility, down to the most picayune, like brushing their children's hair. Forty-odd years later, *Slate* writer and academic Rebecca Onion wrote an essay in 2014 about how she would only consider motherhood if she and her husband made a Shulman-style agreement. But hair brushing is far less of a problem than travel planning.

Start by being as honest as possible with yourself and each other about your deepest career aspirations. If you could wave a magic wand, where would you ideally find yourself in twenty or thirty years? Whom do you wish you could be? How ambitious are you? What will you consider a life well lived? What life goals do you have other than career success?

Then ask yourselves about your family plans. Do you want children? Do you—as is often the case with men—simply assume that you will have them someday? Do you imagine yourselves caring for your parents when they reach that stage of life?

If you see caring for loved ones in your future, particularly for children, and you both aspire to careers that will require you to work largely on someone else's time and at someone else's direction, here are some scenarios you should consider along with some questions you should ask each other:

- I come home all excited because my boss has told me that he really thinks I am leadership material and he wants to promote me. In my company, however, the top managers have all had line experience in many different parts of the company across the country and around the world. My next job will certainly require a move. Will you move with me? Even if that means taking a step down or sideways in your career? And when we move, will you be willing to reweave the fabric of our own and our children's lives in terms of schools, friends, doctors, and activities while I try to get a handle on my new job?

- We *both* come home all excited because we each see a fabulous promotion on the horizon. Your boss has had a similar conversation with you, but if we move for my new job, you will not be able to work in another branch of the same firm and your boss really hates the idea of your working remotely. Will you defer your promotion so I can take mine?

- If I take a job that requires lots of travel, will *you* be the available parent for everything from teacher conferences to snow and sick days, not to mention after-school activities requiring parental involvement? Will you be the lone dad among the moms on the school trip? Will you still love and support me when the kids are crying and the house is a mess and I walk out the door to head for the airport?

- Are you comfortable hiring a great deal of outside help to raise our children? If not, are you willing to move to my family's hometown (or your family's) so that we have grandparents and siblings nearby to help make it work?

- If one of our children has special needs, or a particularly stormy adolescence, or would be more likely to flourish with more parental attention, will you consider being the parent who downshifts to be at home more? Will you still think I'm a good parent too, even though I am providing more cash than care? Will you believe that we can seesaw up and down over the course of our marriage and that I will support you when your turn comes?

- Can you handle it if I earn more than you do and have a more conventionally successful career? (This is particularly true if it is a woman asking this question of a man, but it is relevant for many gay couples as well, and for women who have never thought about being financially dependent in any way.) Are you secure enough to accept the denigrating remarks that are likely to come your way from other men, but even more frequently from women, in-laws, and even your own parents?

You probably won't have answers to all of these questions now, but it's essential to have the conversation to focus both your minds on the real issues and trade-offs that combining career and family are likely to entail. If he says that of course he wants you to have your career, but that he cannot actually imagine deferring his own advancement or even changing jobs so that you can reach for the stars, you may want to think again. At the very least, you will both learn something important about yourselves and each other.

Once again, you can of course point to the tiny handful of couples who have equally high-powered careers and seemingly perfect children, but surely you should also consider the millions of women who started out on an equal track with their mates and then found that something had to give. Or look hard at the domestic arrangements of the women you most admire and see how many have an indispensably supportive mate who is the lead parent and either does or oversees much more than half the housework!

You will want to keep having these discussions at regular intervals down the road. And they are relevant even if you aren't sure about having children. It's very hard to anticipate at twenty-five what you will want at thirty-five. Many people also end up having unanticipated caregiving responsibilities for elderly and sick relatives, so it's worth at least beginning to talk about what that might look like for you. You are very likely to find yourselves both making choices that you did not anticipate at the beginning, but you will be far happier if they are explicit and open choices in which each partner recognizes what the other is gaining and what he or she is giving up. You can also plan together about how you will switch places down the road.

IN THE THICK OF IT . . .

THIS CHAPTER WAS ABOUT PLANNING your career, which assumes that you are early enough in your working life to be in the planning stage. For those of us who are already in the middle of "the juggle," the concept of intervals and tours of duty may be lovely, but they have little to do with our daily reality. Moreover, intervals assume a degree of financial stability that many families simply don't have—taking downtime and working on a freelance or consulting basis, in particular, can mean sharp monthly variations in income.

To take advantage of the talent of the millions of women who are doing their best just to hang on, and to make intervals of competition and care a much more realistic option for everyone, it's time to talk more about the future of work and insist on sweeping cultural change of the same magnitude as attitudes about smoking or same-sex marriage.

The good news is that change is already under way. You just have to find the right workplace. . . .

10

THE PERFECT WORKPLACE

How many articles have you read about the amazing benefits of exercise? Hundreds if not thousands have told us that just walking briskly for thirty minutes a day can regulate our weight, lower our blood pressure, reduce stress, boost our immune systems, and stimulate our brain. As journalists routinely write, if a single pill could do all that we would all take it every morning. But somehow many of us find it hard to take the fairly small steps necessary, no pun intended, to become more active.

That's the way I feel about businesses that just don't get it when it comes to the benefits of allowing employees to fit together work and family. Reams of research demonstrate the impact on recruitment, retention, productivity, creativity, and employee morale. Moreover, in an age of continual CEO laments about the war for top talent and of national worries about whether the American workforce is educated enough to be competitive in a digital and global economy, it's astounding that an enormous pool of highly educated and credentialed women in their forties and fifties remain completely shut out of leadership-track positions because they chose at one point to ramp down in order to make time for care.

So why are we still stuck in this rut? Because, as I have argued throughout this book, drawing on decades of work by legal scholars, economists, and feminists, the majority of Americans are mired in a 1950s mindset when it comes to assumptions about when and how we work, what an ideal worker looks like, and when to expect that ideal worker to peak in his or her career. Men who came up through the old system and succeeded in it simply find it very hard to believe that their businesses could flourish any other way.

Fortunately, help is not only on the way, it's here. As the head of human resources for a company where I serve on the board recently told us, millennials want to be able to work "anywhere, anytime, anyhow." The U.S. economy is also evolving in ways that are already changing working conditions for hundreds of thousands of Americans. Further, a growing number of traditional companies are starting to get it and are finding new ways of working that allow their employees much more flexibility and even cash support for parental leave and daycare, and in some cases even eldercare.

These large-scale changes are important. Over time, they will affect how each of us lives and works, but it is hard for us to figure out how to effect them. At the other end of the spectrum are the small changes that each of us can make on a daily basis in terms of how we think, talk, and plan. The workplace offers a middle ground where economic and social forces and individual efforts can meet at a practical level. Workers and managers can decide, separately and together, to create an environment that allows everyone to fit care and career together in ways that benefit both.

THE FUTURE OF WORK

THE LANDSCAPE OF WORK IN the United States is changing as radically as it did in the move from the agricultural to the industrial age. Digital technology pushes the workplace away from centralized offices and toward distributed networks. No one can actually foresee the full scope and scale of these changes, although commentators and prognosticators abound. I will oversimplify a mass of complex processes that are already under way to identify at least some of the biggest changes that I see coming, so you can understand what kind of workplace you want to be in and take charge of your own career trajectory.

The On-Demand Economy

IN THE ON-DEMAND ECONOMY, INDEPENDENT contractors—freelancers—work on demand for whoever needs their services rather than for fixed periods of time for a single employer. They are connected only by a platform that matches them with customers and provides verification, security, and payment systems. This is the world of Uber, Lyft, Airbnb, and TaskRabbit. It will increasingly be the world of just about everything: handyman services, cooking, laundry, shopping, personal training, coding, doctoring, lawyering, bossing, and creating everything from television ads to Ebola suits.

Providing services on demand is connected to the "sharing economy," which started from the idea that people who have a car they don't use all day or an extra bedroom in their apartment could make money by sharing that extra capacity with those who want it. Instead of everyone owning one of everything, we can generate income by sharing things that we already have. Other labels for the same phenomenon are "project economy" and "gig economy," in the sense that you can earn income project by project rather than at fixed times for fixed sums.

The on-demand economy has already come in for plenty of criticism. An Uber driver who is a housewife or student driving to earn extra income whenever he or she has time is one thing. But drivers who are actually trying to make a living often receive below-minimum-wage pay and no benefits—no health or disability insurance, workers' compensation, unemployment insurance, or retirement plans. That's what it means to be a contractor rather than an employee. Some job is better than no job, but the inequities are stark. As *New York* magazine reports, a platform start-up that connects housecleaners to customers ends up employing homeless people to clean the homes of the prosperous. Even as the entrepreneurs succeed in attracting hundreds of millions in investments from Silicon Valley investors, they do not provide the pay and benefits necessary to allow the service providers they profit from to rent a home of their own.

That said, the on-demand economy is bound to continue growing, and it has enormous promise—even now, it at least allows low-income workers to stay home when a child is sick or school is closed and not lose their jobs. To make it work for everyone, however, we'll have to find ways to make the sharing economy a caring economy, just as workers in the new factories of the Industrial Revolution turned to unions and strikes to claim their fair share of the wealth they were creating. We have to attend to the needs of all platform workers to ensure that they can earn a living wage, have access to good healthcare and education, and provide for their futures.

New forms will emerge, or rather new adaptations of old forms. MIT professor Thomas Malone, who wrote a prescient book called *The Future of Work* in 2004, predicted that freelancers with a craft or a specific profession would be likely to organize as guilds to exert the power necessary to even the playing field with employers. He used the example of the Screen Actors Guild, now known as SAG-AFTRA, which brings together a wide range of media artists—actors, singers, dancers, broadcast journalists, voiceover artists—who work as independent contractors. SAG members come together on specific creative projects—a play, a movie, a sound recording, a broadcast—and disband again, much as plumbers, electricians, carpenters, roofers, and other small businesses or individuals come together to build a house. The guild itself negotiates and provides health and pension benefits, allowing members to work flexibly on different projects as much as they want or need to.

If we can provide for contractors or freelancers in ways that ensure they can earn a living and provide for their families and their futures, the on-demand economy offers the prospect of far more flexible, self-scheduled work hours. It points to the end of the office as we know it, the place you must go to earn a living. That is exactly what many workers who are trying to fit their work and their caregiving responsibilities together need.

Moving up the income scale, the on-demand economy is likely to be a godsend for professionals who are also caregivers. Lawyers, business executives, bankers, doctors, and many other professional women could continue to advance in their careers or at least stay in the game while being the kind of parents they want to be. Consider Axiom Law and Bliss Lawyers, both of which have a bench of high-quality law firm alumni whom they rent out on a project basis to large companies—doing the same work that law firms do but at a fraction of the cost and a multiple of the flexibility. Topcoder matches freelance computer coders to projects; Eden McCallum provides project-based consulting services; Medicast allows patients to request a doctor through an app, charging a flat fee for a basic visit and paying malpractice insurance for the doctors on their roster. The Business Talent Group, based in Los Angeles, even rents out bosses who use their executive skills to get a specific project done.

If we can provide the right kind of portable social safety net, this deep flexibility will make it far easier for a wide range of platform workers to navigate the phases of life when they need to be caring for family members. But in the meantime, of course, millions of Americans still have day jobs with fixed hours, fixed locations, and bosses who expect fixed amounts of work. How can we change *that* economy to make room for care?

OpenWork

THOUGH MANY OFFICES ARE STILL stuck in a framework that was established over a century ago, some imaginative and innovative workplaces are making dramatic changes today. These workplaces allow employees to shape their own working environment together with their supervisors. They have opened up spaces for conversations that previously took place in secret or not at all and opened the door to an entire array of possibilities that can improve productivity, community, loyalty, and contentment. All of these changes make room for care. All of them are part of something called OpenWork, a platform and movement that I am proud to be a part of.

OpenWork is both a noun and a verb. It means a kind of work, a way of working, a spirit and set of values that animates a particular workplace. Openworkers are employees who have been able to make change from the bottom up, either collaboratively at their employer's invitation or more insistently, helping their superiors see and understand the enormous benefits of trust, mutual respect, flexibility, and mutual accountability. Kathleen Christensen, board chair of OpenWork.org, describes it as a place where "we share stories of organizations shattering the poverty of imagination that limits business productivity and societal well-being."

OpenWork works, for management and workers alike. Ninety-seven percent of openworking companies see increased productivity; 88 percent of employees report greater job satisfaction; and 45 percent have reduced rates of stress and burnout. To see how the elements of OpenWork have been put into practice, the website offers a wide range of examples. These are real places that have made real changes.

At the financial arm of General Motors, for instance, the company wanted to increase engagement and decrease stress at their call centers:

> [GM Financial] handed over the scheduling to employees to figure out the best way to work. They ended up allowing employees to make their own assignments and schedules. They came together and came up with a plan [under which] they could show up within 3 hours of their start time—or compress their hours during the summer—as long as they were working the equivalent of an 8-hour shift every day. It's resulted in significant reported decrease in stress and a 90 percent reduction of tardiness. People can have their home lives, and get stuck in traffic without panicking. It's really reduced attrition rates. They're now below industry average at just 6.2 percent.

Another company that exemplifies OpenWork principles is a multiservice tax firm from Dallas, Texas, called Ryan, LLC. They lost a number of star employees to burnout in 2008 and, in response, created a program called myRyan, which "enables employees to work wherever they want and whenever they want, as long as their work responsibilities are met." They can monitor their own progress through an online dashboard, but they monitor *performance*, measured with a score, instead of hours worked. The goal is to maintain a high score, not to work a certain number of billable hours.

Accounting firms, both big and small, have been particularly innovative—perhaps because women have often been the book-keepers in family businesses and accounting has long featured more women than law or finance. It's a particular plus that at least some of the partners in the Big Four global accounting firms—KPMG, PricewaterhouseCoopers, EY, and Deloitte—were promoted from part-time positions. In 2013, for instance, Ernst & Young (as it was then named) promoted more than two hundred employees "to executive levels while on formal flexible work arrangements." Deloitte has a program of "mass career customization" for all employees, based on a book of that name co-authored by Deloitte vice chairman Cathleen Benko and Anne Cicero Weisberg. It allows each business unit to come up with a set of options for its employees that would allow them to either ramp up or dial down their careers as necessary. Sharon Allen, who was chairman of Deloitte from 2003 to 2011, said of the system, "Over the course of a long career, almost everybody has a need to adjust what they're doing—the pace, the location, whatever that might be."

Beyond accounting, consider 1-800 CONTACTS, a direct-to-consumer retail business with more than nine hundred employees in Utah. It has an ingenious attendance system that is modeled on airline frequent-flier programs. Employees can earn points for "positive attendance behaviors" (like coming to work on time) and then redeem those points for up to one hundred unpaid days off a year and more than thirty paid days. Like an airline system, employees can use fewer points on each redemption if they provide more advance notice. They can also trade, release, or pick up shifts from home or even from their smartphones.

In still other sectors, Delta Air Lines has created a host of flexible options to allow employees to manage their time better and fit together their professional responsibilities with their family lives. Southern California Gas Company has a program called the SmartWork initiative, which offers flexible work hours, telecommuting, and extended-leave options. Other options include collaborative software to help employees work from home. According to Joan Blades and Nanette Fondas, American Express employees who work virtually "produce 43 percent more business than their office counterparts. IBM saves $700 million in real estate costs by allowing 25 percent of its employees worldwide to work from home."

On the more creative side, the software startup Evernote is executing its own version of a supremely flexible work environment. Evernote gives its employees unlimited vacation days. In fact, they don't bother tracking days off at all. One Evernote employee, who had recently returned from a three-week Mount Everest trip of a lifetime, told *Businessweek* in 2012, "It's a trust-based system. . . . It treats people as if they can run their own schedule."

Ironically, the larger challenge can be to get employees to take advantage of the vacation offered. When the Evernote unlimited-vacation benefit was first instituted, some people took *less* vacation than they had before, because they wanted to impress their bosses. So the Evernote CEO began writing thousand-dollar checks to anyone taking a weeklong vacation, so long as she had the ticket stubs to prove it and she shared stories about her travels with colleagues. "Our employees are better after they have traveled," the CEO said to *Businessweek*. "They are more productive; they are more useful to the company."

I had a similar experience at New America. When I took over, many employees had large accrued balances of vacation and personal days that they had not taken but planned to cash out when they left. In fairness, many of the younger people had been working around the clock on important projects that needed to get done, in a culture where they did not feel that they could take a vacation and still deliver what was being asked of them. I believe so strongly in the value of time off, however, that we instituted six weeks of paid time off to be used however and whenever an employee wants, subject to one caveat: you can only roll over two weeks every year. If you don't use the rest, you lose it. I got a lot of pushback from many employees who resented the paternalism. But I am looking after not just their health and well-being but also the health, well-being, and productivity of New America as an organization.

Some new companies have done away with the office altogether. Automattic, the tech company that created the blogging platform WordPress, is a "completely distributed" company. That means that every single one of its two-hundred-plus employees works from home, though they do have a physical headquarters in San Francisco so the company can get mail. Automattic employees work in 170 different cities, and they are given a monthly $250 outlay to invest in a co-working space if they'd like, in addition to a onetime $3,000 home office stipend when they join the company.

CEO Matt Mullenweg says that he is able to get the best work out of the best employees when they work from where they want to be. In an interview with the tech website Mashable, Mullenweg argued that, in an office, if people are dressed for work, show up on time, and look busy, "you assume [they] are working. . . . At home, all you have is your output—did you commit the code, did you write the post, did you make the proposal? There's no theater of physical proximity."

It may seem that this kind of flexibility is limited to digital age companies that create virtual rather than physical products. But a desire to reduce overhead and increase efficiency can arise in any business. After I gave a speech in my hometown of Charlottesville, Virginia, a woman came up to tell me that she too had a completely distributed flexible workplace, that her boss had created a network whereby the office employees could all work from home. Her business? A construction company!

These attitudes and the resulting flexibility in the tech start-up sector are one major reason that Wall Street financial firms are beginning to lose the competition for top recruits. In the fall of 2013 *The Wall Street Journal* reported that firms like Goldman Sachs and Barclays were responding by reducing weekend hours for their junior staffers. On the other hand, Morgan Stanley's chief executive, James P. Gorman, was honest enough to say what every investment banker I know was likely thinking: "I'm not sure that's the right answer because I'm not sure how you stop work if there's a deal on."

The answer is that you don't. Clients expect round-the-clock service when a deal is being done. But it is possible to come up with much more creative solutions, like letting employees take short days and days off equivalent to the amount of time they were completely immersed in a particular deal. Or create regular leaves and sabbaticals. Academics are used to working very intensively for three to four months at a time during the semester and then switching rhythms to a much more sustainable pace during breaks and summers. If even the most intense workplaces made it more possible for employees to adjust their own rhythms, individual bonuses might go down, but the quality of life and employee retention would go up.

TAKING CHARGE

You may be thinking that the only way to find yourself in an open workplace is to quit your job and move to one, that your boss or your company is never going to be willing to make the kind of changes that would allow you to fit your family and career together. Not so. The whole point of OpenWork is to have honest conversations that will lead to change. You can initiate those conversations and make changes yourself that will have a tremendous impact.

Train Your Boss

ONE GOOD APPROACH FOR EMPLOYEES is to "manage up." Many of the wonderful people who have worked for me over the years have learned how to filter my requests and prioritize the tasks that are most important, knowing that my reach sometimes exceeds my grasp. The very best people who've worked for me have also learned how to remind me, gently, that they are human. If I give them more than they can do, or should reasonably try to do within a limited time period, they look up and say, "If I can't get to everything, what is most important?"

I'm actually very grateful when they do that, because it forces me to think through what *is* most important. Equally valuable, these employees no longer risk spending their time working on something that was a lower priority and not getting to something I was expecting and needed more urgently.

Of course, they could stay up all night for a week and try to get everything done. But then they would be less sharp and less productive, and they likely wouldn't last in the job for very long. I'm not saying that all-nighters aren't necessary from time to time; as I have made clear, I've pulled plenty. Real crises do come up, and it's important to signal that you can be counted on in a crunch. Some of us also procrastinate until the adrenaline kicks in with a sufficient rush to allow us to get a huge amount done in a short period. But working continually in crisis mode takes a tremendous toll over time. It's perfectly fine to set limits and make clear that while you will get the important stuff done and will go the extra mile when necessary, you are not prepared to sacrifice other important things in your life to someone's fifth or sixth priority.

You may also be helping your boss become a healthier and more productive person himself. When my current assistant, Hana Passen, began working for me in the fall of 2012, I was amazed when she left the office at six o'clock even if I was still there. She had just graduated from college and she and I were getting to know each other; I would go through a long list of things to do and she would take it down but then start to pack up to go—to either rugby practice or other activities that she had scheduled after work.

At first, I found myself thinking, *I would never have left before my boss*. Quite the contrary, I would stay as late as he did and generally much later. But over the first few months we worked together, I discovered that Hana was almost always available if I needed her and got prodigious amounts done. After a while, I started wondering what was wrong with my time management that I was still there after she had left!

Have the Conversation with Your Boss

ONE OF MY FORMER STUDENTS at the Woodrow Wilson School, Fatema Sumar, worked for then-senator, now–secretary of state John Kerry on the staff of the Senate Foreign Relations Committee. When she returned from maternity leave after having her second child, she proposed to her staff director that she be able to work from home on Fridays in order to fit her new caregiving responsibilities together with her continuing professional responsibilities. Critically, she also said she thought she could produce better results for the committee this way. He agreed on a limited trial basis and quickly found that she became one of the most productive members of the office. This arrangement lasted even after she had her third child, and it allowed others to make more flexible choices about when and where they worked as well.

Fatema found the courage to have a direct conversation with her boss about what she needed. You should have this conversation too—after all, you can't really expect your manager to know what you want if you don't ask for it. But there are more and less successful ways of asking. Here are some pointers to make it easier.

Do your research. Check your employee handbook to see what the company's policies are on flexibility. If the company advertises the possibility of flexible arrangements, then your pitch should be less about whether you can take advantage of them than about how to ensure that you stay on track for promotion—even if on a slower track—if you do. Presume that the company's values are in the right place, but tackle flexibility stigma head-on.

Have a plan. Whether you're making a proposal in line with existing company policy or proposing a customized arrangement, make sure you have a specific plan in mind that will make it possible for you to fit the different pieces of your life together. It might be working a four-day week, telecommuting on Mondays or Fridays, leaving work at 5:45 every day so that you can pick your kids up from daycare and come back online after they're asleep, or whatever other arrangements will reduce your stress and increase your productivity.

Make an appointment. Don't just spring your suggestion on your boss at the office coffee machine. Signal that you and your partner have been talking about how to best maintain your commitments to your careers while making time for caregiving.

Highlight the benefits to your company. Be sure that

when you map out your plan, you make it clear to your boss how this new arrangement will benefit the company as well. Explain how you think you'll be more productive. Working from home can allow you, for instance, to focus on bigger projects that require concentrated thinking for hours at a time, which can be very difficult to do in the office. If your boss is hesitant, suggest a trial period—career experts recommend three months—after which, if it's not working out, you can reassess. And be sure to agree on metrics for evaluating the results of the experiment.

If at first you don't succeed . . . Asking doesn't guarantee receiving, of course. But even if your boss says no, you don't have to let the issue drop. In a *Woman's Day* article about requesting flextime, Sara Sutton Fell, the CEO of FlexJobs, suggests that if you've been turned down, bring the issue back up at an annual review. She even offers a potential script: "I know we discussed this a while ago, and it's still on my radar. I see it as a benefit not just for me personally, but for business," and follow it up with an explanation about what you're bringing to the table as an employee.

I'll be frank. When employees at the Woodrow Wilson School asked for more flexible schedules when I was a dean, I was willing but backed down in the face of staunch opposition from existing supervisors. The argument was always the same: "If we do it for this person we will have to do it for everyone and we won't be able to maintain any kind of control or discipline." Or else resentment that the person in question would be getting special treatment.

At New America the question has been more one of linking teleworking to agreed standards of performance and of navigating the tensions between one set of standards for administrative staff and another for the program staff who work on policy analysis and research. In both cases, as in the State Department, the issue has been how to make the transition from an old system to a new one. I come from an academic culture where I am used to getting lots of work done in many different places—where my office was a place I went to mainly for meetings. But for people who come from more traditional office cultures, home or a café or even a library is a place you go when you are *not* working. This transition may need to be made gradually, one experiment at a time, with clear measures of success or failure.

One final note. It's important to remember that your boss isn't necessarily your adversary; you may be pleasantly surprised at how he or she reacts to situations in which you have to adapt your work to fit your family. One week in the State Department, Deputy Secretary of State Jim Steinberg repeatedly missed or came late for Secretary Clinton's 8:45 meeting. On the fourth day, she raised an eyebrow at his assistant. But the minute his assistant explained that Jim's wife was traveling (she also worked for the government) and he was taking their daughters to school, Clinton's potential irritation turned to respect and support for his willingness to be an equal parent.

In general, your boss wants you to be the best employee you can be, and that means making you a happy employee. British economists have even found that happy workers are about 12 percent more productive (something you might want to mention casually to your boss!). It's going to take some time to revolutionize the workplace, but every step an individual employee takes sets a precedent; the women and men following in your footsteps will thank you.

If You Are Caught Up on Your Email, Your Priorities Are Wrong

EVEN IF YOUR WORKPLACE GIVES you maximum control over when, where, and how you do your work, it's still up to you to put your family first. Over a decade ago, I formulated what has been my work mantra ever since: "If you are caught up on your email, your priorities are in the wrong place." I realized that I could spend another hour at the office every night knocking down the daily pile of email—at least a third of which was unnecessary to anyone and all of which would quickly pile up again no matter what I did—or I could go home and read to my sons before bed. When I thought about what really mattered, the answer was obvious.

No one at a memorial service will ever remember if you answered all your email. Quite the contrary. When I worked in the State Department I noted an inverse relationship between how high up people were and how much email they actually answered—they simply had more important work on their plates. Cheryl Mills, Hillary Clinton's chief of staff, read all her email but did not respond unless a response was absolutely necessary, and then she had it down to one letter—"k" instead of "okay."

Email is just the most obvious manifestation of a much bigger issue: the 24/7 work culture and its associated feelings of responsibility and guilt. Many of us try so hard to respond to an ever-increasing set of demands from an ever-growing number of people who can now reach us at all hours. The key is to stop long enough to think through what your real priorities are. What's really most important to you? If you don't set your own priorities and draw the boundaries that will help you achieve them, no one else will do it for you.

IF FAMILY COMES FIRST . . .

IF CEOs, SUPERVISORS, AND MANAGERS want to avoid missing out on the next great wave of productivity increases and morale improvements, they too need to adopt policies that provide true flexibility. It might seem daunting, but all it takes is understanding, vision, and a little bit of nerve.

When I took my first big management job as dean of the Woodrow Wilson School in 2002, our sons were five and three. If one of them had a problem—from falling sick at school or daycare to a more sustained learning issue that might require diagnosis and outside assistance—that family matter came first.

The situation I've just described probably confirms many managers' worst fears about hiring a mother. But since I had no doubt about my own commitment to my work and my ability to focus, reason, and lead while I was a mother, and since I was the boss, I rejected the stereotype. After some trial and error, I found that if I attended to the family issue first, subject of course to meeting important obligations that could not be postponed or delegated, then I would be far more focused, productive, and determined when I turned back to my work.

Once, during a daylong meeting I had with the Woodrow Wilson School's advisory board, I told the board members that my associate dean would take over from eleven to noon while I went down the road to attend a teacher's conference. It would've been better, of course, to schedule the teacher's conference on a different day, but for whatever reason that was not possible and it was important that I be there. The world did not come to an end; my associate dean was perfectly capable of taking over; and although some of my board members may have been bemused, others recognized that missing one hour out of eight with them mattered far less than missing a crucial hour with my child's teacher.

Over time, I developed a slogan: "If family comes first, work does not come second. Life comes together." This slogan applied equally to me, my colleagues, and my employees. If anyone working for me had a family issue—with a child, a parent, a spouse, a grandparent, aunt, uncle, niece, nephew, or cousin—she should attend to it. We, her managers and co-workers, would cover for her and support her in any way we could. In return, we expected her to take responsibility for meeting her professional obligations, for making up any work she could not delegate, and for ensuring that important issues or assignments did not fall through the cracks.

I have applied this philosophy at the Woodrow Wilson School, at the State Department, where I managed some thirty-five people in the Office of Policy Planning, and now at New America. Indeed, within my first year at New America, on the eve of a trip to Chicago to meet with the head of a foundation that funds our work, the director of one of our programs wrote to me to say that his wife had been covering for him with their children for the past two weeks but she now had an important case and he simply had to step up.

I could have told him that this was an important trip (it was) and that he could not simply bow out on such short notice. It would have been completely within my rights as president of the organization going to meet a funder. But as a working spouse myself, I knew exactly the kind of interspousal negotiation he was going through and thought better of him as a husband and father that he was doing his fair share. His presence at my side was a nice-to-have rather than a need-to-have; the trip went off fine without him. For him, however, the entire incident affirmed his commitment to New America as an organization that lives its values and allows him to be both a family man and a working man. He is a very valuable member of our team, and I now know I can breathe a bit easier the next time a headhunter calls.

I certainly cannot claim to be a perfect manager; management is a process of continual learning and course correction. But I've witnessed firsthand that when I create the space for all the people who work for me, regardless of rank, to put their families first, their work never comes second. They put the two together in a way that both get done. Responsible people do not limit their obligations to the workplace. Indeed, I would not hire a job candidate who told me that his work would always come before his family. I would question his character.

Focus on Results

THE MOST EXTREME FORM OF flexibility that I have come across is the results-only work environment, or ROWE, an approach pioneered by Cali Ressler and Jody Thompson, authors of *Why Work Sucks and How to Fix It: The Results-Only Revolution.* As they describe it, ROWE means "people can do whatever they want, whenever they want, as long as the work gets done." That means no set hours at all. The only thing that matters is that your work is getting done, and getting done well.

ROWE is harder than it looks, and, inevitably, has some unintended consequences and problems of its own. To begin with, some employees have jobs that require them to be physically present at designated times, and even when work can be done effectively at home, lots of empty offices, particularly those of managers, can erode morale. Worse still, a two-tier class system can quickly develop whereby lower-level employees resent having to be present to do their jobs when higher-level staff can stay home.

ROWE has also had mixed reviews in large companies. It was famously adopted by Best Buy but was stopped later by new CEO Hubert Joly, who thought the approach was too one-size-fits-all. In an op-ed in the Minneapolis *Star Tribune* he wrote, "This program was based on the premise that the right leadership style is always delegation [to the employee]. Anyone who has led a team knows that delegation is not always the most effective leadership style." On the other hand, the Gap adopted ROWE and has claimed remarkable early success with the program.

Regardless of whether ROWE works as a formal, detailed program to be implemented, I find that the ROWE mindset has a positive impact on how managers manage. Ressler and Thompson insist that supervisors be clear about their expectations for employees as well as how results will be measured. Overseeing who comes in on time (or better yet, early) and leaves on time (or better yet, late) is much easier than thinking hard about how to set goals that can be met precisely. That process, in turn, requires setting clear priorities and communicating those priorities to your team, with measurable benchmarks and deadlines against them.

Sabrina Parsons, the CEO of Palo Alto Software, has applied these principles to her workplace with great results. Although the firm did not officially roll out ROWE, it uses similar principles. All of Parsons's employees have flexible schedules. "We very much focus on results and setting real tangible goals and objectives for every job and every employee," she says. If you work for her, you're "judged on what you do, not how many hours you're at the office. We think people do better work and more innovative work if they come in fresh every morning."

Parsons is a mother of three boys, ages ten, eight, and five. She has taken her focus on results a step further, transforming the workplace itself. When her children were infants, she brought them into the office, and she has allowed employees to do the same. Though Palo Alto employees get three months of maternity leave, a handful of employees have wanted to come back earlier, and they are allowed to bring their infants with them. "We've given them a place for the baby to be," Parsons explains. It's primarily a place of work, so if an employee had a colicky or special needs infant, Parsons says she would work out some other arrangement, whether it was working from home or something else. But otherwise, as long as employees can get their work done, why is an infant snoozing away a problem? Parsons's commitment to these principles has paid off: her company has grown from twenty-eight to sixty employees in the past three years and their revenue has increased 40 to 50 percent each year.

Thinking and working this way requires an even deeper mind shift about how we get good results in the first place. It's a strange analogy, but I always think of my rice cooker. Traditional rice cookers operate on clear input and output principles—one cup rice, two cups water, thirty-five minutes' cooking. But mine determines the cooking time based on the quality of the rice, the weather, and any other factor that might affect the outcome.

It sounds odd, and requires additional calculation on the part of the machine, so the cooking time always varies. But the result is so much better! So too is the work that is done when we determine assignments and time based on the quality of the work we need done and the individual characteristics of the people who are going to do that work.

Invest in Caregivers

THE FINAL STEP TOWARD CREATING a workplace in which all employees can be their best and most productive selves requires managers and executives to see caregiving itself as an asset. Radical as it may seem, it's time for CEOs, supervisors, and team leaders to assume that the experience of caring for children, aging parents, or any loved one will give your employees experience and insights that will help them on the job. To begin with, they will be extremely efficient; working caregivers do not have time to waste.

And remember, from chapter 5, all the attributes that care helps develop: knowledge, patience, adaptability to different rhythms, honesty, courage, trust, humility, and hope.

Believing that care is just as valuable and formative an experience as competition means making paternity leave mandatory, or at least the default option, so that new fathers would have to opt out of taking it rather than opting in. It also means welcoming whatever arrangements allow workers who are also caregivers not only to stay on the job, but also to stay on a leadership track, even though their rise will likely be slower and more irregular than workers who are not caregivers.

Even more important, managers must recognize the enormous talent pool of women in their late forties and fifties who have taken time out for caregiving.

The McKinsey Global Institute predicts that by 2020 the world will face a "skills gap" of nearly 40 million people, meaning that employers will need that many workers with a college degree or higher than the global labor force can supply. In their words, "Businesses operating in this skills-scarce world must know how to find talent pools with the skills they need and to build strategies for hiring, retaining, and training the workers who will give them competitive advantage." Part of the answer is right in front of them. All those women currently missing from the ranks of top management—the ones who keep disappearing between entry level and the C-suite—are actually still there. You just have to have eyes to see them and the foresight and wisdom to give them a real chance and hire them again.

So take some risks and invest in caregivers. Even more broadly, invest in care itself: in the many ways that our caring sides and our competitive sides can come together brilliantly and productively. Take your cue from Bill Gates, who amassed one of the world's biggest fortunes before being influenced by his wife,

Melinda, to give most of it away. One of the key moments for me in writing this book was reading a speech that he gave at the World Economic Forum in 2008, where he identified self-interest and caring for others as the twin forces of human nature. He sees those same forces as the drivers of what he calls "creative capitalism," the harnessing of market forces to lift billions of people out of poverty. Figure out how to mesh competition and care in your own business, and create the perfect workplace of your own.

11

CITIZENS WHO CARE

WE AMERICANS LOVE SELF-HELP. *The New York Times* DEVOTES AN entire separate bestseller list to self-help books. Manuals that tell us to lean in or stand up or climb over others as a way to enhance our personalities, overcome our flaws, and assure our progress speak to a national religion of self-improvement. After all, if it's only up to us, then change is within our control. It doesn't depend on organizing or mobilizing others within a political system that many of us see as dysfunctional.

Don't get me wrong. I've bought as many of those books as anyone else has—from how to lose weight to how to find inner peace. But when we're talking about the kinds of changes I am calling for, the only way each of our lives is going to get better is if we work together. We can't do it on our own; we have to exercise our collective political power to change the system. We've done it before, and we can do it again now.

I'm trained as a lawyer and a policy expert; I know as well as anyone that "policy" is just another word for a set of guidelines as to what we should do in a particular situation—e.g., "Honesty is the best policy." Public policy means the principles we decide as citizens that we want to live by, principles that our elected representatives translate into regulations and laws. It's the crystalliza-tion of what we can do if we come together and decide how we want our tax dollars to be spent. We can renew America, in line with the best of our history and ourselves, as a country that values work and family equally and enables its citizens to live full and happy lives.

BUILDING AN INFRASTRUCTURE OF CARE

Businesses cannot compete and create value for themselves and society as a whole without roads, bridges, tunnels, ports and airports, railroad tracks, electricity, water, waste disposal, and, today, high-speed broadband. That is what "infrastructure" means: the skeleton of a functioning economy that everyone needs but individual citizens either cannot or will not provide on their own. The infrastructure of travel and transport—either through physical or virtual space—is the infrastructure of eco-nomic competition. We need an equal infrastructure of care: a set of arrangements and institutions that allows citizens to flourish not only in the pursuit of their individual goals but also in their relationships to one another.

We used to have an infrastructure of care: it was called women at home. But with almost 60 percent of those women in the work-force, that infrastructure has crumbled and it's not coming back. We need to build a new infrastructure of care for the twenty-first century, one that meets the demands of our society and our econ-omy. Writing about the "elder boom" and its enormous impact on the growing need for care in the United States, Ai-jen Poo makes the point that although "an infrastructure for care may seem different than an infrastructure for railroads, highways, electricity or the Internet . . . care always comes first." If you can't "feed, bathe, or clothe yourself," none of the rest of it matters.

Poo talks about the "Care Grid," just like the energy grid. I like the image. Just as we draw on different types of energy delivered through a variety of different grids, we will need many different approaches to providing and supporting care. Here are some of the possible elements of such an infrastructure, drawing on the policies of the United States and other countries:

- High-quality and affordable childcare and eldercare
- Paid family and medical leave for women and men
- A right to request part-time or flexible work
- Investment in early education comparable to our investment in elementary and secondary education
- Comprehensive job protection for pregnant workers
- Higher wages and training for paid caregivers
- Community support structures to allow elders to live at home longer
- Legal protections against discrimination for part-time workers and flexible workers
- Better enforcement of existing laws against age discrimination
- Financial and social support for single parents
- Reform of elementary and secondary school schedules to meet the needs of a digital rather than an agricultural economy and to take advantage of what we now know about how children learn

The specifics of policy proposals on each of these issues differ from state to state and often by party affiliation and political philosophy; a comprehensive catalogue is thus impossible. But for those of you who want to know more, you can find plenty of additional information in the endnotes of this book, including links to organizations where you can get directly involved and campaigns that you can support.

A major argument in favor of building a universal infrastructure of care by mandating things like paid leave and job protection for pregnant and even part-time workers is that it levels the playing field for those businesses that are trying to do the right thing. Putting these policies into place in an individual business, rather than achieving the same results through a tax-financed insurance program, can be expensive. In an economy of tight margins and litigious shareholders, taking on those expenses may cede a crucial advantage to the competition. A short-term advantage, to be sure, as firms determined to do right by their employees find themselves rewarded with higher engagement, productivity, and retention rates. But still, enough of an edge that we can't rely on corporations to make the necessary changes themselves, business by business. We need the kind of political change that establishes a new floor and a new set of standards to aspire to.

THE POLITICS OF CARE

OKAY. YOU KNOW I'M A Democrat. So if you are a Republican you may well be thinking that I'm in left-wing la-la land. But the politics of care are not so predictable. Consider Megyn Kelly, a Fox News anchor and working mother, who strongly agrees on the need for paid maternity leave. In a live segment on her Fox show, she reminded Mike Gallagher, a conservative talk show host who had called her three-month maternity leave "a racket," that the

United States is one of only four countries in the world that does not require paid maternity leave, adding, for good measure, that his reaction was "moronic." "We're populating the human race," she said. "It's not a vacation. It's hard, important work."

Strengthening American families and supporting caring communities garners support across the political spectrum. On the left, President Obama put forward proposals to expand access to affordable, high-quality childcare in his 2015 budget. Right now, only 10 percent of children receive what's known as "high-quality care." Childcare workers make a median annual salary of less than twenty thousand dollars a year, yet families with two children in center-based care pay more money for childcare than they do for rent in all fifty states. Obama also called for more states to expand paid sick and family leave.

On the right, one of the few states that currently offers paid family leave (workers pay the cost out of a small increase in their payroll tax) is New Jersey, under Republican governor Chris Christie. Republican senators have sponsored a law that would allow employers to offer employees paid leave hours instead of overtime pay; some polls show that a majority of Republican women voters support paid family leave. Republican senator Kelly Ayotte co-chairs a bipartisan caucus across both the Senate and the House devoted to assisting family caregivers. She follows in the footsteps of Senator Kay Bailey Hutchison, who successfully sponsored legislation to allow homemakers to contribute to retirement accounts the same way that salaried workers can.

We Americans differ, as always, on ways and means. The specific disagreement around care is not as much about whether we should be devoting resources to caring as it is about who, in fact, should be doing the caring. Conservatives prefer family, church, and community. Liberals worry that those approaches let far too many Americans fall through the cracks, that they reinforce inequalities for those who are often most vulnerable and in need, with no family, church, or community to turn to.

My feeling is that our problems in this arena are so severe that we need to be trying both at the same time, recognizing a role for government *and* business, church *and* state, states *and* the federal government (and municipalities too). Moreover, why not encourage a little competition over care? Left and right should challenge each other to see whether market solutions or government solutions for the care crisis work better. Different states can adopt different solutions; we can develop common metrics to see where children, seniors, and others needing care are better off. Different cities can do the same. Whatever works best.

At the federal level, Congress should be able to pass a variety of measures that will allow states and workplaces to develop competing approaches. To get there, however, we will need compromise—recognition of the validity of multiple points of view and at least the *possibility* that a plan other than the one you favor just might work better. To get that compromise, in turn, we need more members of Congress with direct experience of caregiving.

Indeed, given the wide-ranging support from everyday Americans of both parties for more government help for caregivers, it often seems as if our legislators are the only ones who aren't getting the message. There's a simple reason for that: we are electing too many men. When I write that sentence, you may well read it as a sexist, essentialist claim about how men care about national defense and the state of the stock market and women care about families and a social safety net. It's never comfortable when reality confirms stereotypes, but at least for the moment, strong empirical evidence documents that it's the women in Congress who are pushing for affordable daycare and paid leave.

What is new is that we now have reason to believe that reaching a critical mass of women in any group that operates by majority rule, including a legislature, may well cause *men* to behave differently.

Vote for More Women

AMERICA'S REVOLUTIONARY RALLYING CRY WAS "no taxation without representation." We still haven't really achieved that goal. Men can represent women, of course, just as women can represent men, African Americans can represent European Americans, and older Americans can represent younger Americans. Still, the radical under-representation of women in our legislative bodies has dramatic implications.

If asked why we should vote for more women, most voters would be likely to think about the distinctive qualities they associate with women over men. In *The Athena Doctrine*, John Gerzema and Michael D'Antonio surveyed 64,000 women and men in thirteen countries about what is most important to "leadership, success, morality, and happiness today." In all thirteen countries, people of both genders picked stereotypically feminine traits— like collaboration, sharing credit, and patience—as the ones that will solve today's global challenges. The majority also admitted to being worn out by a "world dominated by codes of what they saw as traditionally masculine thinking and behavior: codes of control, competition, aggression and black-and-white thinking." Amazingly, to me at least, two-thirds of respondents believed the world would be a better place if "men thought more like women."

At first glance, these assertions seem just as sexist as claims that the world would be a better place if women thought like men. They are riddled with stereotypes that ultimately do not benefit either sex. On the other hand, after conducting multiple experiments, political scientists Tali Mendelberg and Christopher Karpowitz find that women in politics do in fact tend to pay more attention to caregiving issues and to the disadvantaged in general. But the numbers of women in legislative bodies don't matter on their own, in terms of actually passing laws that move the needle on these issues. As Mendelberg and Karpowitz write in their 2014 book *The Silent Sex*, summarizing their findings, "Women's percentage in deliberating bodies matters little—in itself."

What matters is whether women speak up. If they sit in town hall meetings, policy planning sessions, and general discussions and no one hears their views, nothing will change. Here numbers do matter, but only insofar as the number of women reaches a sufficient critical mass that women are actually prepared to say what they think. Once they do, all sorts of things change.

Mendelberg and Karpowitz conducted an experiment. Participants, both men and women, were separated into groups and told they would be doing tasks to earn money. They would then be deciding, *as a group*, how much of that money to redistribute to the members of the group who had the least. The observers recorded the results and also kept track of the participants' speech: how often speakers mentioned issues of caregiving versus economic issues and how often women spoke.

The results were surprising even to the researchers. First, Mendelberg and Karpowitz found that all-women groups were much more generous than all-male groups—the guaranteed income of all group members was higher by about seven thousand dollars for all-female groups. Indeed, "groups chose a more generous safety net under majority rule as the number of women rose." Unsurprisingly to any woman, they also found that women speak less when they are in the minority.

Most striking, however, Mendelberg and Karpowitz discovered that at least in some circumstances, when women are the majority in the group, *men* speak more about caregiving issues. In groups with one man and four women, 62 percent of the men raised the topic of children, compared with just 19 percent of men in groups of four men and one woman. Of course, an experimental lab setting isn't the same as the floor of Congress. Still, these findings underline the point that when women's voices are not heard, the issues women care about are not considered relevant or essential. They are considered separate women's issues instead of everybody issues.

When women's voices are heard, as Mendelberg and Karpowitz put it, they are doing "more than naming a problem; they are including marginalized or disadvantaged groups in the conception of 'us.'" In other words, women actually represent a broader spectrum of citizens than men do. Equally important, "when women have greater standing, men share the floor more equally, adopt the language of care for children more often, endorse more generous safety net support for the poor, are less likely to interrupt women in hostile ways, and provide more positive forms of support and encouragement to female speakers."

The implications for American politics—and indeed politics all over the world—are stunning. If we can elect enough women— women who will of course have different personalities and political views themselves—we will stand a far better chance of representing who we really are as a nation. By adding enough women to the mix, we will not only add female voices and perspectives, we will make it possible for the *men* we elect to be their true selves, to speak and vote as fathers, sons, husbands, and brothers as well as warriors, competitors, winners. They will not always agree with each other, of course, just as the women we elect will not. That disagreement is what democracy is about. But they will all do a better job of representing the full spectrum of who we are as a people: citizens who both compete and care.

THE CARE ECONOMY

INVESTORS SHOULD BE PAYING AS much attention to care trends as politicians. The demand for jobs in the care sector is growing as a function both of increased awareness of the difference that good care makes and of demographics. Remember that the ratio of retired adults to working-age adults will increase by almost half between today and 2030. Even by 2020, one in six Americans will be over 65 and more than one in three Americans will likely have eldercare responsibilities.

Americans also have strong views about how we want to age; almost 90 percent of us believe that we should not end up in institutions. But aging at home, with dignity, requires an entire industry of home healthcare, which is why the demand for home careworkers is skyrocketing. But if we want higher-quality care, we will have to pay for it. Better wages, higher social value, and regulated working conditions are a good start. If we value the quality of our children's care, our parents' care, and indeed our own care someday, we must pay much more attention to the care economy.

A farsighted group of economists have been working on these issues for decades. The dynamics of the care economy are complicated by the definition of care itself, with its unavoidable intertwining of love and effort, paid and unpaid work. Reducing care to a pure commodity, like grain or steel or anything else we pay for, destroys its value. But pretending its emotional reward is so great that it should not be paid for at all, or paid for at a very low rate, ignores its value and reduces the quantity and quality of its supply. The economist Nancy Folbre and a group of her colleagues in sociology, political science, and demography have outlined an entire agenda for "care policy and research." More studies along these lines are still needed in order for us to build up the intellectual and practical foundations of the care economy as a specialized version of the larger twenty-first-century service economy.

Interestingly, it is our military that already best understands the value of investing in the next generation of American children. Children's brains are shaped most in the first five years of their lives, so it's not an exaggeration to say that the care and education of our children from birth to age five is a national security issue for the United States that ranks alongside the Islamic State, terrorist networks generally, Russian expansionism, and China's rise.

The Pentagon walks the walk. It offsets the cost of high-quality childcare for servicemen by subsidizing on-site daycare. Fees are based on family income. This assistance has been available to military families since 1989. Equally important, the Pentagon pays teachers in its early care and education programs the same wages that other Defense Department employees make based on training, education, seniority, and experience. In other words, the part of the U.S. government most directly responsible for upholding national security recognizes the need to pay wages that can attract and retain college- and graduate-school-educated workers to provide care and early learning to the children of all employees from birth onward.

In the private sector, some farsighted entrepreneurs are already stepping into the breach of the care economy. Sheila Lirio Marcelo, a Harvard MBA/JD who found herself caring for two small children and aging parents at the same time, founded Care .com because she was having trouble finding quality caregivers. Care.com is a marketplace for caregivers of children and the elderly; it matches a caregiver and an employer every two minutes. And it's not just helpful to families and caretakers alike, it's big business. The company raised $91 million in an initial public stock offering, and when it went public in January 2014, Care .com had a market value of over $550 million.

Bright Horizons is another company that successfully monetizes care. They provide a variety of services from high-quality early-education centers to emergency childcare to coordinating on-site daycare at various companies, hospitals, and universities. Bright Horizons is also publicly traded, and when it returned to the market in 2013, it was valued at $1.4 billion.

Real estate developers are also starting to respond to the caregiving needs of American families. In California, for example, developers are creating townhouses geared toward multigenerational families. These townhouses include bathrooms and bedrooms on the ground floor so seniors don't have to use the stairs and then traditional nuclear family layouts on the upper floors. That way, the "sandwich generation" can take care of their parents, and the grandparents can help watch their grandchildren.

Seniors are also banding together so that they can grow old with their friends, *Golden Girls* style. It's called "co-housing," and a housing consultant told *The New York Times* that it will be especially appealing to boomers. The "social consciousness of the 1960's can get re-expressed" through communal living, she predicted. I can personally testify to the pleasure of these arrangements; I share an apartment in Washington two days a week with a dear friend whom I have known since college. She moved from her home base in New York to serve in government; her husband comes down regularly. It's just like having a college roommate again, complete with visits from the boyfriend!

Outside large-scale caregiving companies and real estate developers is a growing army of individual caregivers. Ai-jen Poo's National Domestic Workers Alliance joined with twenty other organizations to create the Caring Across Generations movement. By focusing on changing U.S. demographics, particularly around aging, and pioneering innovations in home- and community-based caregiving, the movement seeks "to transform the way we care in this country."

Caregivers for adults with dementia—Alzheimer's disease and other forms—face special challenges. But as with children, education and specialized training can make a substantial difference both to the individuals being cared for and the caregivers. More broadly, the Family Caregiver Alliance is a community-based nonprofit organization that addresses the needs of the families and friends providing unpaid, long-term care for their loved ones at home.

Look also for an explosion of jobs based on providing different types of specialized care. We have always had doctors and nurses; now we have physician's assistants of many different kinds and nurse-practitioners with multiple specializations. And therapists of every description for body and mind are proliferating: for balance, posture, gait, stress, and recovery from challenges ranging from joint replacements to stroke. These are not jobs that people take when they cannot get into "real careers." They are jobs that require medical knowledge and skills as well as the ability to build a meaningful set of relationships with clients; they are essential to allowing all of us—from youngest to oldest—to lead better lives.

Beyond the market for high-quality paid care is a broader approach to thinking about our entire economy in a way that takes account of the value of care. How should we measure the social capital in our relationships and the human capital that we build through nurture and care? The Caring Economy Campaign is developing economic indicators that track social wealth alongside traditional measures of money and property. At the very least, we should be able to measure the economic value of care for children and adults. After all, the entire idea of the gross domestic product is a human construct; we can measure anything we think is important and seek to increase.

AN EXCEPTIONAL AMERICA

IN THE FOREIGN POLICY WORLD, and the political world generally, entire libraries have been written about American exceptionalism. As a nation, we have thought ourselves to be different from other nations from our very earliest days. In 1630, John Winthrop, who would become governor of Massachusetts Bay Colony, wrote, "We must consider that we shall be as a City upon a hill. The eyes of all people are upon us." We were to be the shining example of people who could govern themselves, who could establish freedom of worship and expression, who could explore and develop what was, to us and to our fellow Europeans, "the new world."

In the realm of care, the United States is largely exceptional for what it is *not* doing. We are alone among all advanced industrial countries (and indeed virtually among all countries) in not mandating paid maternity leave; many of our peer countries in Western Europe, by contrast, provide quite generous maternity and paternity leave. Britain, for example, even under austerity, provides up to a year of leave with at least some pay.

Beyond the early weeks and months of life, other industrialized countries offer an astonishing array of facilities and services to support parents and caregivers more generally, from daycare for children to adult care for the disabled, the senescent, and the dying. Former Norwegian minister of children and family Valgard Haugland sums up his country's philosophy: "We have decided that raising a child is real work, and that this work provides value for the whole society." It is only fair, then, "that the society as a whole should pay for this valuable service."

These countries are already reaping the benefits, in terms of both competitiveness and social mobility. A decade ago, Andy, who has long studied European politics, told me that it was easier to move up from humble origins into the middle class in Europe than in the United States. I just couldn't believe it. It seemed preposterous; our history is replete with examples of immigrants fleeing hidebound class structures and religious prejudice to make it in America.

Today, though, it's impossible to deny. Multiple economic studies from a range of universities, think tanks, and international organizations have concluded that an immigrant to Denmark, Australia, Norway, Finland, Canada, Sweden, or Germany has a better chance of improving his or her lot than in the United States. Poor children in these countries have almost double the chance of climbing out of poverty as they do in the United States. To be sure, some of these countries are smaller and more homogeneous than America. But Canada, for instance, has a higher percentage of foreign-born citizens than the United States does, yet Canadians are twice as likely to move up the social and economic ladder as Americans are. And though multiple factors are correlated with social mobility—segregation, income inequality, schools, and family structure—the ability of families, supported by communities, to maintain a stable and caring environment for children plays a very big part.

We don't have to do exactly what other countries do. In fact, some evidence suggests that the ultra-generous maternity leaves in Europe can actually hurt ambitious women. Claire Cain Miller points out in *The New York Times* that women in Europe are half as likely as men to be managers, while women in the United

States are equally likely to be managers. This disparity is due to a combination of unintended consequences of long maternity leaves: women may put the brakes on their ambitions, and employers may be reluctant to put women of childbearing age in key positions because they fear they will be absent too much.

But here is what we *can* do. We can take our founding credo—"All men are created equal"—and understand it to mean that men and women are equal and that the work that was once divided between men and women—earning income and providing care—is equally necessary and equally valuable. We can also come to appreciate the many ways in which a caring society is a more equal society.

Psychologist Carol Gilligan points out that we hear children yelling "You don't care!" just as much as "That's not fair!" "You don't care" reflects the fear of abandonment that all vulnerable and dependent people fear—young, old, sick, or disabled. "That's not fair" reflects the fear that those who have power will abuse it, will make or break the rules in favor of themselves.

Think about the implication of this point. It means that not being cared for is just as much a marker of inequality as being discriminated against. Both conditions are ways that those with power can take advantage of those without power—the young, the old, the sick, the disabled, the different, the structurally disadvantaged. "That's not fair" can mean "You don't see me or hear me; you don't give me equal rights or regard." "You don't care" can mean "You have abandoned me in my time of need and vulnerability, when I could not assert my equality with my fellow citizens."

As Americans, we should take pride in defining ourselves as citizens who care. Who care about our country and care about one another. Who remember that our past was not just a saga of rugged individuals setting out to conquer the land of opportunity, but also of barn raisings, quilting bees, grazing commons, and one-room schoolhouses. Who understand that we can only compete as a nation if we remember to care.

We can break through our current political logjams. We can reinvent ourselves once again, as we have many times before. We can be exceptional once again, not only for the speed of our computers and the power of our armies, but for the strength of our communities and the quality of our care.

CODA

In many ways this book is a love letter to my own family. They've always been the foundation of everything that I've done and all that I am; it's no surprise that you've met various Slaughters and Moravcsiks within these pages. Still, over the past few years, as I've learned to look at the world through the dual lenses of competition and care, I've come to see many of my own family members differently, with newfound respect.

All my life, I've been keenly aware of how fortunate I am to have been born in the late 1950s instead of the early 1930s, as my mother was, or the 1900s, as my grandmothers were. Until recently, I saw these women in terms of what they could have been if they had only had the opportunities I have had. I'm still grateful that I came of age when those opportunities were expanding dramatically, but I now see these women—my foremothers—as having contributed just as much to society as their husbands did. They invested in their families; they educated and inspired their children, sons and daughters alike, to be what we have become; they cared for those in need, both immediate relatives and beyond. In the dry language of sociology and economics, they were the custodians of human capital. In a richer and more sensitive rhetoric, they were the nurturers of humanity itself.

My Belgian grandmother, Henriette Madeleine De Bluts

Limbosch, married my grandfather, a medical student, in 1932, and had my mother and my uncle in quick succession. When the Germans occupied Brussels in May 1940, my grandfather refused to surrender with the Belgian army and instead managed to join the Allied Forces at Dunkirk and be evacuated to England, where he later joined the Special Air Service. After living under occupation for two years, my grandmother decided she would join him. Thus began a six-month saga worthy of Hollywood. She was an attractive young woman of thirty-four who would not take no for an answer.

My brothers and I grew up on the stories of her flight. She eventually dictated her memories of the entire six-month journey—from France to Switzerland, through Spain to Portugal, and finally by boat to London. Whenever her friends in the Belgian Resistance tried to arrange a way for her to slip across the border from occupied into free France, the response that came back was "Yes, but without the children." On that subject my grandmother was adamant. She had no idea what the war would bring, and she simply would not leave her children behind. As she explained to my mother decades later,

> Looking back now, with some life experience and age, I fully realize that it was total repression of the possible looming dangers. It also was, I guess, because I have a very optimistic personality. Often I have tried to imagine myself in a difficult situation, asking myself how on earth I was going to get out of it, and never would I think that I could not resolve the problem or get out of the plight I would be in. No, I never considered that I would not be successful in this particular endeavor and that it could really be disastrous for myself and my children.

I have to smile when I read that passage. It is so much Grandmère, a woman of such iron determination that when her doctors told her much later in life that she would only hobble due to a loss of cartilage in her ankle, she simply gritted her teeth, endured the pain, and continued to stride the streets of Brussels at a ferocious pace. She managed her household, her husband's surgical practice, and the family's investments, bringing a detailed perfectionism to everything she did. She was often strict and demanding—she used to correct the thank-you letters I sent her in French and send them back to me—but she was also willing to put in an unlimited amount of time with her grandchildren on schoolwork or any other projects to help them succeed.

I have always looked at my grandmother's life and thought that her combination of determination, optimism, management ability, and ingenuity would have made her an amazing CEO—Belgian business might never have been the same! I still wish that she had had a much wider range of choices about how to live her life. But I now see a woman who made it possible for my grandfather to tend countless grateful patients, raised two successful children who have each contributed to the world in their own way, provided a critical safety net for several of her grandchildren, and brightened and improved the lives of many people.

Grandmère understood that the web of care requires work. She was a creature of duty. Her mother had insisted that her spine never touch the back of a chair when she sat (a posture lesson she tried but failed to pass on to her daughter and granddaughters). That same upright acceptance of the roles society assigned her gave shape and purpose to her life, caring not only for her husband and children, but also for her parents, my grandfather's parents, friends, neighbors, and even Marie, her longtime housekeeper. It is society as a whole that assigns value and prestige to what people do; as I see it now, she added every bit as much social value caring for her family and community as her husband did caring for his patients.

My American grandmother, whom I knew as Ma, was cut from quite different cloth. Born Mary McBee Hoke in 1902, she grew up as an only child in Lincolnton, North Carolina, a small town where her family had lived for generations. When her father was named to the supreme court of North Carolina, the family moved to Raleigh. Her mother died suddenly when my grandmother was only eighteen, leaving her to be her father's companion for a few short years until he died as well.

She was a young woman of means with a large circle of friends in the mid-1920s; her house quickly became the center of her set's social life. She had graduated from what was then Saint Mary's College—a school that then ran from elementary school through the first two years of college—and read law briefly with a local attorney. She traveled on her own, to Boston and even to Europe. The picture I have of her is of an independent, energetic, daring young woman ready to shape her own life.

Then she met Edward "Butch" Slaughter, an assistant football coach at North Carolina State University. She fell in love; they married in 1930. Shortly thereafter my grandfather took a job as the line coach at the University of Virginia and eventually moved his young family to Charlottesville, where they lived for the rest of their lives. Charlottesville was just several hours to the north, but in Ma's eyes it was a completely different world: stiffer, more formal, and more socially conscious. She became the coach's wife rather than the judge's daughter; she devoted herself to her family but never recovered her former self-reliant and social self.

At her funeral I talked about her love of words, how her children and grandchildren could recite the poems that she had memorized in her own childhood. I always thought she would have been a wonderful English professor. Or a lawyer, using her phenomenal memory for detail to build her case. She could sit down next to anyone from anywhere in the South, ask a few questions, and figure out how our family and theirs intertwined at some point over the past two centuries. The failure to harness that talent for a more productive use than identifying "kissing cousins" is a classic example of how societies lose out when they do not allow their women to achieve their full potential.

I have thus always thought of Ma's life as a prime example of unfulfilled potential. And yet, to me, her first grandchild and only granddaughter, she was everything a grandmother should be. I wear her Saint Mary's school ring, with the initials MMH, on my little finger; rare is the day that I do not look down at it and re-member her. When I think of how her unconditional love and unflagging support for my every move have been part of the bed-rock on which my own achievements have been built, I value what she did as much as I regret what she could not do.

I've changed my lenses on some of my current family mem-bers as well. After my article came out, a close childhood friend wrote and observed how different my father had always been from hers and from the other fathers we both knew growing up. I wrote Dad an email thanking him and wondering, for the first time, how it was that he came to be so progressive for a man in Virginia in the 1960s. He told me that as a trial lawyer he had handled a certain number of divorce cases in which men left their wives, who then had no means of supporting themselves. He vowed at that point that his daughter would never find herself in that position.

I thus now see my father more in the round. I realize that his support for my career came not just from pride in what he thought I could accomplish but also from care—a determination that I be able to support myself if need be. But as progressive as he was, it never would have occurred to him to raise his sons—my brothers—to embrace caregiving as much as he raised me to be a breadwinner. One of those brothers, Bryan, has a busy legal practice, four children, and a very equal marriage to my sister-in-law Jen, who is also a lawyer. Jen chose to work part-time after their first child was born, but Bryan is a deeply committed father who attributes their division of labor much more to relative earnings than to desire. It would never have occurred to *me* before I wrote this book that Bryan might in fact want to work more flexibly at some point while his children are growing up so he could spend more time with them.

I also once would have interpreted Jen's choice to slow down as a decision to take herself off the fast track, reflecting a level of career ambition that was simply lower than mine. I would have seen her as a "mother who is working part-time" married to a full-time professional—exactly the way the labor market types the millions of women who have made the same decision. I now see her as the talented lawyer and manager she is, one who has chosen to focus more on her family for this period in her life. I see the ways that her choice benefits all of us as a society. And I see that when the frenetic activity of raising four children draws to a close, as it inevitably will, she will still have at least fifteen years of active working life ahead of her.

I hope that after reading this book you will look around and see the world—including your own family members—differently too. Above all, I hope that we can all imagine different and much more equal lives for our children. When I look at our sons, a lump comes to my throat. They were twelve and ten when I left for Washington in 2009, still very much boys. Now they are young men, towering over me in ways I simply cannot get used to, with their own friends and plans and dreams. As I write this, with Edward leaving for college, they are on the edge of the nest.

That makes it a particularly poignant moment to reflect on what has always been one of my deepest fears about having sons. The old saw "A son is a son until he takes a wife; a daughter is a daughter for the rest of her life" does not apply so much with my brothers and sisters-in-law, but I have certainly seen its truth often enough with my friends. When women take over as the caring anchors of their own families, they so often tend the relationships with their parents and siblings much more closely than with their in-laws.

I worry about that with our boys. What I want more than anything for them is that they will bring home wonderful mates who will become part of our family and that they will continue to define themselves as sons, brothers, husbands, and, someday, fathers as much as they embrace their professional identities. I hope that they will find work they love as much as I love mine, but whatever they end up doing, I want them to know that I will be as proud of them for putting in the time and effort necessary to build strong families of their own—however they choose to construct them—as for anything else they might achieve. And I hope that they will be equally willing to support and be supported by their spouses—with both cash and care.

Let's hope that by the time they reach that stage, society will agree with me.

Family is the foundation of our flourishing. At least since the Industrial Revolution, we have split work and family into two different spheres, one the world of men and the other the world of women. As more and more women entered the world of work, the relationship between work and family became one of profound tension, each tugging at the other. In fact, however, family makes work possible in the same way work makes family possible.

It's up to us to create the conditions in which the two can reinforce each other.

I am hopeful for the coming decades. The millennial generation, which includes my sons, seems to understand the value of pushing past what David Brooks calls "the big Me." Emily Esfahani Smith and Stanford marketing professor Jennifer L. Aaker have written about "millennial searchers," drawing on research showing that three-fourths of millennials seek "meaningful work." Although meaning is inevitably subjective, "a defining feature is connection to something bigger than the self. People who lead meaningful lives feel connected to others, to work, to a life purpose, and the world itself." Nourishing human connection is the essence of care.

We can, all of us, stand up for care. We can change how we think, how we talk, how we plan and work and vote. We can come together as women and men. We can finish the business that our mothers and grandmothers began, and begin a new revolution of our own.

ACKNOWLEDGMENTS

THE THINKING IN THIS BOOK IS SOME OF THE HARDEST WORK I HAVE ever done. A week before "Why Women Still Can't Have It All" was published I told my agent that under no circumstances was I going to write a book about work and family. I had a foreign policy book I wanted to write (and still do). Two weeks later I was signing a contract. What changed my mind was the tsunami of response to the article, which convinced me that many more voices need to be heard in this conversation. My first thank-you goes to the thousands of readers who wrote to me directly or who commented, debated, and posted in online conversations after the article came out. Some of you are friends and former students; most of you are complete strangers. I never managed to respond to many of you, which I still regret. But I read what you wrote, including the critiques, and you shaped my thinking.

Your contributions continued through years of what I came to think of as "call and response research." I gave hundreds of speeches to women's groups: septuagenarians in Sarasota, investment bankers, sales representatives, students, diplomats, lawyers, human resources managers, entrepreneurs, and community groups. Every time, after listening to your questions and comments, I would write down my notes and impressions afterward. One of those encounters haunts me still: the quiet woman who hung back amid the crush of people who came up after a public lecture and then pulled me aside just as I was leaving to tell me that twenty-odd years ago she had a son who was severely disabled. She left her job, and her dreams, to care for him. She thanked me for my article and my talk, saying that for those twenty years she had felt like a failure. I can still see her face and remember my own emotion at the thought that someone of such courage and strength should carry the additional burden of not living up to social expectations. She is a different kind of role model, one that U.S. society, at least, could use more of. It is we who should be thanking her and the millions like her who put their families ahead of their careers.

As I embarked on this book, I found myself in an entire new world of academic research, commentary, reporting, public opinion, blog posts, and tweets. I suddenly became a member of an extraordinary group of women and men who have been thinking and writing about work and family issues for years, who included me and sent a steady stream of links to articles, books, and opinion. Thanks to my Twitter buddies Nanette Fondas, Cali Yost, Kristin Maschka, Patrick Fitzgibbons, and many others whom I know only by their Twitter handles; to journalists Maria Shriver, Lisa Belkin, KJ Dell'Antonia, Anand Giridharadas, and Tim Kreider; and to banker and philanthropist Adrienne Arsht. A special thank-you to Deborah Fallows, who published *A Mother's Work* in 1985, a book that was thirty years ahead of its time and that she and I would both call *A Parent's Work* today.

In the academy and think-tank world, I am grateful above all to Joan Williams, author of the classic *Unbending Gender* and one of the first people I called when the media requests poured in. Ellen Galinsky of the Families and Work Institute, Marcie Pitt-Catsouphes of the Sloan Center on Aging & Work at Boston College, Sara McLanahan and her colleagues at the Bendheim-Thoman Center for Research on Child Wellbeing at Princeton,

Stewart Friedman and his Work/Life Integration Project at the Wharton School, Robin Ely at Harvard Business School, Chai Feldblum and Katie Corrigan at Georgetown Law School, and Joanna Barsh and the Centered Leadership Project at McKinsey have all done invaluable work and been particularly helpful. That entire community owes a debt to the Alfred P. Sloan Foundation's Kathleen Christensen, who for decades has systematically funded work on women, work, and families.

Many great scholars in microeconomics, psychology, sociology, political science, and gender studies have devoted their lives to the research, analysis, and hard conceptual and theoretical work that have advanced the boundaries of our thinking and knowledge about gender equality. As an academic in another field, I have had to accept that I could not possibly do your work justice, but let me at least acknowledge here my gratitude and recognize that I stand on your shoulders: Claudia Goldin, Cecilia Rouse, Lawrence Katz, Kathleen Gerson, Pamela Stone, Arlie Hochschild, Stephanie Coontz, Lois Hoffman, Lise Youngblade, Francine Blau, Joan Tronto, Sara Ruddick, Carol Gilligan, David A. J. Richards, Mahzarin Banaji, Leslie Perlow, Sylvia Ann Hewlett, and so many more.

The hard work of writing is distilling so much material from so many different sources into a single set of ideas and stories that make those ideas come alive. I am grateful to a small army of student volunteers who self-organized to help me keep track of all the emails flooding into my inbox: Brett Keller, Cat Moody, Alexandra Utsey, Mica Bumpus, and Carl Westphal. Another group of remarkable young women came out of the woodwork to provide research assistance. To Hannah Safford, Berta Baquer, Rebekah Grindlay, Julie Rose, Anne Frances Durfee, Lili Timmerman, Joyce Zhang, and Julia Taylor Kennedy, this book could not have been written without you.

Jessica Grose was indispensable as a researcher, storyteller, and all-purpose sounding board. Grace Rosen played a brief but helpful role tracking down endnotes. And special thanks to my trusty team of readers: Allison Stanger, Bill Burke-White, Nora Joffe Elish, Janie Battle Richards, and Conor Williams. Tom Hale and Michele Norris-Johnson read critical sections on very short notice, for which I am grateful. Nin Andrews offered valuable advice on the title and the cover; Judy Edersheim lent me her life story.

Bob and Nan Keohane's contributions to this book extend far beyond their wise comments. Their blend of mutual love, support, and accomplishment has long inspired Andy and me, and their friendship, wine, and lively conversation at regular intervals brightened long weekends of writing.

I became president and CEO of New America in September 2013. Special thanks go to my colleagues on the leadership team, who were patient and supportive over the many months when I was "finishing" the book. I am particularly grateful to Lisa Guernsey and her early-education team; they opened my eyes to the dramatic impact of care and education from ages zero through eight; also to Liza Mundy, Elizabeth Weingarten, and Brigid Schulte for their brilliant research and writing in our Breadwinning and Caregiving program; and to David Gray for being another important male voice in this space.

I also want to thank David Bradley and his brilliant team at *The Atlantic*—Corby Kummer, Don Peck, Scott Stossel, and James Bennet—for seeing and believing in what ultimately became "Why Women Still Can't Have It All," without which this book never would have happened. And thanks to my original team of readers—Shirley Tilghman, Martha Minow, Nancy Weiss Malkiel, Kate Reilly, Rebecca Brubaker, and Rebecca Stone.

In a book about care, I must also thank the many people

who have taken care of me in various ways over the past three years: Diane Spiegel, Joyce Hofmann, Steve Kennelly, Aziz el-Badaoui, Jimmy Reed, and my Washington roommates and long-time friends Amy McIntosh and Jeff Toobin.

My editing team at Random House were with me every step of the way. The brilliant, warm, and wonderful woman who convinced me to bring my book to Random House, Susan Kamil, said at our first meeting, "Tell me about your grandmothers," opening the door to a different conception of the book I wanted to write. With her inimitable combination of praise and persuasion, she pushed me to push myself far beyond my *Atlantic* article.

Jessica Sindler and Sam Nicholson worked with Susan and helped sharpen many insights. As the lone man in the enterprise, Sam was particularly helpful. I will also never forget his earnest lecture on "the art of omission," without a trace of the irony that might have accompanied a recent Princeton graduate explaining to a former dean of the Woodrow Wilson School how to write! But I will write better in the future in part due to his efforts. The Random House marketing and publicity teams also deserve great credit: Theresa Zoro, Sally Marvin, London King, Poonam Mantha, Leigh Marchant, Andrea DeWerd, and Max Minckler. My terrific copy editors, Amy Ryan and Beth Pearson; proofreader Nancy Elgin; book designer Susan Turner and jacket designer Ben Wiseman; and production manager Sandra Sjursen. And to so many others at Random House, from president and publisher Gina Centrello to deputy publisher Tom Perry to so many of you whom I never met but who wrestled with different aspects of how to title, present, and market this book. Thanks also to Amanda Panitch at Lippincott Massie McQuilkin for being there in the crunch.

My assistant Hana Passen began working for me in September 2012; she has seen me through every phase of the writing process. I call her my "assistant," but she is really my life manager, organizing everything and everyone from teams of research assistants to impromptu focus groups who reacted to titles and covers. She also read and commented on multiple drafts of the manuscript. Thank you!

Terry Murphy is proof that allowing people who work with you to put their families first will ensure that they do great work and stay with you for life. Terry began working for me at Harvard Law School in the late 1990s; when she brought her son home from Romania I arranged to let her work remotely as needed. Fifteen years later, she has gotten a Ph.D. herself, become a professional editor, raised a son and a daughter, and remained completely indispensable to me. She has read drafts, provided terrific comments, hunted down sources, and checked endnotes. As a mother, she has also *lived* this book.

Will Lippincott at Lippincott Massie McQuilkin is simply the world's best agent. Through visits, emails, and phone calls, he was always there. I am proud to have him represent me and to count him as a friend.

I have written about my family a great deal in these pages. As always, they were my strongest support group, through three years of holidays and vacations punctuated by "How's the book going?" They provided advice, edits, and refuge to get the final draft done. One of my friends once told me that I "won the parent lottery." And so I did: My mother, Anne Slaughter, whose physical and spiritual beauty still lights up a room at eighty. My father, Ned Slaughter, who has taught us all the meaning of character and integrity. My siblings, Bryan and Hoke Slaughter, and my sisters-in-law, Laurel Beckett Slaughter and Jennifer Ciocca Slaughter—long may we dance together! A special shout-out to Hoke, who read the manuscript twice, gave me careful comments, and sent so many emails with suggestions that my Random House team came to know him by name. And to my family on Andy's side: Francesca Moravcsik, who has proved that "phase three" can include becoming a championship senior athlete; my sister-in-law Julia Moravcsik, a strong and resilient single mother; the talented Edward Fletcher, who is cousin and mentor all at once; and Edith Moravcsik, who takes care of us all.

Thanks also to my extended family, who have helped teach me the many meanings of care: Alexander Slaughter, Mary Peeples Slaughter, Mary Hoke Slaughter, David and Jodie Slaughter, Georgean Ciocca, Jean-Michel Limbosch, Christiane Leclère, Caroline Limbosch, Henri Van de Velde, Jean-Frédéric Limbosch, Michèle Werdel, and Patrick Limbosch. And to my nieces and nephews—Jane Slaughter, Libby Slaughter, Cate Slaughter, Michael Slaughter, Gwen Slaughter, and Sean Bowling—I hope that you will read this book when you grow up and that it will help to shape your choices. I am especially proud of my oldest niece, Lilly Slaughter, whose first job was as an assistant kindergarten teacher. She poured the love and lessons her parents taught her directly into her young charges.

Enough. I clearly have *not* learned the art of omission. But this book is dedicated to my three men. Andy, in so many ways this is your story as well as mine: a tale of two strong-willed people with multiple desires and ambitions figuring out what a genuinely equal marriage looks like, with a deep well of love and commitment but plenty of bumps along the way. You have been willing to follow me—to Princeton, to China, to government and back—racking up your own professional successes but also becoming lead parent in ways neither of us fully expected. More than anyone else, you make it possible for me to do what I do. Best of all, you make me laugh—often at myself. Thank you, for everything.

To Edward and Alexander, I have so often felt like the world's biggest hypocrite writing this book. Writing about my decision to come home to be with you, only to be glued to my computer screen trying to get this done! As you know better than anyone, my definition of being "home" has many permutations. "The next two weeks are going to be rough, but after that . . ." Still, I am proud and happy to be your mother. And no matter what you may think (or hope!), the business of parenting is never finished.

NOTES

"It's Such a Pity You Had to Leave Washington"

xx **Within five days**   As of December 3, 2014.

xxi **"I just read your article"**   Email to Anne-Marie Slaughter, June 26, 2012.

Part I: Moving Beyond Our Mantras

3 **She described it as**   Betty Friedan, *The Feminine Mystique*, 50th anniversary edition (New York: W. W. Norton and Company, 2013), eBook, p. 1.

3 **She began to believe**   Ibid., loc. 144 of 8353.

Chapter 1: Half-Truths Women Hold Dear

10 **In the same breath**   "Gender and Generation in the Workplace," Families and Work Institute, 2004, familiesandwork .org/downloads/GenerationandGender.pdf; Jane Leber Herr and Catherine Wolfram, "Work Environment and 'Opt-Out' Rates at Motherhood Across High-Education Career Paths," National Bureau of Economic Research Working Paper Series, February 2009, nber.org/papers/w14717.pdf.

10 **"I was leaving most of the responsibility"**   Email to Anne-Marie Slaughter, December 3, 2012.

11 **Relatively rare**   Karen Z. Kramer, Erin L. Kelly, and Jan B. McCulloch, "Stay-at-Home Fathers: Definition and Characteristics Based on 34 Years of CPS Data," *Journal of Family Issues*, September 12, 2013, jfi.sagepub.com/content/early/2013/09/ 09/0192513X13502479.abstract?papetoc.

12 **"If we didn't start to learn"** Lia Macko and Kerry Rubin, *Midlife Crisis at 30: How the Stakes Have Changed for a New Generation—And What to Do About It* (Emmaus, PA: Rodale, 2004), p. 10.

13 **20 percent of law firm partners** "Women in Law in Canada and the U.S.," Catalyst, March 11, 2013, catalyst.org/knowledge/women-law-us.

13 **24 percent of full-time tenured professors** Martha S. West and John W. Curtis, "AAUP Faculty Gender Equity Indicators 2006," American Association of University Professors, 2006, aaup .org/NR/rdonlyres/63396944-44BE-4ABA-9815-5792D93856F1/0/AAUPGenderEquityIndicators2006.pdf.

13 **21 percent of surgeons** "The Surgical Workforce in the United States: Profile and Recent Trends," American College of Surgeons Health Policy Research Institute, April 2010, acshpri.org/documents/ACSHPRI_Surgical_Workforce_in_US_apr2010.pdf.

13 **8 percent of the most senior bankers** Elena Moya, "Glass Ceiling Is Thicker in Investment Banking than in Other Areas of Finance," *Financial News*, March 28, 2011, efinancialnews.com/story/2011-03-28/glass-ceiling-is-thicker-in-investment-banking-than-in-other-areas-of-finance?ea9c8a2de0ee111045601ab04d673622.

13 **3 percent of hedge and private equity fund managers** Linda Basch and Jacki Zehner, "Women in Fund Management," National Council for Research on Women, June 2009, regender.org/sites/ncrw.org/files/wifm_report.pdf.

13 **6 percent of mechanical engineers** Liana Christin Landivar, "Disparities in STEM Employment by Sex, Race and Hispanic Origin," American Community Survey Reports, September 2013, census.gov/prod/2013pubs/acs-24.pdf.

13 **8.5 percent of the world's billionaires** Erin Carlyle, "The World's Richest Women," *Forbes*, March 7, 2012, forbes.com/sites/erincarlyle/2012/03/07/the-worlds-richest-women.

14 **It's the reason that optimists do better** Martin E. Seligman, *Learned Optimism: How to Change Your Mind and Your Life* (New York: Vintage, 2011), eBook, pp. 144–72.

15   **"tear down the external barriers"**   Sheryl Sandberg, *Lean In: Women, Work, and the Will to Lead* (New York: Knopf, 2013), p. 8.

17   **Afterward, he'd point out**   Katty Kay and Claire Shipman, *The Confidence Code: The Science and Art of Self-Assurance—What Women Should Know* (New York: HarperCollins, 2014), p. xviii.

21   **"I resigned yesterday"**   Email to Anne-Marie Slaughter, June 13, 2013.

22   **"Denial of requests"**   Pamela Stone, *Opting Out? Why Women Really Quit Careers and Head Home* (Berkeley: University of California Press, 2007), p. 115.

22   **Carey Goldberg . . . describes her effort**   Carey Goldberg, "Sheryl Sandberg's Biggest Blind Spot," WBUR, April 2, 2013, cognoscenti.wbur.org/2013/04/02/lean-in-carey-goldberg.

23   **"I aspire to a C-level position"**   Email to Anne-Marie Slaughter, June 22, 2012.

23   **"living one single incident"**   Maria Shriver and the Center for American Progress, "A Woman's Nation Pushes Back from the Brink: Executive Summary," *The Shriver Report*, January 12, 2014, shriverreport.org/a-womans-nation-pushes-back-from-the-brink-executive-summary-maria-shriver.

25   **The divorce rate**   "Marriage and Divorce: Patterns by Gender, Race, and Educational Attainment," *Monthly Labor Review*, October 2013, bls.gov/opub/mlr/2013/article/marriage-and-divorce-patterns-by-gender-race-and-educational-attainment.htm.

26   **the many divorced mothers**   Kenneth A. Couch, Christopher R. Tamborini, Gayle Reznik, and John W. R. Phillips, "Divorce, Women's Earnings, and Retirement over the Life Course," chapter 8 in K. Couch, M. C. Daly, and J. Zissimopoulos, eds., *Lifecycle Events and Their Consequences: Job Loss, Family Change, and Declines in Health* (Stanford, CA: Stanford University Press, 2013), pp. 133–57.

26   **almost three-fourths of boomer women**   Robyn Ely, Pamela Stone, and Colleen Ammerman, "Rethinking What You 'Know' About High-Achieving Women," *Harvard Business Review*, December 2014, hbr.org/2014/12/rethink-what-you-know-about-high-achieving-women.

26 **women still end up carrying**   Kim Parker and Wendy Wang,
    "Modern Parenthood," Pew Research Center Social and
    Demographic Trends, March 14, 2013, pewsocialtrends.org/2013/
    03/14/modern-parenthood-roles-of-moms-and-dads-converge-as
    -they-balance-work-and-family.

27 **these highly successful women**   Carol Hymowitz, "Behind
    Every Great Woman," *Bloomberg Businessweek*, January 4, 2012,
    businessweek.com/magazine/behind-every-great-woman-01042012
    .html.

28 **"Bottom line is"**   Andrea Shalal-Esa, "Hewson's Long Lockheed
    Journey Ends at the Top," Reuters, November 9, 2012, reuters
    .com/article/2012/11/10/us-lockheed-hewson-idUSBRE8A904
    T20121110.

28 **Among the jobs she held**   Marjorie Censer, "After Nearly 30
    Years with Lockheed, Hewson Is Named Chief Executive,"
    Washington Post, November 13, 2012, washingtonpost.com/
    business/capitalbusiness/after-nearly-30-years-with-lockheed
    -hewson-is-named-chief-executive/2012/11/13/173cc04a-2cdc
    -11e2-a99d-5c4203af7b7a_story.html.

28 **"elected to focus"**   Doug Cameron and Joann S. Lublin,
    "Vaulted to Top at Lockheed, and Ready to Navigate Cliff," *Wall
    Street Journal*, November 11, 2012, online.wsj.com/news/articles/
    SB10001424127887324439804578113250113672078.

29 **Her husband has stayed home**   Rebecca Hughes Parker, "The
    Unsteady Rise of the Power Mom and the Diapering Dad,"
    April 12, 2013, rebeccahughesparker.com/2013/04/12/the-unsteady
    -rise-of-the-power-mom-and-the-diapering-dad (originally posted
    at Professionelle.me as part of the Professionelle Talks series in
    May 2013).

30 **She said she broke down crying**   "Makers: Women Who Make
    America, Abby Pogrebin," PBS, February 26, 2013, video.pbs.org/
    video/2331420920.

30 **"If you turn down a promotion"**   Jill R. Aitoro, "Marillyn
    Hewson: Inside Out," *Washington Business Journal*, February 1,
    2013, bizjournals.com/washington/print-edition/2013/02/01/
    marillyn-hewson-inside-out.html?page=2.

31 **"built on the unstated assumption"** Timothy L. O'Brien, "Why Do So Few Women Reach the Top of Big Law Firms?," *New York Times*, March 19, 2006, nytimes.com/2006/03/19/business/yourmoney/19law.html.

33 **Statistically, IVF** "Committee Opinion: Female Age-Related Fertility Decline," American College of Obstetricians and Gynecologists, March 2014, acog.org/Resources-And-Publications/Committee-Opinions/Committee-on-Gynecologic-Practice/Female-Age-Related-Fertility-Decline.

33 **In her book *Creating a Life*** Sylvia Ann Hewlett, *Creating a Life: Professional Women and the Quest for Children* (New York: Talk Miramax, 2002), p. 33.

Chapter 2: Half-Truths About Men

39 **"I'd wanted so badly"** Lily Ledbetter, with Lanier Scott Isom, *Grace and Grit: My Fight for Equal Pay and Fairness at Goodyear and Beyond* (New York: Crown, 2012), pp. 6–7.

39 **That was 1999** "Highlights of Women's Earnings in 2013," U.S. Bureau of Labor Statistics, Report 1051, December 2014, bls.gov/opub/reports/cps/highlights-of-womens-earnings-in-2013.pdf.

40 **"they are somehow not 'macho' enough"** Email to Anne-Marie Slaughter, July 20, 2012.

40 **"Comments were made"** Jennifer L. Berdahl, Vicki J. Magley, and C. R. Waldo, "The Sexual Harassment of Men? Exploring the Concept with Theory and Data," *Psychology of Women Quarterly*, 20 (1996): 527–47.

40 **Seventeen years later** Joan C. William, "The Daddy Dilemma: Why Men Face a 'Flexibility Stigma' at Work," *Washington Post*, February 11, 2013, washingtonpost.com/national/on-leadership/the-daddy-dilemma-why-men-face-a-flexibility-stigma-at-work/2013/02/11/58350f4e-7462-11e2-aa12-e6cf1d31106b_story.html.

40 **men who requested a twelve-week leave** Ibid.

40 **caregiving fathers had** Jennifer L. Berdahl and Sue H. Moon, "Worker Mistreatment of Middle Class Workers Based on Sex,

Parenthood, and Caregiving," *Journal of Social Issues* 69 (2013): 341–66.

41 **men and women valued workplace flexibility equally**   Joan C. Williams, Mary Blair-Loy, and Jennifer L. Berdahl, "Cultural Schemas, Social Class, and the Flexibility Stigma," *Journal of Social Issues* 69 (2013): 209–34.

41 **Overall, the share of companies**   Claire Cain Miller, "Paternity Leave: The Rewards and the Remaining Stigma," *New York Times*, November 7, 2014, nytimes.com/2014/11/09/upshot/paternity -leave-the-rewards-and-the-remaining-stigma.html.

41 **In one case, a management trainee**   *Bates v. 84 Lumber Co.*, No. 05-5554 (6th Cir. 2006).

41 **"You are probably not aware"**   Email to Anne-Marie Slaughter, July 13, 2012.

42 **He tries to mesh**   Andrew Cohen, " 'Having It All'? How About: 'Doing the Best I Can'?," *Atlantic*, June 27, 2012, theatlantic.com/ business/archive/2012/06/having-it-all-how-about-doing-the-best -i-can/258898.

43 **Perusing a biography of Colgate Darden**   Guy Friddell, *Colgate Darden: Conversations with Guy Friddell* (Charlottesville, VA: University Press of Virginia, 1978), p. 100.

45 **Along with Liberia and Papua New Guinea**   Tara Siegel Bernard, "In Paid Family Leave, U.S. Trails Most of the Globe," *New York Times*, February 22, 2013, nytimes.com/2013/02/23/your -money/us-trails-much-of-the-world-in-providing-paid-family -leave.html.

45 **The unpaid leave we do offer**   "Fact Sheet #28: The Family and Medical Leave Act," U.S. Department of Labor, Wage and Hours Division, revised 2012, dol.gov/whd/regs/compliance/whdfs28.pdf.

45 **have been at those companies**   Ibid.

47 **children raised by gay parents**   Stephanie Pappas, "Why Gay Parents May Be the Best Parents," *LiveScience*, January 15, 2012, livescience.com/17913-advantages-gay-parents.html.

47 **Frank Ligtvoet, a gay dad**   Frank Ligtvoet, "The Misnomer of 'Motherless' Parenting," June 22, 2013, nytimes.com/2013/06/23/ opinion/sunday/the-misnomer-of-motherless-parenting.html.

47 **A study from Ohio State**   "Family Stability May Be More

Crucial than Two Parents for Child Success," Research News, Ohio State University, August 31, 2009, researchnews.osu.edu/archive/familystability.htm.

47 **Conversely, a 2013 report** "The First Eight Years: Giving Kids a Foundation for Lifetime Success," Annie E. Casey Foundation, December 2, 2013, aecf.org/~/media/Pubs/Initiatives/KIDS %20COUNT/F/FirstEightYears/AECFTheFirstEightYears2013 .pdf.

48 **Saint Paul writes** I Timothy 5:8, Bible, King James Version (New York: Thomas Nelson Publishers, 1971).

48 **"Men are the protectors"** Verse 4:34, "The Women," English translation, Quranic Arabic Corpus, corpus.quran.com/translation .jsp?chapter=4&verse=34.

49 **a mere 2 million men** Gretchen Livingston, "Growing Number of Dads Home with the Kids; Chapter 2: Why Are Dads Staying Home?," Pew Research Center Social and Demographic Trends, June 5, 2014, pewsocialtrends.org/2014/06/05/chapter-2 -why-are-dads-staying-home.

49 **Only 8 percent of Americans** Wendy Wang, Kim Parker, and Paul Taylor, "Breadwinner Moms," Pew Research Center Social and Demographic Trends, May 29, 2013, pewsocialtrends.org/ 2013/05/29/breadwinner-moms/2.

49 **When asked the same question with a gender flip** Paul Taylor, ed., "The Decline of Marriage and Rise of New Families," Pew Research Center Social and Demographic Trends, November 18, 2010, pewsocialtrends.org/files/2010/11/pew -social-trends-2010-families.pdf.

49 **The resulting shift in economic power** Liza Mundy, *The Richer Sex: How the New Majority of Female Breadwinners Is Transforming Sex, Love and Family* (New York: Simon & Schuster, 2012); Hanna Rosin, *The End of Men: And the Rise of Women* (New York: Riverhead, 2012).

49 **The even bigger story** "United States: The Rich and the Rest," *Economist*, October 13, 2012, economist.com/node/21564418.

49 **Senator Elizabeth Warren** Elizabeth Warren and Amelia Warren Tyagi, *The Two-Income Trap: Why Middle-Class Parents Are Going Broke* (New York: Basic Books, 2004).

49   **average mortgage expenses had risen**   Bradford Plumer, "The Two-Income Trap," *Mother Jones*, November 8, 2004, motherjones .com/politics/2004/11/two-income-trap.

49   **In the intervening years**   Dylan Matthews, "Wages Aren't Stagnating, They're Plummeting," *Washington Post*, July 31, 2012, washingtonpost.com/blogs/wonkblog/wp/2012/07/31/wages-arent -stagnating-theyre-plummeting.

50   **Nearly 50 percent of millennial men**   Eileen Patten and Kim Parker, "A Gender Reversal on Career Aspirations," Pew Research Center Social and Demographic Trends, April 19, 2012, pewsocialtrends.org/2012/04/19/a-gender-reversal-on-career -aspirations.

50   **"I have told Susie"**   "Read an Excerpt of Liza Mundy's 'The Richer Sex,'" ABC News, January 9, 2014, abcnews.go.com/blogs/ politics/2014/01/read-an-excerpt-of-liza-mundys-the-richer-sex.

50   **According to Mundy**   Liza Mundy, "Daddy Track: The Case for Paternity Leave," *Atlantic*, January/February 2014, theatlantic .com/magazine/archive/2014/01/the-daddy-track/355746/2.

Chapter 3: Half-Truths in the Workplace

51   **Numerous books on the subject**   Some of these books accept the idea of balance; others reject balance but promise happiness anyway; still others suggest the helpful idea of fit. See Sharon Meers and Joanna Strober, *Getting to 50/50: How Working Parents Can Have It All* (Berkeley: Cleis Press, 2013); A. Roger Merrill and Rebecca R. Merrill, *Life Matters: Creating a Dynamic Balance of Work, Family, Time, & Money* (New York: McGraw-Hill, 2003); Teresa A. Taylor, *The Balance Myth: Rethinking Work-Life Success* (Austin: Greenleaf Book Group Press, 2013); Matthew Kelly, *Off Balance: Getting Beyond the Work-Life Balance Myth to Personal and Professional Satisfaction* (New York: Hudson Street Press, 2011); Cali Williams Yost, *Work + Life: Finding the Fit That's Right for You* (New York: Riverhead, 2004); and Joan Blades and Nanette Fondas, *The Custom-Fit Workplace: Choose When, Where, and How to Work and Boost Your Bottom Line* (San Francisco: Jossey-Bass, 2010).

51   **American workers**   Kiera Butler, Dave Gilson, Josh Harkinson, Andy Kroll, and Laura McClure, "Harrowing, Heartbreaking Tales of Overworked Americans," *Mother Jones*, July/August 2011, motherjones.com/politics/2011/06/stories-overworked-americans.

51   **Public health experts**   "Stress in America: Paying with Our Health," American Psychological Association, February 4, 2015, apa.org/news/press/releases/stress/2014/stress-report.pdf.

51   **Indeed, the United States**   "Adult Labor and Working Conditions: Rankings," World Policy Forum, 2015, worldpolicyforum.org/topics/adult-labor-and-working-conditions/rankings.

53   **The firm's brass**   Irene Padavic, Robin Ely, and Erin Reid, "The Work-Family Narrative as a Social Defense: Explaining the Persistence of Gender Inequality in Organizations," Harvard Business School Working Paper, March 2015.

53   **"What do I want people to worry about"**   Ibid.

54   **in 2013 women earned 82 cents**   "Highlights of Women's Earnings in 2013," U.S. Bureau of Labor Statistics, Report 1051, December 2014, bls.gov/opub/reports/cps/highlights-of-womens -earnings-in-2013.pdf.

54   **But hidden within that average**   Michelle J. Budig, Joya Misra, and Irene Boeckmann, "The Motherhood Penalty in Cross-National Perspective: The Importance of Work-Family Policies and Cultural Attitudes," *Social Politics: International Studies in Gender, State & Society* 19, no. 2 (2012): 163–93.

54   **Single women without children**   Mark Perry and Andrew G. Biggs, "The '77 Cents on the Dollar' Myth About Women's Pay," *Wall Street Journal*, April 7, 2014, wsj.com/articles/SB10001424052 702303532704579483752909957472.

54   **They make 76 cents**   Claire Cain Miller, "The Upshot: The Motherhood Penalty vs. the Fatherhood Bonus," *New York Times*, September 6, 2014, nytimes.com/2014/09/07/upshot/a-child-helps -your-career-if-youre-a-man.html.

54   **motherhood is now a greater predictor**   Stephanie Coontz, "Progress at Work, but Mothers Still Pay a Price," *New York Times*, June 9, 2013, nytimes.com/2013/06/09/opinion/sunday/coontz

-richer-childless-women-are-making-the-gains.html; Kristin
Rowe-Finkbeiner, "The Real Feminist Nightmare," *Politico*,
November 25, 2013, politico.com/magazine/story/2013/11/the
-real-feminist-nightmare-not-michelle-obama-100339.html#
.VWX-Y0ZBEnM.

54 **women between the ages of twenty-five and thirty-four**
"On Pay Gap, Millennial Women Near Parity—for Now," Pew
Research Center Social and Demographic Trends, December 11,
2013, pewsocialtrends.org/2013/12/11/on-pay-gap-millennial
-women-near-parity-for-now.

54 **But those gains dissipate**   Ibid.

54 **To the majority of men and women**   Wendy Wang, Kim
Parker, and Paul Taylor, "Breadwinner Moms," Pew Research
Center Social and Demographic Trends, May 29, 2013,
pewsocialtrends.org/2013/05/29/breadwinner-moms.

54 **Women are indeed the considerable majority**   Kim Parker
and Wendy Wang, "Modern Parenthood," Pew Research Center
Social and Demographic Trends, March 2013, pewsocialtrends
.org/2013/03/14/modern-parenthood-roles-of-moms-and-dads
-converge-as-they-balance-work-and-family.

54 **the typical caregiver of an elderly relative**   "Family Caregiving:
The Facts," Centers for Disease Control and Prevention, September
2011, cdc.gov/aging/caregiving/facts.htm.

55 **Her decision to leave them**   Amanda Marcotte, "Wendy Davis'
Daughters: Our Mom Did a Great Job," *Slate*, January 21, 2014,
slate.com/blogs/xx_factor/2014/01/28/was_wendy_davis_a_bad
_mother_because_her_husband_contributed_a_lot_of_childcare
.html.

55 **Rahm Emanuel left his young children**   Manny Fernandez
and Laurie Goodstein, "Life Story of Wendy Davis Swings from
Strength to Flash Point in Texas Campaign," *New York Times*,
January 29, 2014, nytimes.com/2014/01/30/us/texas-democrat
-defends-back-story-under-criticism.html.

55 **A physician who had two kids**   Email to Anne-Marie Slaughter,
February 22, 2013.

56 **43 percent of the *men***   "Life Interests—1992 and 2012," Work/

Life Integration Project, Wharton School, University of Pennsylvania, worklife.wharton.upenn.edu/research/life-interests-of-wharton-students/1992-and-2012. For a more descriptive account of the findings, see Stewart D. Friedman, *Baby Bust: New Choices for Men and Women in Work & Family* (Philadelphia: Wharton Digital Press, 2013).

56 **a third of male millennial HBS grads** Robyn Ely, Pamela Stone, and Colleen Ammerman, "Rethinking What You 'Know' About High-Achieving Women," *Harvard Business Review*, December 2014, hbr.org/2014/12/rethink-what-you-know-about-high-achieving-women.

57 **"Most men stress"** Marc Tracy, "Here Come the Daddy Wars," *New Republic*, June 14, 2013, newrepublic.com/article/113490/daddy-wars-will-be-mommy-wars-men.

57 **an almost equal number of fathers and mothers** Kim Parker and Wendy Wang, "Modern Parenthood: Roles of Moms and Dads Converge as They Balance Work and Family," Pew Research Center Social and Demographic Trends, March 14, 2013, pewsocialtrends.org/files/2013/03/FINAL_modern_parenthood_03-2013.pdf.

58 **Or more precisely** Joan Williams, *Unbending Gender: Why Family and Work Conflict and What to Do About It* (New York: Oxford University Press, 2000), p. 22.

58 **"the face-time warrior"** Brigid Schulte, *Overwhelmed: Work, Love and Play When No One Has the Time* (New York: Sarah Crichton Books, 2014), p. 77.

58 **The firm's key HR problem** Padavic, Ely, and Reid, "The Work-Family Narrative as a Social Defense," p. 19.

59 **As Padavic, Ely, and Reid wryly conclude** Ibid., p. 20.

59 **"'Fixing the women's problem'"** Debora L. Spar, *Wonder Women: Sex, Power, and the Quest for Perfection* (New York: Sarah Crichton Books, 2013), p. 201.

59 **"I am beyond tired"** Email to Anne-Marie Slaughter, April 8, 2013.

60 **Twenty percent of U.S. companies** Ariane Hegewisch and Yuko Hara, "Maternity, Paternity, and Adoption Leave in the

United States," Institute for Women's Policy Research, May 2013, iwpr.org/publications/pubs/maternity-paternity-and-adoption -leave-in-the-united-states-1.

60   **36 percent allow employees**   Kenneth Matos and Ellen Galinksy, "2014 National Study of Employers," Families and Work Institute, April 2014, familiesandwork.org/downloads/ 2014NationalStudyOfEmployers.pdf.

61   **The HR department may roll out flex policies**   Ibid., p. 30.

61   **the National Study of Employers finds a virtual chasm**   Ibid.

61   **"can't get someone right there"**   Fredric R. Van Deusen, Jacquelyn B. James, Nadia Gill, Sharon P. McKechnie, "Overcoming the Implementation Gap," Boston College Center for Work and Family, February 2007, p. 30, bc.edu/content/dam/files/centers/ cwf/research/publications/pdf/BCCWF%20Flex%20Study %202007.pdf.

62   **"Girls don't ask"**   Patrick Jenkins and Harriet Agnew, "Sexism and the City," *Financial Times,* January 17–18, 2015, ft.com/intl/ cms/s/2/7c182ab8-9c33-11e4-b9f8-00144feabdc0.html #axzz3UTFyp2mH.

62   **"flexibility stigma"**   Joan C. Williams, Jennifer Glass, Shelley Correll, and Jennifer L. Berdahl, Special Issue: The Flexibility Stigma, *Journal of Social Issues,* 69, no. 2 (2013).

62   **"flexibility is as valuable as compensation"**   Email to Anne-Marie Slaughter, June 21, 2012.

62   **a law firm associate named Carlos**   Joan Blades and Nanette Fondas, p. 48.

63   **even if his firm had said yes**   Scott Coltrane, Elizabeth C. Miller, Tracy DeHaan, and Lauren Stewart, "Fathers and the Flexibility Stigma," *Journal of Social Issues* 69, no. 2 (2013): 279–302.

63   **Patterns like these**   Anna Beninger and Nancy M. Carter, "The Great Debate: Flexibility vs. Face Time," Catalyst, July 2013, catalyst.org/knowledge/great-debate-flexibility-vs-face-time -busting-myths-behind-flexible-work-arrangements.

64   **More than 70 percent**   Maria Shriver, "The Female Face of Poverty," *Atlantic,* January 8, 2014, theatlantic.com/business/ archive/2014/01/the-female-face-of-poverty/282892.

64   **Consider the case of Rhiannon Broschat**   Jon Graef, "Fired
      Whole Foods Worker Rhiannon Broschat-Salguero: 'I'm Not
      Going to Choose My Job Over My Son,'" *Chicagoist*, February 9,
      2014, chicagoist.com/2014/02/09/fired_whole_foods_worker
      _rhiannon_b.php.

64   **"Why Women's Economic Security Matters"**   Transcript,
      "Why Women's Economic Security Matters for All," Center for
      American Progress, Washington, D.C., September 18, 2014,
      cdn.americanprogress.org/wp-content/uploads/2014/09/09.18.14
      -CAP-Womens-Economic-Security-transcript.pdf.

65   **Walmart, Jamba Juice**   Jenny Brown, "Enough with the Just In
      Time Schedules, Say Retail Workers," *Labor Notes*, November 19,
      2012, labornotes.org/2012/11/enough-just-time-schedules-say
      -retail-workers#sthash.sFnhjWIq.dpuf.

65   **"Hotel housekeepers"**   Susan J. Lambert, "When Flexibility
      Hurts," *New York Times*, September 20, 2012, nytimes.com/2012/
      09/20/opinion/low-paid-women-want-predictable-hours-and
      -steady-pay.html.

66   **She and her son lost two homes**   Jodi Kantor, "Working
      Anything but 9 to 5," *New York Times*, August 13, 2014, nytimes
      .com/interactive/2014/08/13/us/starbucks-workers-scheduling
      -hours.html.

66   **The day after Kantor's article**   Jodi Kantor, "Starbucks to
      Revise Policies to End Irregular Schedules for Its 130,000
      Baristas," *New York Times*, August 14, 2014, nytimes.com/2014/
      08/15/us/starbucks-to-revise-work-scheduling-policies.html.

67   **"Mr. Darman sometimes managed"**   Maureen Dowd,
      "Campaign Profile; A Primer: How the White House Budget Czar
      Not Only Survives, but Thrives," *New York Times*, September 22,
      1992, nytimes.com/1992/09/22/us/1992-campaign-campaign
      -profile-primer-white-house-budget-czar-not-only-survives.html.

67   **Virginia Rometty**   Andrew Nusca, "IBM's Rometty: 'Growth
      and Comfort Don't Coexist,'" *Fortune*, October 7, 2014, fortune
      .com/2014/10/07/ibms-rometty-growth-and-comfort-dont-coexist.

68   **"I was lying on the floor"**   Arianna Huffington, *Thrive: The
      Third Metric to Redefining Success and Creating a Life of Well-Being,
      Wisdom, and Wonder* (New York: Harmony Books, 2014), p. 1.

70   **The moral of the ad**   "The First Ever 2014 Cadillac ELR:
Poolside," YouTube video, posted by Cadillac, February 7, 2014,
youtube.com/watch?v=qGJSI48gkFc.

70   **"You know what really needs attention?"**   Brigid Schulte, "5
Reasons Why You Shouldn't Work Too Hard," *Washington Post*,
February 21, 2014, washingtonpost.com/blogs/she-the-people/
wp/2014/02/21/5-things-you-get-from-working-too-hard/
?tid=pm_pop.

70   **Cadillac was disparaging**   Diana T. Kurylko, "Mercedes Beats
BMW in Luxury Race," *Automotive News*, January 6, 2014,
autonews.com/article/20140106/RETAIL01/301069959/mercedes
-beats-bmw-in-luxury-race.

70   **Last I checked**   Rebecca Ray, Milla Sanes, and John Schmitt,
"No Vacation Nation Revisited," Center for Economic Policy,
May 2013, cepr.net/documents/publications/no-vacation-update
-2013-05.pdf.

71   **led Henry Ford to establish**   Robert Asher and Ronald
Edsforth, with Stephen Merlino, eds., *Autowork* (Albany, NY: State
University of New York Press, 1995), p. 156.

71   **After he cut hours**   Schulte, *Overwhelmed*, p. 161.

71   **Futurist Sara Robinson**   Ibid., p. 162.

71   **we should change the rhythm**   Mihaly Csikszentmihalyi,
Creativity: Flow and the Psychology of Discovery and Invention (New
York: HarperCollins, 1996), pp. 129–30.

71   **Without play**   Douglas Thomas and John Seely Brown, *A New
Culture of Learning: Cultivating the Imagination for a World of
Constant Change* (Scott's Valley, AZ: Create Space Independent
Publishing Platform, 2011), eBook, loc. 1370–89.

71   **Timothy Keller**   Timothy Keller, *Every Good Endeavor* (New
York: Dutton, 2012), p. 41.

72   **Americans think about leisure**   Ibid., p. 42.

72   **"simply contemplate"**   Ibid., p. 41. I owe these insights to
Anand Giriharadas, "Keeping One's Work in Perspective," *New
York Times*, December 29, 2012, nytimes.com/2012/12/29/us/
29iht-currents29.html.

72   *World Happiness Report*   John F. Helliwell, Richard Layard, and

Jeffrey Sachs, eds., *World Happiness Report 2015* (New York: United Nations Sustainable Development Solutions Network, 2015), worldhappiness.report/ed/2015.

73   **"As soon as that baby's lips"**   "Paul Tudor Jones Comments on the Lack of Female Traders," *Washington Post*, May 23, 2013, washingtonpost.com/local/education/paul-tudor-jones-comments-on-the-lack-of-female-traders-during-u-va-event/2013/05/07/871a3fc4-b723-11e2-aa9e-a02b765ff0ea_story.html.

73   **women spoke up for his overall character**   Michelle Celarier, "Hedge Fund Women Not Bashing Paul Tudor Jones for Saying Having Babies Makes Women Lousy Traders," *New York Post*, May 25, 2013, nypost.com/2013/05/25/hedge-fund-women-not-bashing-paul-tudor-jones-for-saying-having-babies-makes-women-lousy-traders.

73   **others said they were grateful**   Jacki Zehner, "Can Mothers Be Traders?," LinkedIn Post, May 25, 2013, linkedin.com/today/post/article/20130525134605-25295057-can-mothers-be-traders.

73   **Moreover, Jones explained**   "Paul Tudor Jones Comments on the Lack of Female Traders."

73   **Here Jones is simply wrong**   Brad M. Barber and Terrence Odean, "Boys Will Be Boys: Gender, Overconfidence and Common Stock Investment," *Quarterly Journal of Economics* 16, no. 1 (2001): 261–92; Meredith Jones, "Women in Alternative Investments: A Marathon, Not a Sprint," Rothstein Kass, December 2013, kpmg-institutes.com/content/dam/kpmg/kpmginstitutes/pdf/2014/women-in-alternative-investments.pdf.

74   **in a book entitled *Scarcity***   Sendhil Mullainathan and Eldar Shafir, *Scarcity: The New Science of Having Less and How It Defines Our Lives* (New York: Henry Holt, 2013).

74   **Financial expert and neuroscientist John Coates**   John Coates, *The Hour Between Dog and Wolf: Risk-Taking, Gut Feelings and the Biology of Boom and Bust* (New York: Penguin Press, 2012).

74   **"their call on the market"**   Ibid., pp. 273–74.

76   **"If you've lived a life"**   Joan C. Williams, "Why Men Work So Many Hours," *Harvard Business Review*, May 29, 2013, blogs.hbr.org/cs/2013/05/why_men_work_so_many_hours.html.

Chapter 4: Competition and Care

81   **the "sticky floor"**   Barbara Presley Noble, "At Work: And Now the 'Sticky Floor,'" *New York Times*, November 22, 1992, nytimes .com/1992/11/22/business/at-work-and-now-the-sticky-floor.html.

81   **But the growing numbers of talented women**   Judith Warner, *Perfect Madness: Motherhood in the Age of Anxiety* (New York: Riverhead Books, 2005).

82   **Women hold less than 15 percent**   "Statistical Overview of Women in the Workplace," Catalyst, March 3, 2014, catalyst.org/ knowledge/statistical-overview-women-workplace.

82   **Almost two-thirds**   Maria Shriver and Olivia Morgan, *The Shriver Report: A Woman's Nation Pushes Back from the Brink* (New York: Palgrave Macmillan, 2014); Laryssa Mykyta and Trudi J. Renwick, "Changes in Poverty Measurement: An Examination of the Research SPM and Its Effects by Gender," U.S. Census Bureau Working Paper, January 2013; Suzanne M. Bianchi, "Feminization and Juvenilization of Poverty: Trends, Relative Risks, Causes, and Consequences," *Annual Review of Sociology* 25 (1999): 307–33; Sara McLanahan and Erin Kelly, "The Feminization of Poverty: Past and Future," in *Handbook of the Sociology of Gender* (New York: Plenum Publishing Corp., 1999), pp. 127–45; Diane Pearce, "The Feminization of Poverty: Women Work and Welfare," *Urban & Social Change Review* 11, nos. 1–2 (1978): 28–36.

83   **"Elite or poor"**   Alison Wolf, *The XX Factor: How the Rise of Working Women Has Created a Far Less Equal World* (New York: Crown Publishers, 2013), eBook, pp. 17–18.

84   **"along with language"**   Sarah Blaffer Hrdy, "The Past, Present and Future of the Human Family," Tanner Lectures on Human Values, delivered at the University of Utah, February 27 and 28, 2001, tannerlectures.utah.edu/_documents/a-to-z/h/Hrdy_02.pdf.

84   **"It was like all of a sudden"**   Pamela Stone, *Opting Out? Why Women Really Quit Careers and Head Home* (Berkeley: University of California Press, 2007), p. 145.

85   **Half of single moms**   "Single Motherhood in the United States—A Snapshot," Legal Momentum, Women's Legal Defense

and Education Fund, 2012, legalmomentum.org/sites/default/files/
reports/single-mothers-snapshot_0.pdf.

85   **American single parents**   Timothy Casey and Laurie
Maldonado, "Worst Off—Single Parent Families in the United
States: A Cross-National Comparison of Single Parenthood in the
U.S. and 16 Other High Income Countries," Legal Momentum,
Women's Legal Defense and Education Fund, December 2012,
legalmomentum.org/sites/default/files/reports/worst-off-single
-parent.pdf; Matt Bruenig, "The Poorest Norwegian Children Are
Twice as Rich as the Poorest American Children," Demos: An
Equal Say and An Equal Chance for All, January 12, 2015, demos
.org/blog/1/12/15/poorest-norwegian-children-are-twice-rich
-poorest-american-children.

85   **Ranie Sherr**   Terrie Morgan-Besecker, "Minimum Wage
Earners Struggle to Survive," *Times-Tribune*, December 22, 2013,
thetimes-tribune.com/news/minimum-wage-earners-struggle-to
-survive-1.1605234.

85   **María, a single mom in Providence**   Ajay Chaudry, Juan
Pedroza, and Heather Sandstrom, "How Employment Constraints
Affect Low-Income Working Parents' Child Care Decisions,"
Urban Institute, Brief 23, February 2012, urban.org/
UploadedPDF/412513-How-Employment-Constraints-Affect
-Low-Income-Working-Parents-Child-Care-Decisions.pdf.

86   **the entire reform of U.S. welfare programs**   "1996 Welfare
Amendments," Social Security History, ssa.gov/history/tally1996
.html; Mary B. Larner, Donna L. Terman, and Richard E.
Behrman, "Welfare to Work: Analysis and Recommendations," *The
Future of Children* 7, no. 1 (Spring 1997), futureofchildren.org/
futureofchildren/publications/docs/07_01_Analysis.pdf; Mary Daly
and Joyce Kwok, "Did Welfare Reform Work for Everyone? A
Look at Young Single Mothers," Federal Reserve Bank of San
Francisco Economic Letter, August 3, 2009, frbsf.org/economic
-research/publications/economic-letter/2009/august/welfare
-reform-single-mothers.

86   **The result is that a mother with dependent children**   Joan
Entmacher, Katherine Gallagher Robbins, Julie Voghtman, and

Lauren Frohlich, "Insecure & Unequal: Poverty and Income Among Women and Families 2000–2012," National Women's Law Center, September 2013, nwlc.org/sites/default/files/pdfs/final_2013_nwlc_povertyreport.pdf; Casey and Maldonado, "Worst Off."

86 **Gayle Pritchard**   Elizabeth Warren and Amelia Warren Tyagi, *The Two-Income Trap: Why Middle-Class Mothers and Fathers Are Going Broke* (New York: Basic, 2003), pp. 97–122.

87 **motherhood is "the single biggest risk factor"**   Ann Crittenden, *The Price of Motherhood: Why the Most Important Job in the World Is Still the Least Valued* (New York: Henry Holt, 2001), p. 6.

88 **gave a commencement address at Vassar**   Gloria Steinem, "'Women's Liberation' Aims to Free Men Too," *Washington Post*, June 7, 1970.

88 **Alice Walker coined the term "womanism"**   Alice Walker, *In Search of Our Mothers' Gardens: Womanist Prose* (San Diego: Harcourt Brace Jovanovich, 1983); Patricia Hill Collins, "What's in a Name? Womanism, Black Feminism, and Beyond," *Black Scholar* 26, no. 1 (Winter/Spring 1996): 9–17.

89 **"From Private Woman"**   Catherine Rottenberg, "Hijacking Feminism," Al Jazeera, March 25, 2013, aljazeera.com/indepth/opinion/2013/03/201332510121757700.html.

89 **"equal rights, justice"**   Catherine Rottenberg, "Happiness and the Liberal Imagination: How Superwoman Became Balanced," *Feminist Studies* 40, no. 1 (2014), bgu.ac.il/~rottenbe/FeministStudies40-1-Rottenberg.pdf.

89 **"It's been more than forty years"**   Susan Faludi, "Feminism for Them?," *The Baffler*, no. 24 (2014), thebaffler.com/past/feminism_for_them.

90 **"As a mother to four"**   Email to Anne-Marie Slaughter, August 10, 2012.

91 **hundred million–plus hours**   Riane Eisler and Kimberly Otis, "Unpaid and Undervalued Care Work Keeps Women on the Brink," *The Shriver Report*, January 22, 2014, shriverreport.org/unpaid-and-undervalued-care-work-keeps-women-on-the-brink/#_edn2.

91   **"the pauperization of motherhood"**   Nancy Folbre, "The
Pauperization of Mothers: Patriarchy and Public Policy in the
United States," *Review of Radical Political Economics*, 16, no. 4
(1985): 72–88.

91   **in a 2012 volume on care provision**   Nancy Folbre, ed., *For
Love and Money: Care Provision in the United States* (New York:
Russell Sage Foundation, 2012), p. xiv.

92   **that difference has a far greater impact**   Michelle Budig and
Melissa Hodges, "Differences in Disadvantage: How the Wage
Penalty for Motherhood Varies Across Women's Earnings
Distribution," *American Sociological Review* 75, no. 5 (2010):
705–28; Michelle Budig, "The Fatherhood Bonus and the
Motherhood Penalty," Third Way Next, 2013, content.thirdway
.org/publications/853/NEXT_-_Fatherhood_Motherhood.pdf.

92   **"A stay-at-home mother"**   Warren and Tyagi, *The Two-Income
Trap*, p. 59.

93   **I asked Pew Research to crunch the numbers**   Email from
Richard Fry/Gretchen Livingston at Pew Research to Anne-Marie
Slaughter, June 24, 2014.

93   **traditionally "feminine" skills**   Hanna Rosin, *The End of Men*
(New York: Riverhead Books, 2012), pp. 4–5.

94   **"women dominate twenty"**   Ibid., p. 85; Liza Mundy, *The
Richer Sex*, pp. 62–68.

94   **9 percent of nurses in the United States**   "Male Nurses
Becoming More Commonplace, Census Bureau Reports," United
States Census Bureau, February 25, 2013, census.gov/newsroom/
press-releases/2013/cb13-32.html.

95   **"There has never been a national effort"**   Lonnae O'Neal
Parker, "Four Years Later, Feminists Split by Michelle Obama's
'Work' as First Lady," *Washington Post*, January 18, 2013,
washingtonpost.com/lifestyle/style/feminists-split-by-michelle
-obamas-work-as-first-lady/2013/01/18/be3d636e-5e5e-11e2
-9940-6fc488f3fecd_story.html.

95   **"I declared myself a womanist"**   Taigi Smith, "What Happens
When Your Hood Is the Last Stop," in Daisy Hernández and
Bushra Rehman, eds., *Colonize This! Young Women of Color on Today's
Feminism* (New York: Seal, 2002), pp. 54–64.

96   **"to some power in herself"**   Mary Helen Washington, ed., *Invented Lives: Narratives of Black Women 1860–1960* (Garden City, NY: Anchor, 1987), p. 395.

96   **"It is not my child who tells me"**   Alice Walker, "One Child of One's Own: A Meaningful Digression Within the Work(s)," *Ms.*, August 1979, p. 75.

97   **"You get home way too late"**   Kate Bolick, "Single People Deserve Work-Life Balance, Too," *Atlantic*, June 28, 2012.

97   **"Granted, single people"**   Email to Anne-Marie Slaughter, June 24, 2012.

98   **"low-income African American and immigrant women"** Folbre, *For Love and Money*, p. xi.

99   **She has been organizing immigrant women**   "Ai-jen Poo," National Domestic Workers Alliance, domesticworkers.org/aijen-poo.

99   **her work led**   "Domestic Workers' Bill of Rights," New York State Department of Labor, labor.ny.gov/legal/domestic-workers-bill-of-rights.shtm.

99   **"winning coalition"**   Ai-jen Poo, with Ariane Conrad, *The Age of Dignity: Preparing for the Elder Boom in a Changing America* (New York: New Press, 2015), p. 115.

99   **"Your chances of"**   Atul Gawande, *Being Mortal* (New York: Henry Holt, 2014), p. 79.

Chapter 5: Is Managing Money Really Harder than Managing Kids?

101   **"that people internalize"**   Email to Anne-Marie Slaughter, April 29, 2013.

103   **"When a four-year-old tipped over a glass of milk"**   Ann Crittenden, *The Price of Motherhood: Why the Most Important Job in the World Is Still the Least Valued* (New York: Henry Holt), p. 73.

104   **"requires this capacity"**   Megan Gunnar, "Worthy Work, STILL Unlivable Wages: The Early Childhood Workforce 25 Years After the National Child Care Staffing Study," New America, Panel Discussion, November 18, 2014, newamerica.org/education-policy/worthy-work-still-unlivable-wages.

105 **"From the time of conception"** Committee on Integrating the Science of Early Childhood Development, *From Neurons to Neighborhoods: The Science of Early Childhood Development* (Washington, DC: National Academies Press, 2000), pp. 3–4.

105 **A more recent study** Sabrina Tavernise, "Project to Improve Poor Children's Intellect Led to Better Health, Data Show," *New York Times*, March 28, 2014, nytimes.com/2014/03/28/health/project-to-improve-intellect-of-poor-children-led-to-better-health-too-research-finds.html.

105 **Four decades later** Frances A. Campbell, Elizabeth P. Pungello, Kirsten Kainz, et al., "Adult Outcomes as a Function of an Early Childhood Educational Program: An Abecedarian Project Follow-Up," *Developmental Psychology* 48, no. 4 (July 2012): 1033–43.

105 **they were also physically healthier** Frances Campbell, Gabriella Conti, James J. Heckman, Seong Hyeok Moon, Rodrigo Pinto, Elizabeth Pungello, and Yi Pan, "Early Childhood Investments Substantially Boost Adult Health," *Science* 343, no. 6178 (March 28, 2014): 1478–85.

107 **supporting people to do what they want to do** Keren Brown Wilson, drawn from Atul Gawande, *Being Mortal* (New York: Henry Holt, 2014), pp. 103–7; quote is on p. 105.

107 **"it's also been laughter"** Allison Stevens, "Working Moms Not Exhausted? Oh Yes We Are," *Women's e-News*, July 10, 2012.

107 **The "wonder" part** Alison Gopnik, *The Philosophical Baby: What Children's Minds Tell Us About Truth, Love, and the Meaning of Life* (New York: Farrar, Straus and Giroux, 2009), p. 72.

109 **"give us a reprieve from etiquette"** Jennifer Senior, *All Joy and No Fun: The Paradox of Modern Parenting* (New York: HarperCollins, 2014), p. 102.

109 **Grant then asks the same question** Adam Grant, *Give and Take: A Revolutionary Approach to Success* (New York: Viking, 2013).

109 **Abraham Lincoln's political career** Ibid., p. 32.

110 **Edu sent me a small book** Milton Mayeroff, *On Caring* (New York: Harper & Row, 1971).

110 **"in a new era of evolutionary history"** Ruth Nanda Anshen,

"What This Series Means," afterword in Mayeroff, *On Caring*, p. 107.

111 **The book's central message** Mayeroff, *On Caring*, p. 1.

111 **"In caring"** Ibid., p. 7.

112 **Knowledge, because** Ibid., p. 19.

113 **True patience** Ibid., p. 24.

113 **Google could not have said it better** James B. Stewart, "Looking for a Lesson in Google's Perks," *New York Times*, March 15, 2013, nytimes.com/2013/03/16/business/at-google-a -place-to-work-and-play.html.

113 **Patience is also involved** Mayeroff, *On Caring*, p. 21.

113 **"Nobody has a great idea the first time"** Eric Ries interview with Gavin Newsom, quoted in *Citizenville: How to Take the Town Square Digital and Reinvent Government* (New York: Penguin, 2013), p. 99.

115 **"the cultivation of character"** David Brooks, *The Road to Character* (New York: Random House, 2015).

116 **"park our cars"** Gunnar, "Worthy Work, STILL Unlivable Wages."

116 **She did it by creating** Michael Winerip, "A Chosen Few Are Teaching for America," *New York Times*, July 11, 2010, nytimes .com/2010/07/12/education/12winerip.html; Fiona Glisson, "Breaking: Admissions Numbers Released," *Daily Pennsylvanian*, March 26, 2014, thedp.com/article/2014/03/breaking-admissions -numbers-released.

119 **"In the United States"** Crittenden, *The Price of Motherhood*, p. 1.

119 **A video circulated** "World's Toughest Job—#worldstoughestjob— Official Video," YouTube video, posted by cardstore, April 14, 2014, youtube.com/watch?v=HB3xM93rXbY.

119 **"My commanding officer"** Email to Anne-Marie Slaughter, October 31, 2012.

123 **"For the past two years"** Email to Anne-Marie Slaughter, June 30, 2012.

124 **In January 2013** Margaret Fortney, "What Princeton Women Want," *Daily Princetonian*, January 7, 2013, dailyprincetonian.com/ opinion/2013/01/what-princeton-women-want.

Chapter 6: The Next Phase of the Women's Movement
Is a Men's Movement

126 **"It started the way"**   Matt Villano, "I Hate Being Called a Good Dad," *New York Times*, November 9, 2012, parenting.blogs.nytimes.com/2012/11/09/i-hate-being-called-a-good-dad.

127 **"soft bigotry"**   Andrew Romano, remarks at Princeton Club seminar "Why Women Still Can't Have It All," April 10, 2013. (Romano borrowed the term from a George W. Bush speech to the NAACP Annual Convention on July 10, 2000.)

128 **"How Brad Pitt"**   Simon Kuper, "How Brad Pitt Brings Out the Best in Dads," *Financial Times*, October 10, 2014.

128 **"an African American male"**   Email to Anne-Marie Slaughter, June 21, 2012.

131 *The Atlantic* **published another article**   Ryan Park, "What Ruth Bader Ginsburg Taught Me About Being a Stay-at-Home Dad," *Atlantic*, January 8, 2015, theatlantic.com/features/archive/2015/01/what-ruth-bader-ginsburg-taught-me-about-being-a-stay-at-home-dad/384289.

132 **"Raising children"**   Kunal Modi, "Man Up on Family and Workplace Issues: A Response to Anne-Marie Slaughter," *Huffington Post*, July 12, 2012, huffingtonpost.com/kunal-modi/man-up-on-family-and-work_b_1667878.html?utm_hp_ref=media.

132 **Dean Martha Minow**   Email to Anne-Marie Slaughter, September 4, 2011.

133 **Daniel Murphy**   Jessica Grose, "The Lesson from Baseball's Paternity Leave Controversy: Paternity Leave Is Not Controversial," *Slate*, April 7, 2014, slate.com/blogs/xx_factor/2014/04/07/mlb_paternity_leave_controversy_a_happy_ending_to_the_boomer_esiason_flap.html.

133 **In 2012 Kimberly-Clark**   "Huggies—Dad Test Trailer," Vimeo video, posted by Vince Soliven, 2013, vimeo.com/49980480.

133 **A stay-at-home father**   Chris Routly, "We're Dads, Huggies. Not Dummies," Change.org, March 2012, change.org/petitions/we-re-dads-huggies-not-dummies.

133 **Huggies eventually pulled the ad**   Ibid.

133 **Chevrolet aired an ad**   Chevrolet Malibu TV commercial,

"The Car for the Richest Guys on Earth," iSpot.tv, last aired September 14, 2014, ispot.tv/ad/7j2u/2014-chevrolet-malibu-the -car-for-the-richest-guys-on-earth.

133   **an ad for Dove Men+Care**   "New 2015 Commercial— #RealStrength Ad I Dove Men+Care," YouTube video, posted by dovemencareus, January 20, 2015, youtube.com/watch?v= QoqWo3SJ73c.

134   **Mothers are still spending**   Kim Parker and Wendy Wang, "Modern Parenthood: Roles of Moms and Dads Converge as They Balance Work and Family," Pew Research Center Social and Demographic Trends, March 14, 2013, pewsocialtrends.org/files/ 2013/03/FINAL_modern_parenthood_03-2013.pdf.

135   **"a glimpse"**   "About Us," GoodMen Project, undated, goodmenproject.com/about.

135   **"starting to feel this pull"**   Betsy Bury, Dartmouth Class of 1987, *25th Reunion Class Book* (Hanover, NH: Dartmouth College, 2012), p. 27.

136   **"My daughter can go"**   Email to Anne-Marie Slaughter, January 20, 2015.

136   **"Girls are surpassing boys"**   Michael Kimmel, "Solving the 'Boy Crisis' in Schools," *Huffington Post*, April 30, 2013, huffingtonpost .com/michael-kimmel/solving-the-boy-crisis-in_b_3126379.html.

137   **girls have actually done better**   Thomas A. DiPrete and Claudia Buchmann, *The Rise of Women: The Growing Gender Gap in Education and What It Means for American Schools* (New York: Russell Sage Foundation, 2013).

137   **upper-middle-class boys**   Sean F. Reardon, "The Widening Academic Achievement Gap Between the Rich and the Poor: New Evidence and Possible Explanations," in Greg J. Duncan and Richard J. Murnane, eds., *Whither Opportunity? Rising Inequality, Schools, and Children's Life Chances* (New York: Russell Sage Foundation, 2011).

138   **The real crisis in the United States**   Sharon Lewis, Michael Casserly, Candace Simon, et al., "A Call for Change: Providing Solutions for Black Male Achievement," Council of the Great City Schools, December 2012, cgcs.org/cms/lib/DC00001581/

Centricity/Domain/4/A%20Call%20For%20Change_FinaleBook
.pdf.

138 **"only 12 percent of Black fourth-grade boys"** Ibid.

138 **psychologist Wayne Martino** Wayne Martino, "Gendered
Learning Practices: Exploring the Costs of Hegemonic Masculinity
for Girls and Boys in Schools," in *Gender Equity: A Framework for
Australian Schools* (Canberra, Australia: Ministerial Council for
Employment, Education, Training, and Youth Affairs, 1997).

138 **"It's not cool"** Kimmel, "Solving the 'Boy Crisis' in Schools."

138 **Particularly for working-class boys** DiPrete and Buchmann,
The Rise of Women, chapter 6.

139 **"To begin," Jim writes** Email to Anne-Marie Slaughter,
February 19, 2013.

140 **the "resentment towards my wife"** Email to Anne-Marie
Slaughter, May 21, 2014.

140 **in early human groupings** Sarah Blaffer Hrdy, *Mothers and
Others: The Evolutionary Origins of Mutual Understanding*
(Cambridge, MA: Belknap Press of Harvard University Press,
2009), p. 134.

140 **In the book *Sex at Dawn*** Christopher Ryan and Cacilda Jethá,
Sex at Dawn: The Prehistoric Origins of Modern Sexuality (New York:
Harper Perennial, 2011), eBook, p. 132.

141 **"women's sexual psychology"** Paul Seabright, *The War of the
Sexes* (Princeton, NJ: Princeton University Press, 2012), p. 16.

142 **She found plenty of husbands** Bebe Moore Campbell,
Successful Women, Angry Men (New York: Random House, 1987), p.
68.

142 **"Men's breadwinning"** Marianne Bertrand, Emir Kamenica,
and Jessica Pan, "Gender Identity and Relative Income Within
Households," National Bureau of Economic Research Working
Paper, May 2013, faculty.chicagobooth.edu/emir.kamenica/
documents/identity.pdf; Liana C. Sayer, Paula England, Paul
Allison, and Nicole Kangas, "She Left, He Left: How
Employment and Satisfaction Affect Men's and Women's
Decisions to Leave Marriages," *American Journal of Sociology* 116,
no. 6 (May 2011): 1982–2018, ncbi.nlm.nih.gov/pmc/articles/

PMC3347912; Wendy Wang, Kim Parker, and Paul Taylor, "Breadwinner Moms," Pew Research Center Social and Demographic Trends, May 29, 2013, pewsocialtrends.org/2013/05/29/breadwinner-moms.

143 **Sara Blakely** "Spanx Speaks: Founder Sara Blakely," 2013 Women in the World Summit, April 2013, livestream.com/womenintheworld/womenintheworld/videos/15577625; Ralph Gardner, Jr., "Alpha Women, Beta Men," *New York*, 2003, nymag.com/nymetro/news/features/n_9495.

143 **"During my time as a stay-at-home dad"** Park, "What Ruth Bader Ginsburg Taught Me."

144 **more than half of American stay-at-home dads** Gretchen Livingston, "Growing Number of Dads Home with the Kids; Chapter 2: Why Are Dads Staying Home?," Pew Research Center Social and Demographic Trends, June 5, 2014, pewsocialtrends.org/2014/06/05/chapter-2-why-are-dads-staying-home.

144 **"to experience with my daughter"** Mohamed El-Erian, "Father and Daughter Reunion," *Worth*, May/June 2014, worth.com/index.php/component/content/article/4-live/6722-father-and-daughter-reunion.

145 **"I recognize"** Max Schireson, "Why I Am Leaving the Best Job I Ever Had," Max Schireson's blog, August 5, 2014, maxschireson.com/2014/08/05/1137.

145 **These men are in rarefied positions** Jeremy Adam Smith, *The Daddy Shift: How Stay-at-Home Dads, Breadwinning Moms, and Shared Parenting Are Transforming the American Family* (Boston: Beacon Press, 2009).

145 **"The happiest day of my life"** Shirley Leung, "A Welcome Role Reversal," *Boston Globe*, June 13, 2014, bostonglobe.com/business/2014/06/12/number-stay-home-dads-rising/OnmubpLSzZgC5XLzaO93uM/story.html.

146 **Bronnie Ware, an Australian blogger** Bronnie Ware, *The Top Five Regrets of the Dying* (New York: Hay House, 2012).

146 **"I wish I'd had the courage"** Bronnie Ware, "Top 5 Regrets of the Dying," *Huffington Post*, January 21, 2012, huffingtonpost.com/bronnie-ware/top-5-regrets-of-the-dyin_b_1220965.html.

146 **The second was** Ibid.

146 **"My deepest fear"**   Park, "What Ruth Bader Ginsburg Taught Me."

146 **"Everything else is unfulfilled"**   Barack Obama, "Remarks by the President at Morehouse College Commencement Ceremony," May 19, 2013, whitehouse.gov/the-press-office/2013/05/19/remarks-president-morehouse-college-commencement-ceremony.

Chapter 7: Let It Go

150 **"So many women want to control"**   Lisa Miller, "The Retro Wife," *New York*, March 17, 2013, nymag.com/news/features/retro-wife-2013-3.

151 **"who claim to be overworked"**   Aaron Gouveia, "It's Time to Stop Treating Dads Like Idiots," *Huffington Post*, May 20, 2013, huffingtonpost.com/aaron-gouveia/its-time-to-stop-treating-dads-like-idiots_b_3179351.html.

152 **stereotypes can be both cultural and situational**   Claude Steele, *Whistling Vivaldi: How Stereotypes Affect Us and What We Can Do* (New York: W. W. Norton, 2010), eBook, pp. 131–32.

152 **"If a man is told repeatedly"**   Email to Anne-Marie Slaughter, September 8, 2012.

152 **"even the most senior male chief executive"**   Jack O'Sullivan, "The Masculinity Debate," *Guardian*, May 21, 2013, theguardian.com/commentisfree/2013/may/21/masculinity-debate-men-fear-ridicule-matriarchy.

153 **Women produce big doses**   Navneet Magon and Sanjay Kalra, "The Orgasmic History of Oxytocin: Love, Lust, and Labor," *Indian Journal of Endocrinology and Metabolism*, 15, suppl. 13 (September 2011): 5156–61, ncbi.nlm.nih.gov/pmc/articles/PMC3183515.

153 **only 5 percent of male mammals**   T. H. Clutton-Brock, *The Evolution of Parental Care* (Princeton, NJ: Princeton University Press, 1991), p. 132.

153 **motherhood makes rats smarter**   Craig Howard Kinsley and Kelly G. Lambert, "The Maternal Brain," *Scientific American*, January 2006, www2.sunysuffolk.edu/benharm/Articles/the%20maternal%20brain%20-%20kinsley.pdf.

153 **similar changes**   Kelly G. Lambert, "The Parental Brain: Transformations and Adaptations," *Physiology & Behavior*, 107 (2012), 792–800, ncbi.nlm.nih.gov/pubmed/22480732.

153 **Endocrine systems and neural circuitry**   Benedetta Leuner, Erica R. Glasper, and Elizabeth Gould, "Parenting and Plasticity," *Trends in Neurosciences*, 33, no. 10 (October 2010): 465–73, ncbi.nlm.nih.gov/pubmed/20832872.

153 **More recent neuroimaging research**   Pilyoung Kim, Paola Rigo, Linda C. Mayes, et al., "Neural Plasticity in Fathers of Human Infants," *Social Neuroscience* 9, no. 5 (2014): 522–35, tandfonline.com/doi/abs/10.1080/17470919.2014.933713.

154 **"When you become a dad"**   Christian Jarrett, "How Becoming a Father Changes Your Brain," *Wired*, July 17, 2014, wired.com/2014/07/how-becoming-a-father-changes-your-brain.

154 **"If nature teaches anything"**   Brigid Schulte, "With Exposure to Babies, Rodent Dads' Brains, Like Moms', Become Wired for Nurture," *Washington Post*, June 15, 2013, washingtonpost.com/local/with-exposure-to-babies-rodent-dads-brains-like-moms-become-wired-for-nurture/2013/06/15/8f0758ea-d3e6-11e2-a73e-826d299ff459_story.html.

155 **we've beaten that subject to death**   Jennifer Senior, *All Joy and No Fun: The Paradox of Modern Parenting* (New York: HarperCollins, 2014).

156 **From 1970 to 2006**   T. J. Mathews and Brady E. Hamilton, "Delayed Childbearing: More Women Are Having Their First Child Later in Life," NCHS Data Brief No. 21, August 2009, cdc.gov/nchs/data/databriefs/db21.pdf.

156 **"Because so many of us"**   Senior, *All Joy and No Fun*, p. 7.

156 **"We ourselves want to be needed"**   Milton Mayeroff, *On Caring* (New York: Harper & Row, 1971), p. xv, quoting Andras Angyal.

157 **On her trips back home**   Katrin Bennhold, "When Dad Becomes the Lead Parent," *New York Times*, July 9, 2013, nytimes.com/2013/07/10/world/europe/When-Dad-Becomes-the-Lead-Parent.html.

159 **In 2010, when Pew Research**   Paul Taylor, ed., "The Decline

of Marriage and Rise of New Families," Pew Research Center Social and Demographic Trends, November 18, 2010, pewsocialtrends.org/files/2010/11/pew-social-trends-2010 -families.pdf.

159 **"Yeah, he haunts me"** Hanna Rosin, *The End of Men* (New York: Riverhead Books, 2012), p. 15.

159 **"Even in the most open-minded communities"** Guy Raz, "An NPR Host's Other Job: Stay-At-Home Dad," *Atlantic*, March 17, 2011, theatlantic.com/national/archive/2011/03/an -npr-hosts-other-job-stay-at-home-dad/72588.

159 **more than 2 million people have bought *Lean In*** Gianna Palmer, "What Impact Has 'Lean In' Had on Women?," BBC News, March 5, 2015, bbc.com/news/business-31727796.

159 **more than 100 million readers** Mary-Ann Russon, "50 Shades of Grey Joins Top 10 Bestselling Books: How Many Have You Read?," *International Business Times*, February 27, 2014, ibtimes.co .uk/50-shades-grey-joins-top-10-bestselling-books-how-many -have-you-read-1438234.

161 **women who outearn their husbands** Marianne Bertrand, Emir Kamenica, and Jessica Pan, "Gender Identity and Relative Income Within Households," National Bureau of Economic Research Working Paper Series, May 2013, nber.org/papers/w19023.

161 **"are striving to be superwomen"** Betsy Polk and Maggie Ellis Chotas, *Power Through Partnership: How Women Lead Better Together* (San Francisco: Berett-Koehler, 2014), p. 14.

161 **She says, forthrightly** Debora L. Spar, *Wonder Women: Sex, Power, and the Quest for Perfection* (New York: Farrar, Straus and Giroux, 2013), p. 234.

161 **"We took the struggles and victories"** Ibid.

162 **"force field of highly unrealistic expectations"** Ibid., p. 233.

162 **She may be completely exhausted** Betsey Stevenson and Justin Wolfers, "The Paradox of Declining Female Happiness," *American Economic Journal: Economic Policy* 1, no. 2 (2009): 190–225.

163 **As she tells the story** Gro Harlem Brundtland, *Madam Prime Minister: A Life in Power and Politics* (New York: Farrar, Straus and Giroux, 2002), p. 57.

163   A HOUSE MUST BE CLEAN ENOUGH   Nancy Gibbs, "Norway's Radical Daughter," *Time*, June 24, 2001, content.time.com/time/magazine/article/0,9171,152609,00.html.

164   **"Among my friends"**   Miller, "The Retro Wife."

166   **Your spouse might**   Senior, *All Joy and No Fun*, p. 79.

166   **an immediate emotional response**   Ibid., p. 87.

166   **While single fathers**   Gretchen Livingston, "The Rise of Single Fathers: A Ninefold Increase Since 1960," Pew Research Center Social and Demographic Trends, June 2013, pewsocialtrends.org/files/2013/07/single-fathers-07-2013.pdf; Kelly Musick and Ann Meier, "Are Both Parents Always Better than One? Parental Conflict and Young Adult Well-being," *Social Science Research* 39, no. 5 (2010): 814–30.

166   **Interracial marriage**   "Loving v. Virginia: The Case Over Interracial Marriage," ACLU, aclu.org/racial-justice/loving-v-virginia-case-over-interracial-marriage.

167   **"traditional idealized family"**   Mary Francis Berry, "The Mother of All Debates; The Father's Hour," *New York Times*, February 10, 1993, nytimes.com/1993/02/10/opinion/the-mother-of-all-debates-the-father-s-hour.html.

167   **"[Fathers] not only directed"**   Ibid.

167   **Home economics**   Viviana A. Zelizer, *Pricing the Priceless Child: The Changing Social Value of Children* (Princeton, NJ: Princeton University Press, 1994), pp. 62–64.

168   **"The useful labor"**   Ibid., pp. 97–98.

168   **"manhood flowed out of [men's] utility"**   Susan Faludi, *Stiffed: The Betrayal of the American Man* (New York: HarperCollins, 2010), eBook, p. 816.

168   **"a cloth-diapering wizard"**   Abigail Rine, "Feminist Housedude," *Mama Unabridged*, March 21, 2013, mamaunabridged.com/2013/03/21/feminist-housedude.

Part III: Getting to Equal

171   **Ginsburg once gave an interview**   Jeffrey Rosen, "The New Look of Liberalism on the Court," *New York Times*, October 5,

1997, nytimes.com/1997/10/05/magazine/the-new-look-of
-liberalism-on-the-court.html.

172 **"You may think it can't happen"**   Anne-Marie Slaughter, "Can
We All 'Have It All'?," TEDGlobal 2013, June 2013, ted.com/
talks/anne_marie_slaughter_can_we_all_have_it_all.

Chapter 8: Change the Way You Talk

176 **"This new feature"**   Rich Ferraro, "Facebook Introduces
Custom Gender Field to Allow Users to More Accurately Reflect
Who They Are," GLAAD, February 13, 2014, glaad.org/blog/
facebook-introduces-custom-gender-field-allow-users-more
-accurately-reflect-who-they-are.

177 **"backing away from [my] State Department job"**   Gloria
Feldt, "Why Women Must Seize This Moment," CNN, March 14,
2013, cnn.com/2013/03/10/opinion/feldt-women-balance.

177 **in the genre of women "dropping out"**   Tara Sophia Mohr,
"Slaughter's Story Made the Cover—What Stories Got Left Out?,"
Huffington Post, July 9, 2012, huffingtonpost.com/tara-sophia
-mohr/having-it-all_b_1658131.html.

178 **"leaving to spend time with your family"**   Laura Rozen,
"Policy Planning's Anne-Marie Slaughter Signs Off," *Politico*,
February 3, 2011, politico.com/blogs/laurarozen/0211/Policy
_Planning_chief_AnneMarie_Slaughter_signs_off.html.

178 **"Ms. Flournoy's announcement"**   Elizabeth Bumiller, "One of
the Pentagon's Top Women Is Stepping Down," *New York Times*,
December 11, 2011, nytimes.com/2011/12/13/us/michele-flournoy
-resigns-as-a-top-pentagon-adviser.html.

179 **" 'I can absolutely and unequivocally state' "**   Ibid.

180 **"law firms trip all over themselves"**   Email to Anne-Marie
Slaughter, September 14, 2011.

182 **"Women don't want to be singled out"**   White House Working
Families Summit, Part 2, Washington, D.C., June 23, 2014, c-span
.org/video/?320109-101/white-house-working-families-summit
-part-2.

186 **good "work/life fit"**   Cali Williams Yost, *Work + Life: Finding*

the Fit That's Right for You (New York: Riverhead Books, 2004); Dan Schwabel, "Cali Williams Yost: Why We Have to Rethink Work Life Balance," *Forbes*, January 8, 2013, forbes.com/sites/danschawbel/2013/01/08/cali-williams-yost-why-we-have-to-rethink-work-life-balance.

186 **"custom-fit workplace"**   Joan Blades and Nanette Fondas, *The Custom-Fit Workplace: Choose When, Where, and How to Work and Boost Your Bottom Line* (San Francisco: Jossey-Bass, 2010), pp. 10–11; E. Kelly Moen and R. Huang, " 'Fit' Inside the Work/Family Black Box: An Ecology of the Life Course, Cycles of Control Reframing," *Journal of Occupational and Organizational Psychology* 81 (2008): 411–33; Judy Casey and Karen Corday, "Work-Life Fit and the Life Course: An Interview with Phyllis Moen," Sloan Work and Family Research Network, *Network News* 11, no. 9 (September 2009).

Chapter 9: Planning Your Career (Even Though It Rarely Works Out as Planned)

188 **"Plans are worthless"**   From Eisenhower's speech to the National Defense Executive Reserve Conference in Washington, D.C., November 14, 1957; in National Archives and Records Service, *Public Papers of the Presidents of the United States, Dwight D. Eisenhower, 1957* (Washington, DC: Government Printing Office, 1958), p. 818.

188 **If you're an American woman**   Social Security Online, "Life Expectancy Calculator," Social Security Administration, socialsecurity.gov/cgi-bin/longevity.cgi.

188 **will live to nearly 95**   Felicitie C. Bell and Michael L. Miller, "Life Tables for the United States Social Security Area 1900–2100," Social Security Administration, April 7, 2009, socialsecurity.gov/oact/NOTES/s2000s.html.

188 **your life expectancy is 82**   Social Security Online, "Life Expectancy Calculator."

188 **due to the epidemic of obesity**   Barry Bosworth and Kathleen Burke, "Differential Mortality and Retirement Benefits in the Health and Retirement Study," Brookings Institution, April 8,

2014, brookings.edu/research/papers/2014/04/differential
-mortality-retirement-benefits-bosworth.

190 **"people in their twenties"** "Welcoming the Age of the
Explorer," Future of Work Research Consortium, October 2014,
hotspotsmovement.com/uploads/newsletters/theexplorer.html;
Lynda Gratton, *The Shift: The Future of Work Is Already Here* (New
York: HarperCollins Business, 2011).

191 **working at a "portfolio" of part-time jobs** Barrie Hopson and
Katie Ledger, *And What Do You Do? Ten Steps to Creating a Portfolio
Career* (London: A & C Black, 2009).

193 **David Brooks contrasts "résumé virtues"** David Brooks,
"The Moral Bucket List," *New York Times*, April 12, 2015, nytimes
.com/2015/04/12/opinion/sunday/david-brooks-the-moral-bucket
-list.html.

193 **interviewing ten Princeton graduates** Lisa Belkin, "The
Opt-Out Revolution," *New York Times*, October 26, 2003, nytimes
.com/2003/10/26/magazine/26WOMEN.html.

194 **"Fund-raising for a Manhattan private school"** Judith
Warner, "The Opt-Out Generation Wants Back In," *New York
Times*, August 7, 2013, nytimes.com/2013/08/11/magazine/the-opt
-out-generation-wants-back-in.html.

196 **"seesaw marriages"** Hanna Rosin, *The End of Men* (New York:
Riverhead Books, 2012).

197 **a new model of employer-employee relations** Reid Hoffman,
Ben Casnocha, and Chris Yeh, *The Alliance: Managing Talent in the
Networked Age* (Boston: Harvard Business Review Press, 2014),
eBook, p. 12.

197 **"'employees are our most valuable resource'"** Ibid.

198 **"talent really is the most valuable resource"** Ibid., p. 19.

199 **"if retention in critical skills sets"** "Career Intermission Pilot
Program Update," U.S. Navy official website, October 2009,
public.navy.mil/bupers-npc/reference/messages/Documents/
NAVADMINS/NAV2009/NAV09301.txt; Rear Adm. Tony Kurta,
"Career Intermission Pilot Program Updated," Navy Live, May 16,
2013, navylive.dodlive.mil/2013/05/16/career-intermission-pilot
-program-updated.

199 **The air force is planning** Stephen Losey, "Air Force to Offer 3

Years Off for Airmen to Start Families," *Air Force Times*, May 15, 2014, airforcetimes.com/article/20140515/CAREERS/305150044/ Air-Force-offer-3-years-off-airmen-start-families.

199 **"Some women leave the Air Force"** Ibid.

199 **McKinsey has a program** McKinsey & Company, "Take Time," Agile Future Forum, November 2014, agilefutureforum.co .uk/wp-content/uploads/2014/11/Case-Study-McKinsey.pdf.

202 **This hypothetical applies equally** Abbie E. Goldberg, Julianna Z. Smith, and Maureen Perry-Jenkins, "The Division of Labor in Lesbian, Gay, and Heterosexual New Adoptive Parents," *Journal of Marriage and Family* 74 (2012): 812–28, wordpress.clarku.edu/ agoldberg/files/2012/03/Goldberg-Smith-Perry-Jenkins-2012 -JMF.pdf; Lawrence A. Kurdek, "The Allocation of Labor by Partners in Gay and Lesbian Couples," *Journal of Family Issues* 28, no. 1 (2007): 132–48.

203 **a now-famous essay** Alix Kates Shulman, "A Marriage Agreement," *Up from Under* 1, no. 2 (August–September 1970): 5–8.

203 **Slate writer and academic Rebecca Onion** Rebecca Onion, "The Pre-Pregnancy Contract," *Slate*, July 10, 2014, slate.com/ articles/double_x/doublex/2014/07/pre_pregnancy_contract _signing_on_the_dotted_line_to_avoid_household_conflict.single .html.

Chapter 10: The Perfect Workplace

209 **It will increasingly be the world** "Future of Work: There's an App for That," *Economist*, January 3, 2015, economist.com/news/ briefing/21637355-freelance-workers-available-moments-notice -will-reshape-nature-companies-and?fsrc=scn/tw_ec/there_s_an _app_for_that.

210 **they do not provide the pay and benefits** Kevin Roose, "Does Silicon Valley Have a Contract-Worker Problem?," *New York*, September 18, 2014, nymag.com/daily/intelligencer/2014/09/ silicon-valleys-contract-worker-problem.html.

210 **a prescient book** Thomas W. Malone, *The Future of Work: How the New Order of Business Will Shape Your Organization, Your*

Management Style, and Your Life (Cambridge, MA: Harvard Business School Press, 2004), p. 74. For information on SAG-AFTRA, see sagaftra.org/union-information.

211 **Bliss Lawyers** Deborah Epstein Henry, Suzie Scanlon Rabinowitz, and Garry A. Berger, *Finding Bliss: Innovative Legal Models for Happy Clients and Happy Lawyers* (Chicago: American Bar Association, 2015).

211 **Topcoder matches freelance computer coders** "Future of Work: There's an App for That."

212 **"we share stories"** Email to Anne-Marie Slaughter, April 2, 2015.

212 **Ninety-seven percent of openworking companies** Openwork .org.

213 **"[GM Financial] handed over"** Interview with Kathleen Christensen, program director, Alfred P. Sloan Foundation, October 9, 2014.

213 **Ryan, LLC** Ellen Galinsky and Mike Aitken, "2013 Guide to Bold New Ideas for Making Work Work," When Work Works, 2012, p. 6, familiesandwork.org/downloads/2013GuidetoBoldNew Ideas.pdf. All of the companies listed as winners are the Families and Work Institute's and the Society for Human Resources' When Work Works awardees. The selection process is rigorously designed to survey both employers and employees on effective and flexible workplaces. It uses the employees' ratings to account for two-thirds of the winning score.

214 **Ernst & Young** Ibid., p. 62.

214 **Deloitte has a program** Cathy Benko and Anne Weisberg, "Mass Career Customization™: A New Model for How Careers Are Built," *Ivey Business Journal*, May/June 2008, iveybusinessjournal .com/publication/mass-career-customization-a-new-model-for -how-careers-are-built.

214 **"Over the course of a long career"** Renee McGaw, "Life Balance Issues Are Gender-Neutral," *Denver Business Journal*, January 18, 2009, bizjournals.com/denver/stories/2009/01/19/ focus1.html.

214 **consider 1-800 CONTACTS** Openwork.org.

214 **Delta Air Lines has created** "Workplace Awards: Delta Air

Lines," *When Work Works*, Families and Work Institute and the Society for Human Resource Management, 2014, whenworkworks .org/workplace-awards/delta-air-lines.

215 **Southern California Gas Company** "Workplace Awards: Southern California Gas Company," *When Work Works*, Families and Work Institute and the Society for Human Resource Management, 2014, whenworkworks.org/workplace-awards/ southern-california-gas-company.

215 **American Express employees** Joan Blades and Nanette Fondas, *The Custom-Fit Workplace: Choose When, Where, and How to Work and Boost Your Bottom Line* (San Francisco: Jossey-Bass, 2010), pp. 58–59, citing "Telework Facts & Stats," Telework Coalition, telcoa.org/resources/references/telework-tools/telework-facts -stats; "Workspace Utilization and Allocation Benchmark," GSA Office of Government-wide Policy, July 2011, gsa.gov/graphics/ ogp/Workspace_Utilization_Banchmark_July_2012.pdf.

215 **the software startup Evernote** Douglas MacMillan, "To Recruit Techies, Companies Offer Unlimited Vacation," *Businessweek*, July 19, 2012, businessweek.com/articles/2012-07-19/to-recruit -techies-companies-offer-unlimited-vacation.

215 **the Evernote unlimited-vacation benefit** Ibid.

216 **In an interview with the tech site** Todd Wasserman, "Coming to a Couch Near You: A New Wave of Telecommuting," *Mashable*, April 10, 2014, mashable.com/2014/04/10/the-telecommuting -dream-is-dead.

217 **firms like Goldman Sachs** Shayndi Raice, "Goldman Seeks to Improve Working Conditions for Junior Staffers," *Wall Street Journal*, October 28, 2013, online.wsj.com/news/articles/ SB10001424052702303471004579164051099280722.

217 **Morgan Stanley's chief executive** William Alden and Sydney Ember, "Banks Ease Hours for Junior Staff, but Workload Stays Same," *New York Times*, April 9, 2014, dealbook.nytimes.com/2014/ 04/09/banks-ease-hours-for-junior-staff-but-workload-stays-same.

221 **"I know we discussed this a while ago"** Stephanie Emma Pfeffer, "10 Steps to Negotiating for a Flexible Work Arrangement," *Woman's Day*, July 10, 2013, womansday.com/life/work-money/ tips/a7013/flex-time.

222 **British economists** Andrew J. Oswalk, Eugenio Proto, and Daniel Sgroi, "Happiness and Productivity," University of Warwick Working Paper, February 10, 2014, www2.warwick.ac.uk/fac/soc/economics/staff/eproto/workingpapers/happinessproductivity.pdf.

226 **the results-only work environment** Cali Ressler and Jody Thompson, *Why Work Sucks and How to Fix It: The Results-Only Revolution* (New York: Portfolio, 2008), eBook, p. 10.

226 **"This program was based on the premise"** Hubert Joly, "Best Buy CEO on Leadership: A Comment I Made Was Misconstrued," *Star Tribune*, March 17, 2013, startribune.com/opinion/commentaries/198546011.html.

227 **the Gap adopted ROWE** "Diversity and Inclusion," Gap Inc., *Social & Environmental Responsibility Report 2011/2012*, gapinc.com/content/csr/html/employees/diversity-and-inclusion.html.

227 **insist that supervisors be clear** Cali Ressler and Jody Thompson, "How to Get Employees to Manage Themselves," ChangeThis, issue 106-01, June 5, 2013, changethis.com/manifesto/show/106.01.ManageWork/.

227 **"We very much focus on results"** Interview with Sabrina Parsons, chief executive officer, Palo Alto Software, December 17, 2014.

227 **"We've given them a place"** Ibid.

229 **"Businesses operating in this skills-scarce world"** Richard Dobbs, Anu Madgavkar, Dominic Barton, et al., "The World at Work: Jobs, Pay, and Skills for 3.5 Billion People," McKinsey Global Institute, McKinsey & Company, June 2012, mckinsey.com/insights/employment_and_growth/the_world_at_work.

230 **He sees those same forces** Bill Gates, "Bill Gates—2008 World Economic Forum—Creative Capitalism," Bill & Melinda Gates Foundation, January 24, 2008, gatesfoundation.org/media-center/speeches/2008/01/bill-gates-2008-world-economic-forum.

Chapter 11: Citizens Who Care

232 **We used to have an infrastructure of care** "Latest Annual Data," United States Department of Labor, 2013, dol.gov/wb/stats/recentfacts.htm.

232　**"an infrastructure for care"**　Ai-Jen Poo, with Ariane Conrad, *The Age of Dignity: Preparing for the Elder Boom in a Changing America* (New York: New Press, 2015), p. 143.

233　**High-quality and affordable childcare**　The Family Care Alliance includes a Family Care Navigator on their website that helps caregivers find support services in their states, Link2Care, an online discussion and support group managed by the Alliance and the National Center on Caregiving, which is a clearinghouse for all federal legislation on caregiving policy and can be a resource for those who want to get involved. They have a free electronic newsletter available at caregiver.org, where you can subscribe to a twice-monthly briefing on the legislation, programs, and funding. See "About FCA," Family Caregiver Alliance, caregiver.org/about-fca, and "Newsletters," Family Caregiver Alliance, caregiver.org/newsletters.

233　**Investment in early education**　The United States is barely managing to invest in state-funded pre-K, meaning two years of school before students enter kindergarten. The percentage of four-year-olds enrolled in state-funded pre-K has doubled in the past decade, but it is still only at 28 percent. Ten states have no public pre-K options at all. See W. Steven Barnett, Megan E. Carolan, James H. Squires, and Kirsty Clarke Brown, "The State of Preschool 2013," National Institute for Early Education, 2013, nieer.org/sites/nieer/files/yearbook2013.pdf.

Oklahoma is the shining light of universal pre-K that can illuminate a path for other states to follow. All pre-K teachers in Oklahoma have a college degree, a certificate in early-childhood education, and they're paid the same as elementary, middle, and high school teachers. See Robin Young interview with Steven Dow, "Why Oklahoma's Universal Pre-K Is Successful," *Here & Now*, February 20, 2014, hereandnow.wbur.org/2014/02/20/universal-pre-kindergarten.

Oklahoma treats pre-K like any other grade in the system, and the state has allowed school districts to partner with federal programs like Head Start and other outside organizations in order to shore up funding. See "Oklahoma," National Institute for Early Education, 2013, nieer.org/sites/nieer/files/Oklahoma_0.pdf.

Oklahoma even sends social workers to coach stressed-out
parents on how to raise their kids. See Nicholas Kristof,
"Oklahoma! Where the Kids Learn Early," *New York Times*,
November 9, 2013, nytimes.com/2013/11/10/opinion/sunday/
kristof-oklahoma-where-the-kids-learn-early.html.

The Center for American Progress (CAP) has a plan for getting
two years of universal pre-K for all children. Under CAP's plan, the
federal government would match state expenditures up to $10,000
per child annually. Preschool would be free for poor families, and
wealthier families would be charged on a sliding scale depending
on their financial circumstances. Universal childcare won't come
cheap, but as a society we'll reap the benefits. See Cynthia G.
Brown, Donna Cooper, Juliana Herman, et al., "Investing in Our
Children: A Plan to Expand Access to Preschool and Child Care,"
Center for American Progress, 2013, americanprogress.org/issues/
education/report/2013/02/07/52071/investing-in-our-children.

Georgia also has universal pre-K, and other states like New
York and Minnesota are working on it. See Reid Wilson, "New
York Will Begin Universal Pre-kindergarten," *Washington Post*,
March 31, 2014, washingtonpost.com/blogs/govbeat/wp/2014/
03/31/new-york-will-begin-universal-pre-kindergarten.

233 **Comprehensive job protection**   "Supreme Court Backs
Pregnant UPS Worker," *Forbes*, March 25, 2015, forbes.com/sites/
ashleaebeling/2015/03/25/supreme-court-backs-pregnant-ups
-worker. Though there are already some federal legal protections
for pregnant women—through the Americans with Disabilities
Act, the Pregnancy Discrimination Act, and the Family and
Medical Leave Act—judicial interpretations of these laws still have
plenty of loopholes. As a result, pregnant women are often denied
leave or accommodations. See "It Shouldn't Be a Heavy Lift: Fair
Treatment for Pregnant Workers," National Women's Law Center,
June 2013, nwlc.org/sites/default/files/pdfs/pregnant_workers.pdf.

This report describes the ways in which pregnant women have
not been accommodated by their employers, despite the existing
laws that are meant to protect them. For example, a fast food
worker in Washington, D.C., was barred from taking extra
bathroom breaks and disciplined for drinking water on the job; a

Rent-a-Center employee was forced to go on unpaid leave and ultimately fired; and a UPS employee was not allowed light duty even though nonpregnant injured workers were given light duties when they had similar physical restrictions.

To extend job protections for pregnant workers, the Pregnant Workers Fairness Act should be passed. See "S.942: Pregnant Workers Fairness Act," Congress.gov, 2013, congress.gov/bill/ 113th-congress/senate-bill/942.

On the state and local levels, twelve states and two cities have passed laws requiring businesses to provide "reasonable accommodations" to pregnant workers, ranging from a transfer to a less strenuous position to additional bathroom and water breaks. See "Reasonable Accommodations for Pregnant Workers: State Laws," National Partnership for Women & Families, April 2014, nationalpartnership.org/research-library/workplace-fairness/ pregnancy-discrimination/reasonable-accommodations-for -pregnant-workers-state-laws.pdf.

In March 2015 the Supreme Court handed down an important decision in *Young v. United Parcel Service* 135 S. Ct. 1338 (2015), ruling that employers must at least provide pregnant workers with the same kinds of accommodations they provide to other groups of workers who are temporarily prevented from doing their normal jobs. *Young v. United Parcel Service* 135 S. Ct. 1338 (2015).

233 **Higher wages and training** See Caring Across Generations, an organization building a national movement of the "caring majority" by executing on four major program areas: culture change work; local, state and federal policy advocacy; online campaigning; and field activities and civic engagement, caringacross.org/about-us.

According to the second edition of AARP's State Scorecard, the costs of eldercare are unmanageable for the vast majority of Americans. On average, nursing home costs are 246 percent of the median household income for seniors. Even in the five most affordable states, the cost is 171 percent of median income. Home care is more affordable, but it's still 84 percent of median income, and as AARP puts it, "The typical older family cannot sustain these costs for long periods." See Susan C. Reinhard, Enid Kassner, Ari Houser, et al., "Raising Expectations: A State Scorecard on

Long-Term Services and Supports for Older Adults, People with Physical Disabilities, and Family Caregivers," AARP, 2014, aarp .org/content/dam/aarp/research/public_policy_institute/ltc/2014/ raising-expectations-2014-AARP-ppi-ltc.pdf.

233 **Community support structures**   Atul Gawande provides a frank and in-depth discussion of the issues involved in aging and the end of life, offering options that maximize well-being. See Atul Gawande, *Being Mortal: Medicine and What Matters in the End* (London: Profile Books, 2014).

233 **Legal protections**   In the United Kingdom, the Part-Time Workers (Prevention of Less Favourable Treatment) Regulations 2000 "prohibit an employer treating part-time workers less favourably in their contractual terms and conditions than comparable full-time workers, unless different treatment can be justified on objective grounds." If a part-time worker believes she has been treated unlawfully, she can file a complaint with an Employment Tribunal. See FindLaw UK, findlaw.co.uk/law/ employment/discrimination/500293.html.

In Ireland, the Protection of Employees (Part-Time Work) Act of 2001 ensures that a part-time employee cannot be treated less favorably than a comparable full-time employee regarding conditions of employment. Complaints can be heard by a rights commissioner. See Citizens Information Board, Public Service Information, Ireland, citizensinformation.ie/en/employment/ types_of_employment/employment_rights_of_part_time_workers .html.

In the United States, H.R.675—the Part-Time Worker Bill of Rights Act—was introduced in 2013 by Representative Janice D. Schakowsky. The bill would have corrected an unintended consequence of the Affordable Care Act (ACA) that gives employers an incentive to drop healthcare coverage for part-time workers. That bill was not enacted. See congress.gov/bill/113th -congress/house-bill/675.

However, some states and cities are beginning to take action on their own. California and Connecticut require sick leave for part-time workers. Washington, D.C.; Seattle, Washington; Portland, Oregon; New York, New York; and Jersey City, New Jersey, have also passed legislation. See Reid Wilson, "California on Brink of Requiring Paid Sick Days for Part-Time Workers," *Washington Post*, September 2, 2014, washingtonpost.com/blogs/govbeat/wp/ 2014/09/02/california-on-brink-of-requiring-paid-sick-days-for -part-time-workers.

233 **Better enforcement**   The Age Discrimination in Employment Act of 1967 (Pub. L. 90-202) (ADEA), prohibits employment discrimination against persons forty years of age or older. The law "forbids discrimination when it comes to any aspect of employment, including hiring, firing, pay, job assignments, promotions, layoff, training, fringe benefits, and any other term or condition of employment." See "Age Discrimination," U.S. Equal Employment Opportunity Commission, eeoc.gov/laws/statutes/adea.cfm.

   In addition, the Age Discrimination Act of 1975 prohibits discrimination on the basis of age in programs and activities receiving federal financial assistance; and Section 188 of the Workforce Investment Act of 1998 (WIA) prohibits discrimination against applicants, employees, and participants in WIA Title I financially assisted programs and activities on the basis of age. See "Age Discrimination," U.S. Department of Labor, dol.gov/dol/ topic/discrimination/agedisc.htm.

   In the area of policy, AARP advocates on behalf of persons over the age of fifty. The organization provides research and information to policy leaders regarding the needs, market conditions, and trends that impact this population. See "Age Discrimination Fact Sheet," AARP, April 2014, aarp.org/work/employee-rights/info-02 -2009/age_discrimination_fact_sheet.html.

233 **Reform of elementary and secondary school**   See Alice Park, "School Should Start Later So Teens Can Sleep, Urge Doctors," *Time*, August 14, 2014, time.com/3162265/school-should-start -later-so-teens-can-sleep-urge-doctors; National Association for Year Round Learning, nayre.org; "Learning Time in America: Trends to Reform the American School Calendar: A Snapshot of Federal, State, and Local Action," Education Commission of the States, 2011, ecs.org/docs/LearningTimeinAmerica.pdf; Charles Ballinger and Carolyn Kneese, *School Calendar Reform: Learning in All Seasons* (Lanham, MD: R&L Education, 2006).

233 **But for those of you who want**   For an accessible, powerfully argued overview of all these proposals and more, see Madeleine Kunin, the first woman governor of Vermont, *The New Feminist Agenda: Defining the Next Revolution for Women, Work, and Family* (White River Junction, VT: Chelsea Green Publishing, 2012).

234 **In a live segment on her Fox show**   KJ Dell'Antonia, "Fox News Anchor Pushes Paid Family Leave," *New York Times*, December 12, 2011, parenting.blogs.nytimes.com/2011/12/12/fox-news-anchor-pushes-paid-family-leave.

235 **Childcare workers**   Jonathan Cohn, "The Hell of American Day Care," *New Republic*, April 15, 2013, newrepublic.com/article/112892/hell-american-day-care; "Parents and the High Cost of Child Care: 2014 Report," Child Care Aware of America, 2014.

235 **Republican senators**   Brigid Schulte, "'Mad Men' Era of U.S. Family Policy Coming to an End?," *Washington Post*, February 12, 2014, washingtonpost.com/blogs/she-the-people/wp/2014/02/12/mad-men-era-of-us-family-policy-coming-to-an-end.

235 **a majority of Republican women**   "American Women Applauds President Obama's Action on Paid Family Leave and Paid Sick Days," American Women, January 15, 2015, americanwomen.org/news/american-women-applauds-president-obamas-action-on-paid-family-leave-and-paid-sick-days.

235 **Republican senator Kelly Ayotte**   Jamie Bulen, "Family Caregiving Caucus Co-Chaired by U.S. Senator Ayotte," AARP, March 3, 2015, states.aarp.org/family-caregiving-caucus-co-chaired-by-us-senator-ayotte.

235 **Senator Kay Bailey Hutchison**   Jana Kasperkevic, "Kay Bailey Hutchison: Not a Feminist, but an Advocate for Women," *Guardian*, August 12, 2014, theguardian.com/money/us-money-blog/2014/aug/12/kay-bailey-hutchison-not-feminist-senator-business.

236 **it's the women in Congress**   "The Family and Medical Insurance Leave Act (The FAMILY Act) Fact Sheet," National Partnership for Women and Families, 2014, nationalpartnership.org/research-library/work-family/paid-leave/family-act-fact-sheet.pdf; "H.R. 3712—Family and Medical Insurance Leave Act of 2013," congress.gov/bill/113th-congress/house-bill/3712; "State

Paid Family Leave Insurance Laws," National Partnership for Women & Families, October 2013, nationalpartnership.org/research-library/work-family/paid-leave/state-paid-family-leave-laws.pdf; Betsy Firestein, Ann O'Leary, and Zoe Savitsky, "A Guide to Implementing Paid Family Leave: Lessons from California," Labor Project for Working Families, 2011, paidfamilyleave.org/pdf/pfl_guide.pdf.

237 **In all thirteen countries** John Gerzema and Michael D'Antonio, *The Athena Doctrine: How Women (and Men Who Think Like Them) Will Rule the Future* (San Francisco: Jossey-Bass, 2013), eBook, loc. 204 of 5309.

237 **two-thirds of respondents** Ibid., loc. 181 of 5309.

238 **women in politics** Christopher F. Karpowitz and Tali Mendelberg, *The Silent Sex: Gender, Deliberation, and Institutions* (Princeton, NJ: Princeton University Press, 2014), p. 19.

238 **"Women's percentage in deliberating bodies matters little"** Ibid., p. 16.

238 **all-women groups** Ibid., p. 259.

238 **"groups chose a more generous safety net"** Ibid., p. 260.

238 **women speak less** Ibid., pp. 137–38.

238 **Most striking, however** Ibid., p. 188.

239 **"more than naming a problem"** Ibid., p. 198.

239 **"when women have greater standing"** Ibid., p. 318.

240 **one in six Americans** Ai-jen Poo, *The Age of Dignity*, pp. 2–4, 24.

240 **one in three Americans** Nancy Folbre, ed., *For Love and Money: Care Provision in the United States* (New York: Russell Sage, 2012), p. 187.

240 **the demand for home careworkers is skyrocketing** Ai-jen Poo, *Age of Dignity*, p. 4.

240 **"care policy and research"** Nancy Folbre, Candace Howes, and Carrie Leana, "A Care Policy and Research Agenda," in Nancy Folbre, ed., *For Love and Money: Care Provision in the United States* (New York: Russell Sage, 2012), pp. 183–204.

241 **It offsets the cost of high-quality childcare** "Military Child Care: DOD Is Taking Actions to Address Awareness and Availability

Barriers," Government Accountability Office, February 2012, gao.gov/assets/590/588188.pdf.

241 **the Pentagon pays teachers** Marcy Whitebook, Deborah Phillips, and Carollee Howes, *Worthy Work, STILL Unlivable Wages: The Early Childhood Workforce 25 Years after the National Child Care Staffing Study*, Center for the Study of Child Care Employment, Institute for Research on Labor and Employment, University of California, Berkeley, 2014, irle.berkeley.edu/cscce/wp-content/uploads/2014/11/ReportFINAL.pdf.

241 **Sheila Lirio Marcelo** "Sheila Lirio Marcelo: Founder, Chairwoman & CEO," Care.com, care.com/sheila-marcelo.

241 **The company raised $91 million** Michael B. Farrell, "Care .com's IPO Raises About $91m," *Boston Globe*, January 24, 2014, bostonglobe.com/business/2014/01/24/care-com-raises-million -ipo/N5navjOBBhUWRM1y0p0IBL/story.html.

242 **it was valued at $1.4 billion** Chris Deiterich, "Bright Horizons Blazes in Its Debut," *Wall Street Journal*, January 25, 2013, online .wsj.com/news/articles/SB100014241278873235398045782639328 97208500.

242 **townhouses geared toward multigenerational families** Aaron Glantz, "Multigenerational Housing Is a Real Estate Growth Niche," *New York Times*, April 21, 2011, nytimes.com/2011/04/22/us/22cncmultigenerational.html.

242 **"social consciousness of the 1960's"** Patricia Leigh Brown, "Growing Old Together, in New Kind of Commune," *New York Times*, February 27, 2006, nytimes.com/2006/02/27/national/27commune.html.

242 **the Caring Across Generations movement** "What Is Caring Across Generations?," Caring Across Generations, caringacross .org/about-us.

243 **the Family Caregiver Alliance** "About FCA," Family Caregiver Alliance, caregiver.org/about-fca.

243 **The Caring Economy Campaign** "About," Caring Economy Campaign, caringeconomy.org.

244 **"a City upon a hill"** John Winthrop, "A Model of Christian Charity (1630)," Gilder Lehrman Institute of American History,

gilderlehrman.org/sites/default/files/inline-pdfs/A%20Model
%20of%20Christian%20Charity.pdf.

244 **Britain, for example** "Maternity Pay and Leave," Gov.uk, gov
.uk/maternity-pay-leave/pay.

244 **other industrialized countries** Gretchen Livingston, "Among
38 Nations, U.S. Is the Outlier When It Comes to Paid Parental
Leave," Pew Research Center, December 12, 2013, pewresearch
.org/fact-tank/2013/12/12/among-38-nations-u-s-is-the-holdout
-when-it-comes-to-offering-paid-parental-leave; Sarah Thompson,
Robin Osborn, David Squires, and Miraya Jun, eds., "International
Profiles of Health Care Systems, 2012," Commonwealth Fund,
November 2012, commonwealthfund.org/~/media/Files/
Publications/Fund%20Report/2012/Nov/1645_Squires_intl
_profiles_hlt_care_systems_2012.pdf.

As previously noted, the United States is one of the few wealthy
countries that does not have universal healthcare or paid maternity
leave. However, there are several countries that provide paternity
leave as well, some of it fairly ample. Norway, Ireland, Iceland,
Slovenia, Sweden, and Germany all give new fathers eight weeks or
more of paid parental leave.

When it comes to care for the elderly and chronically ill,
Denmark treats its citizens wonderfully. According to the
Commonwealth Fund, institutionalized care has been de-
emphasized over the years because of "conscious policy efforts" to
allow people to stay in their own homes, which the vast number of
chronically ill people prefer (this is also true of the elderly in the
United States). In Denmark, "Home nursing (*hjemmesygepleje*) is
fully funded after medical referral. Permanent home care
(*hjemmehjælp*) is free of charge, while temporary home care can
qualify for cost-sharing if income is above DKK138,600
(US$23,776) for singles and DKK208,200 (US$35,715) for
couples."

244 **"We have decided that raising a child"** T. R. Reid, "Norway
Pays Price for Family Values," *Washington Post*, November 1, 1998,
cited in Ann Crittenden, *The Price of Motherhood: Why the Most
Important Job in the World Is Still the Least Valued* (New York: Henry
Holt, 2002), p. 192.

245 **an immigrant to Denmark** "A Family Affair: Intergenerational
Social Mobility across OECD Countries," OECD Economic
Policy Reforms, Going for Growth, 2010, oecd.org/tax/public
-finance/chapter%205%20gfg%202010.pdf.

245 **Canada, for instance** Raj Chetty, Nathaniel Hendren, Patrick
Kline, Emmanuel Saez, and Nick Turner, "Is the United States
Still a Land of Opportunity? Recent Trends in Intergenerational
Mobility," *American Economic Review Papers and Proceedings* 104,
no. 5 (2014): 141–47; Miles Corak, "Social Mobility and Social
Institutions in Comparison: Australia, Canada, the United
Kingdom, the United States," Sutton Trust/Carnegie Foundation
Seminar on Social Mobility, London, May 21–22, 2012, milescorak
.files.wordpress.com/2012/05/social_mobility_summit_v3.pdf;
Rana Foroohar, "What Ever Happened to Upward Mobility?,"
Time, November 14, 2011, content.time.com/time/magazine/
article/0,9171,2098584,00.html; Fareed Zakaria, "The Downward
Path of Upward Mobility," *Washington Post*, November 9, 2011,
washingtonpost.com/opinions/the-downward-path-of-upward
-mobility/2011/11/09/gIQAegpS6M_story.html; Fareed Zakaria,
"Social Immobility Erodes the American Dream," *Washington Post*,
August 14, 2013, washingtonpost.com/opinions/fareed-zakaria
-social-immobility-erodes-american-dream/2013/08/14/c2fc6092
-04fa-11e3-88d6-d5795fab4637_story.html.

245 **maintain a stable and caring environment** Raj Chetty,
Nathaniel Hendren, Patrick Kline, and Emmanuel Saez, "Where
Is the Land of Opportunity? The Geography of Intergenerational
Mobility in the United States," *Quarterly Journal of Economics* 129,
no. 4 (2014): 1553–1623.

245 **women in Europe** Claire Cain Miller, "Can Family Leave
Policies Be Too Generous? It Seems So," *New York Times*,
August 10, 2014, nytimes.com/2014/08/10/upshot/can-family
-leave-policies-be-too-generous-it-seems-so.html.

246 **unintended consequences of long maternity leaves**
Francine D. Blau and Lawrence M. Kahn, "Female Labor Supply:
Why Is the US Falling Behind?," Institute for the Study of Labor
Discussion Paper No. 7140, January 2013, ftp.iza.org/dp7140.pdf.
Blau and Kahn show that while women's labor force participation

overall has fallen in the United States because of our lack of paid family leave, we are more likely to be managers and professionals because of this same phenomenon. They conclude: "On the one hand, such policies likely facilitate the labor force entry of less career-oriented women (or of women who are at a stage in the life cycle when they would prefer to reduce labor market commitments). On the other hand, entitlements too long, paid parental leaves and part-time work may encourage women who would have otherwise had a stronger labor force commitment to take part-time jobs or lower-level positions. Moreover, on the employer side, such policies may lead employers to engage in statistical discrimination against women for jobs leading to higher-level positions, if employers cannot tell which women are likely to avail themselves of these options and which are not."

246　**"You don't care!"**　Carol Gilligan, *Joining the Resistance* (Cambridge, UK: Polity Press, 2011), p. 25.

246　**"That's not fair" can mean**　Christopher L. Eisgruber and Lawrence G. Sager, *Religious Freedom and the Constitution* (Cambridge, MA: Harvard University Press, 2007), eBook, loc. 53 of 3816. Legal scholars Eisgruber and Sager coined a term called "Equal Liberty" to discuss two ideas they believe are necessary for religious equality and freedom, one of which is the concept of "equal regard."

Coda

256　**"the big Me"**　David Brooks, *The Road to Character* (New York: Random House, 2015), p. 6.

256　**"a defining feature"**　Emily Esfahani Smith and Jennifer L. Aaker, "Millennial Searchers," *New York Times*, November 30, 2013, nytimes.com/2013/12/01/opinion/sunday/millennial -searchers.html.

INDEX

ABOUT THE AUTHOR

ANNE-MARIE SLAUGHTER is the president and CEO
of New America. She is the Bert G. Kerstetter '66
University Professor Emerita of Politics and International Affairs at Princeton University and the
former dean of its Woodrow Wilson School of Public and International Affairs. In 2009 Secretary of
State Hillary Clinton appointed Slaughter director
of policy planning for the U.S. State Department,
the first woman to hold that job. A foreign policy
analyst, legal and international relations scholar,
and public commentator, Slaughter was a professor
at the University of Chicago Law School and Harvard Law School and is a former president of the
American Society of International Law.

Facebook.com/annemarie.slaughter.5
@SlaughterAM